Good design

for ease of revision

Subheads break content into manageable units

Diagrams of useful or difficult ideas

Worked examples

The *key facts* for the exam

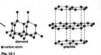

Real **GCSE questions: Hone your skills on the real thing**

Self check pages
- tell you how you are doing
- see how you cope with higher grade material

Full answers and Guide at end of chapter

More questions for you to try

Explanations to help you follow answers in italics

Revision
hints for passing

1 Check your syllabus

On page vi is a table analyzing the syllabuses of the different Boards. The next thing you must do is to obtain a copy of the syllabus and some specimen papers from your Exam Board so that you know exactly what you have to learn. Many topics are common to the syllabuses of all of the Boards but there is no point at this stage in your course in learning things that you will not be asked about. Your syllabus may not include everything in each chapter - it's worth checking your syllabus first. The addresses of the Exam Boards are given below the table on page vi.

2 Plan your revision early

You should start by making a revision plan to cover the last few months before the exam. Having made the plan, you must keep to it!

Your revision should be active - try to write out definitions, equations and key points from memory. Every 20 minutes or so get up and stretch: this may sound silly but it really does help you to concentrate and revise more effectively. Shorten your notes to a few headings, definitions and equations for each topic and learn them thoroughly. There is no excuse for losing marks through not knowing a definition.

Work through questions from the specimen papers in the same way as you do for the self-test sections of this book to give yourself extra practice.

Finally remember that advance planning is always better than last-minute cramming.

3 Don't leave it all to the last minute

Pack everything you need on the night before the examination and avoid the temptation to stay up late trying to revise. Get up early enough the next morning to enable you to get to the examination room without rushing and becoming flustered.

4 Questions: benefit from choice

If the examiner gives you a choice of questions, read the paper carefully before deciding which ones to answer - you may regret it if you choose in a hurry. In all papers, keep an eye on the time and do not spend too long on a difficult question. It is better to leave it and try again later. If you finish early, check your paper - there is always room for improvement.

Do remember that there are a few questions for which no revision is possible - this should not be used as an excuse to do no revision at all! All that is needed to answer these questions is a good dose of common sense. One example is Example 1.5. There are several possible answers to the question about the function of the roof tiles. Think what would happen if the tiles were not there - the rain could wash the salt away, the wind could blow it away, and so on. All you have to do is use your common sense and choose a suitable answer.

Answer the question which is asked! This may sound obvious but many candidates throw away marks by not attending to the wording of the question. If you are asked to *name* a substance, then giving its formula will earn you nothing. If you are asked to *describe* a reaction, the examiner will expect you to mention colour change. fizzing, production of heat, etc. Do not 'waffle' - in other words do not write a great deal on a topic just because you know it well. The examiner will award you marks only if you write what has been asked for.

Contents

Topic

Acknowledgements

The author and publishers wish to thank the following for permission to use copyright material: London East Anglian Group, Midland Examining Group, Northern Examining Association comprising Associated Lancashire Schools Examining Board, Joint Matriculation Board, North Regional Examinations Board, North West Regional Examinations Board and Yorkshire and Humberside Regional Examinations Board; Southern Examining Group and Welsh Joint Education Committee for questions from specimen and past examination papers.

Worked examples and answers included in the text are the sole responsibility of the author, and have not been provided or approved by examining boards or groups.

Every effort has been made to trace all the copyright holders, but if any have been inadvertently overlooked the publishers will be pleased to make the necessary arrangement at the first opportunity.

First published 1986
Reprinted 1986 (twice)
Second edition 1987
Third edition 1990

Published by
MACMILLAN PRESS LTD
Houndmills, Basingstoke, Hampshire RG21 6XS
and London
Companies and representatives
throughout the world

ISBN 0-333-53692-4

A catalogue record for this book is available from the British Library.

Printed in Great Britain by Biddles Ltd,
Guildford and Kings Lynn

10 9 8 7 6 5 4
00 99 98 97 96 95

Alan Barker and Kathryn Knapp

Chemistry GCSE

MACMILLAN

What
the exam boards want

Topic

	ULEAC	ULEAC Nuffield	MEG	MEG Nuffield	MEG Salters	NEAB	NICCEA	SEG	SEG Nuffield	WJEC	NEAB Nuffield
1 Some Simple Ideas	X	X	X	X	X	X	X	X	X	X	X
2 Atoms and Molecules	X	X	X	X	X	X	X	X	X	X	X
3 The Periodic Table	X	X	X	X	X	X	X	X	X	X	X
4 Bonding and Structure	X	X	X	X	X	X	X	X	X	X	X
5 Moles, Formulae and Equations	X	X	X	X	X	X	X	X	X	X	X
6 Electrochemistry	X	X	X	X	X	X	X	X	X	X	X
7 Energy Changes in Chemistry	X	X	X	X	X	X	X	X	X	X	X
8 Rate of Reaction	X	X	X	X	X	X	X	X	X	X	X
9 Atmosphere and Combustion	X	X	X	X	X	X	X	X	X	X	X
10 Water and Hydrogen	X	O	X	X	X	X	X	O	O	O	O
11 Acids, Bases and Salts	X	X	X	X	X	X	X	X	X	X	X
12 The Metals	X	X	X	X	X	X	X	X	X	X	X
13 Carbon	X	X	X	X	X	X	X	X	X	X	X
14 Nitrogen	X	X	X	X	X	X	X	X	X	X	X
15 Oxygen and Sulphur	X	O	X	X	X	X	X	X	X	X	X
16 The Halogens	X	X	X	X	X	X	X	X	X	X	X
17 Some Industrial Processes	X	X	X	X	X	X	X	X	X	X	X
18 Organic Chemistry	X	X	X	X	X	X	X	X	X	X	X
19 Chemistry Analysis	X		X	X						X	

Chapter 10 X Water and hydrogen   O Water only   **Chapter 15** X Oxygen and sulphur   O Oxygen only

Exam Board Addresses

For syllabuses and past papers contact the Publications office at the following addresses:

Midland Examining Group (MEG)
c/o University of Cambridge Local
Examinations Syndicate
1 Hills Road
CAMBRIDGE
CB1 2EU
Tel. 01223 553311

Southern Examining Group (SEG)
Publications Department
Stag Hill House
GUILDFORD
Surrey
GU2 5XJ
Tel. 01483 302302 (Direct line)

**Northern Examinations and
  Assessment Board (NEAB)**
12 Harter Street
MANCHESTER
M1 6HL
Tel. 0161 953 1170
(Also shop at the above address)

**University of London Examinations
  and Assessment Council (ULEAC)**
Stewart House
32 Russell Square
LONDON
WCIB 5DN
Tel. 0171 331 4000

**Northern Ireland Council for the
  Curriculum, Examinations and
  Assessment (NICCEA)**
Beechill House
42 Beechill Road
BELFAST
BT8 4RS
Tel. 01232 704666

**Welsh Joint Education Committee
  (WJEC)**
245 Western Avenue
Llandaff
CARDIFF
CF5 2YX

Scottish Examination Board (SEB)
  for full syllabuses
Ironmills Road
Dalkeith
Midlothian EH22 1LE
Tel. 0131 636 6601

or recent papers from the SEB's agent
Robert Gibson & Sons Ltd
17 Fitzroy Place
Glasgow G3 7SF
Tel. 0141 248 5674

**Remember to check your syllabus
number with your teacher!**

How you will be assessed and graded

Three types of question

The Exam Boards use 3 main types of question. The table opposite tells you which ones your Board uses.

Multiple choice questions require you to choose one correct answer from five alternatives.

- Take your time and real *all* of the possible answers given before making your choice. It is very easy to make mistakes in these questions, either by not reading all of the alternatives or by misreading one of them.
- If you are not sure of the correct answer, you can usually eliminate two or three that are definitely wrong. You can then make a guess from the remainder with a better chance of being right.
- *Never* leave an answer blank.

In any papers containing this type of question try first answering the questions which you find easy. Then go back and tackle the more difficult ones if you have time.

Structured questions consist of a series of questions, usually related to one another and requiring short answers (see Example 2.7). Clues to the length of answer and the detail required can be found

- in the amount of space allowed on the paper for you to write and
- by the number of marks allocated, which is quoted in a bracket. For example, if 5 marks are to be awarded, a one-word answer cannot be enough.

Free response questions require longer answers (see Example 4.1), and it is worth making a check-list of main points and an outline plan before beginning.

In the last two types of question it is especially important to keep to a time schedule. Draw diagrams only if they are asked for or if they really clarify a point. Draw them neatly but do not spend too long on them as they are rarely worth many marks. Give equations wherever possible because they often earn marks, even when they are not specifically mentioned in the question.

The Exam Boards use a number of systems for assigning grades.

- MEG set two compulsory papers which give access to grades G to C; to have the chance of an A or B grade then you must sit an extension paper which obviously contains harder questions (marked *).
- The LEAG exam has a compulsory paper 1 and then you must choose between paper 2 (for grades G to C) or paper 3 (for grades D to A); you cannot take both.

Do remember that the grades we give in this book are only approximate. The number of marks needed for a particular grade will vary from question to question and from Board to Board. When you are marking the questions note that there are no half marks and so there are no marks for an answer that is only half right!

School-based assessment of practical skills

The assessment of practical skills forms 20% of the GCSE exam. It will be carried out by your teacher over a period of several months. Your teacher will train you to work carefully and efficiently, but it is worth remembering the following points:

- follow exactly all the instructions and use the apparatus and chemicals with care
- make measurements accurately and record *all* observations.

For example, if you are asked to heat copper(II) sulphate crystals and describe what happens, it is not sufficient to say, 'The crystals got hot and a gas was given off.' A better answer would be, 'The blue crystals turn to a white powder; a steamy vapour is given off and this condenses to a colourless liquid at the top of the tube.'

When planning experiments in the practical course:

- think carefully about what you are trying to achieve.

Board	Paper	Length	Type of question
LEAG	1	1 hour	Multiple choice
	2	2 hours	Structured
	3	2 hours	Structured and free response
	4		School-based assessment
Grades A-D	Papers 1,3 and 4		
C-G	Papers 1,2 and 4		
MEG	1	1 hour	Multiple choice
	2	1 hour	Structured
	3	1¼ hours	Structured and free response
	4		School-based assessment
Grades A-B	Papers 1,2,3 and 4		
C-G	Papers 1,2 and 4		
MEG Nuffield	1	1½ hours	Multiple choice and structured
	2	1½ hours	Structured and free response
	3		School-based assessment
Grades A-B	Papers 1,2 and 3		
C-G	Papers 1 and 3		
MEG Salters	1	2 hours	Multiple choice and structured
	2	2¼ hours	Structured and free response
	Practical/Projects		School-based assessment
Grades A-C	Papers 1,2 and practical/projects		
C-G	Paper 1 and practical/projects		
NEA	1	2 hours	Multiple choice and structured
	2	1½ hours	Structured and free response
			School-based assessment
Grades A-G	Papers 1,2 and school-based assessment		
C-G	Paper 1 and school-based assessment		
NISEC	1	1 hour	Multiple choice
	2	1½ hours	Structured
	3	1½ hours	Free response
			School-based assessment
Grades A-B	Papers 1,2,3 and school-based assessment		
C-G	Papers 1,2 and school-based assessment		
SEG	1	2 hours	Structured
	2		School-based assessment
	3	1½ hours	Structured and free response
Grades A-G	Papers 1,2 and 3		
C-G	Papers 1 and 2		
SEG Nuffield	1	1 hour	Multiple choice
	2	1 hour	Structured
	3		School-based assessment
	4	1¼ hours	Structured
Grades A-G	Papers 1,2,3 and 4		
C-G	Papers 1,2 and 3		
WJEC	1	2 hours	Multiple choice and structured
	2	2 hours	Structured and free response
			School-based assessment
Grades A-C	Papers 1,2 and school-based assessment		
C-G	Paper 1 and school-based assessment		

8

SOME SIMPLE IDEAS

Topic Guide

1.1 Elements, Compounds and Mixtures

An **element** is a substance which cannot be split up into two or more simpler substances by chemical means, e.g. aluminium or sulphur. It contains atoms of only one type.

There are over 100 elements which are grouped into two main classes – metals and non-metals. The differences between the classes are investigated in later chapters (12–16) and Example 12.3.

A **compound** is a substance which consists of two or more elements chemically combined together, e.g. copper(II) sulphate crystals, $CuSO_4.5H_2O$, contain copper, sulphur, oxygen and hydrogen.

A **mixture** consists of two or more elements or compounds which have not been chemically combined, e.g. water and ethanol, aluminium and sulphur.

The main differences between compounds and mixtures are summarised in Table 1.1.

Table 1.1

	Compound	Mixture
Composition	Fixed	Variable
Properties	Different from constituent elements	Similar to constituents
Separation	Cannot be separated into constituent elements by physical means	Can be separated into constituents by physical means

(a) Abundance of the Elements in the Earth's Crust and Atmosphere (Fig. 1.1)

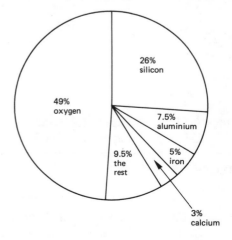

Fig. 1.1

Oxygen is found in the air, combined with hydrogen in water and combined with other elements (e.g. silicon and aluminium) in rocks and soils.

(b) Abundance of the Elements in the Human Body (Fig. 1.2)

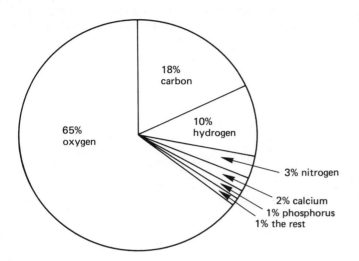

Fig. 1.2

Oxygen, carbon and hydrogen are the main elements in fats, proteins and carbohydrates. Three-quarters of our body weight is water, which accounts for more hydrogen and oxygen. Nitrogen is found in proteins, whereas calcium, together with phosphorus and oxygen, is found in bones.

1.2 Symbols

A system of symbols was developed so that chemical reactions could be written down in shorthand form. The initial letter, or the initial plus one other letter, of an element is used to represent one atom of it, e.g. C is the symbol for carbon and Ca is the symbol for calcium. In some cases, the Latin names are used, e.g. Fe is the symbol for iron (ferrum). A full list of symbols will be in your course text.

1.3 Chemical Changes and Changes of State

When a new substance is made we say that a **chemical change** has taken place or that a chemical reaction has occurred, e.g.

$$2Mg(s) + O_2(g) \rightarrow 2MgO(s)$$

Magnesium oxide is a new substance formed by the reaction of magnesium with oxygen.

Heating some substances simply produces a change of state and no new substance is formed (see Example 1.3).

1.4 The Separation of Mixtures

The separation of mixtures is generally comparatively easy, the method chosen depending on the nature of the substances to be separated.

(a) To Obtain a Solute from a Solution

(i) Evaporation

A **solution** consists of a **solute** dissolved in a **solvent**, e.g. sea water is a solution of salt (the solute) in water (the solvent). If sea water is heated in the apparatus shown in Fig. 1.3 (a), the water evaporates and salt is left. The final heating may be carried out using a steam bath (Fig. 1.3 (b)) to avoid loss of salt by spitting.

(a)

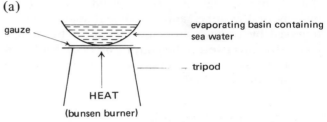

(b)

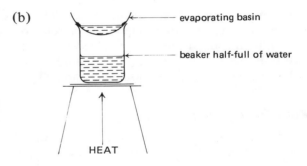

Fig. 1.3

(ii) Crystallisation

The main disadvantage of evaporating all of the solvent from a solution in order to obtain the solute is that if there are any dissolved impurities present, they will be obtained with the solid at the end of the experiment. This problem is avoided if crystallisation is carried out. The solution is evaporated to crystallisation point, i.e. the point at which crystals of solute will form on cooling the solution to room temperature. Drops of solution are removed at intervals and allowed to cool; the formation of crystals in one of these drops indicates that the solution is at crystallisation point. If the solution is allowed to cool, crystals form and can then be filtered out, washed and dried.

(b) To Separate a Solid from a Liquid

(i) Filtration

This method uses the apparatus shown in Fig. 1.4 to separate a solid from a liquid. The solid is left on the filter paper as the residue while the liquid passes through and is collected in the evaporating basin as the filtrate.

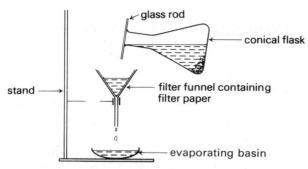

Fig. 1.4

A centrifuge can also be used. A tube of mixture is spun round at high speed. The solid settles to the bottom of the tube, and the liquid may then be removed by using a dropping pipette or by decantation. **Decantation** is the pouring off of a clear liquid after a substance held in suspension has settled to the bottom of the container.

(c) To Separate Two Solids

(i) Sublimation

Sublimation is the direct conversion of a solid to a vapour on heating and of a vapour to a solid on cooling, without going through the liquid state.

Since only a few solids sublime (e.g. ammonium chloride), this method of separation is very limited.

(ii) Paper Chromatography

Paper chromatography is used to separate a mixture of similar solids dissolved in a solvent (see Example 1.4), e.g. it can be used to separate the dyes in ink. A small drop of ink is placed in the centre of a piece of filter paper. Water passes over the ink and the dyes separate into rings of different substances. The separation depends on differences in (a) the solubilities of the dyes in water, and (b) the tendencies of the dyes to stick to the surface of the paper. Chromatography can also be used to separate colourless substances but in this case the paper must be developed by spraying it with another chemical so that the position of the solids can be seen.

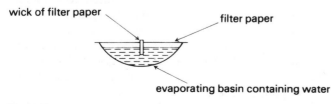

Fig. 1.5

(d) To Separate a Solvent from a Solution

(i) Distillation

For this separation the apparatus shown in Fig. 1.6 is used.

When the solution is boiled, the solvent changes to vapour. The vapour passes down a condenser where it is converted back to liquid and is collected as the distillate in the beaker.

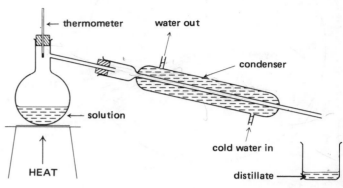

Fig. 1.6

(e) To Separate Two Liquids

(i) Fractional Distillation

Miscible liquids (i.e. ones that mix together completely and do not form layers) may be separated by fractional distillation provided that their boiling points are different.

Important applications of fractional distillation include:
(a) the separation of liquid air into oxygen, nitrogen, etc. (see Section 9.2);
(b) the separation of crude oil into petrol, paraffin, etc. (see Section 18.4);
(c) the manufacture of spirits (e.g. gin, whisky, brandy) (see Section 18.5).

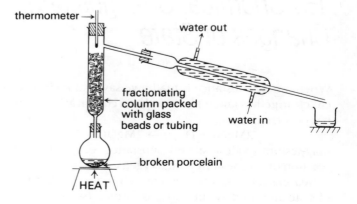

Fig. 1.7 Apparatus for fractional distillation

1.5 Tests for Purity

Pure substances usually have definite sharp melting points and boiling points and the addition of only a trace of an impurity will alter these values. The presence of dissolved solid impurities raises the boiling point of a liquid and lowers the melting point of a solid, making it less sharp.

1.6 Worked Examples

Example 1.1

Which one of the following groups consists only of compounds?

A Cl_2 HCl $MgCl_2$ C_6H_5Cl
B $CaSO_4$ H_2S S_8 Na_2S
C MnO_2 PH_3 XeF_4 O_2
D $KMnO_4$ H_2SO_4 HNO_3 HCl
E NH_3 N_2 $NaNO_3$ CH_3NH_2

The answer is **D**.

> Cl_2, S_8, O_2 and N_2 are all the formulae for elements because each one consists of atoms of the same type.

Example 1.2

The table below gives some information about five elements.

	Element	Melting point/°C	Boiling point/°C
A	Calcium	850	1487
B	Gold	1063	2970
C	Silicon	1410	2360
D	Sulphur	113	445
E	Zinc	420	907

Which element is a liquid at 1000°C?

The answer is **A**.

> At 1000°C calcium has melted but has not yet boiled; it must be a liquid.

Example 1.3

Classify the following as chemical changes or changes of state:

(i) the boiling of water;
This is a change of state; the water has changed to steam.
(ii) the decaying of plants on a compost heap;
This is a chemical change; the plants rot on the compost heap and become totally new substances.
(iii) the melting of lead.   **(6)**
This is a change of state; solid lead has turned to liquid but no new substance has been formed.

Example 1.4

(a) From the list below choose the process shown by each diagram.
chromatography   distillation   evaporation   filtration

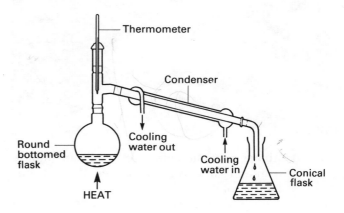

Process **A** is *distillation*.   **(1)**

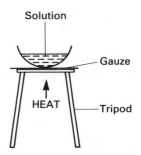

Process **B** is *evaporation*.   **(1)**

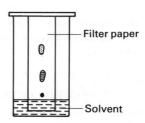

Process **C** is *chromatography*.   **(1)**

(b) Choose which process, **A**, **B** or **C**, you could use to separate:

(i) pure water from sea water;   **(1)**

Process **A**

(ii) a blue dye from a mixture of dyes.   **(1)**

Process **C**

(SEG, June 1988, Paper 1, Q1)

Example 1.5

(a) (i) Above is a photograph of a pile of impure common salt covered with tiles. The salt contains insoluble impurities.

From the processes listed below choose and then write in the correct order those which you would use to obtain crystals of pure common salt.

> crystallise
> evaporate
> filter
> mix with water

Mix with water, filter, evaporate.

(ii) Give one reason why the salt is covered with tiles.   **(4)**

To protect the salt from rain.

> Salt is soluble in water.

(b) Give one reason why common salt is used in the food industry.   **(1)**

Flavouring (or preserving).

(c) An insoluble magnesium compound is added to table salt to make it 'free running'. The magnesium compound gives off carbon dioxide when an acid is added to it. Name the magnesium compound.   **(1)**

Magnesium carbonate.

> Carbonate + acid → a salt + carbon dioxide + water

(d) When the magnesium compound in table salt is eaten it reacts with the dilute hydrochloric acid in the stomach. Name the magnesium salt formed in this reaction.   **(1)**

> $MgCO_3(s) + 2HCl(aq) \rightarrow MgCl_2(aq) + H_2O(l) + CO_2(g)$

(MEG, June 1988, Paper 2, Q2)

Magnesium chloride.

Example 1.6

Name the methods you would use to carry out each of the following separations, explaining briefly the principles upon which your methods rely:

(i) a sample of elderberry wine from a mixture of it with solid yeast residues;   **(2)**

Filtration (see Section 1.4). The elderberry wine will pass through the filter paper but the yeast residues, being insoluble, will remain in the filter paper.

(ii) reasonably pure ethanol from elderberry wine;   **(3)**

Elderberry wine will contain ethanol and water together with a number of other substances. Since these substances have different boiling points they may be separated by fractional distillation (see Section 1.4).

(iii) blue copper sulphate crystals from aqueous copper sulphate.   **(2)**

Crystallisation. Some of the water must be evaporated so that crystals will form on cooling the solution to room temperature.

(OLE)

Example 1.7

Which of the following would be the best way to show that a sample of water was pure?

A   Measure its pH.
B   Measure its boiling point.
C   Add it to a sample of pure water to see if the two were miscible.
D   Use cobalt chloride paper.
E   Use white copper(II) sulphate.

The answer is **B**.

> Cobalt chloride paper turns pink and white copper (II) sulphate turns blue in the presence of water (see Section 10.1). The water may not be pure, however. *Pure* water boils at 100°C at 1 atm pressure.
> **A** is incorrect because many aqueous solutions have the same pH as pure water.

1.7 Self-test Questions

Question 1.1

In the following diagrams ● and ○ represent different atoms.

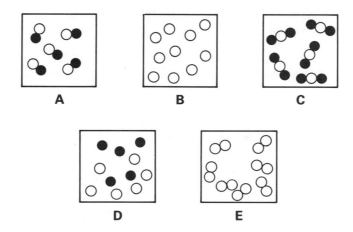

Which diagram represents a mixture of atoms?

(Welsh, June 1988, Paper 1, Q19)

Question 1.2

Use the following list of substances to answer the questions that follow: air, carbon, chlorine, hydrogen, mercury, rock salt, sodium, sulphur, water.
(a) Which metal is a liquid at room temperature and pressure?
(b) Name the two elements present in common salt.
(c) Name a non-metal present in oil.
(d) Which element is yellow in colour?
(e) Name an element used in street lighting.
(f) Name a compound.
(g) Name a mixture.   (7)

Question 1.3

Complete the following statements:
(a) _____ is the process of separating a liquid from a solid sediment by pouring.
(b) _____ is used to separate cream from milk.
(c) A _____ is the solid left on a filter paper.
(d) The _____ is the liquid that passes through a filter paper.
(e) The process of _____ a liquid and then _____ the vapour is known as _____ .   (7)

Questions 1.4–1.7 are about practical procedures:

    A   Distillation
    B   Electrolysis
    C   Filtration
    D   Paper chromatography
    E   Titration

Select from the list above the most suitable procedure for carrying out the following processes.

Question 1.4

In food analysis, to show that a bottle of fruit squash may contain several water soluble dyes.   **(1)**

Question 1.5

In the laboratory, to make salts by the exact neutralisation of an alkali by an acid.   **(1)**

Question 1.6

In industry, to separate nitrogen and oxygen from liquid air.   **(1)**

Question 1.7

In a sewage works, to remove insoluble material from water.   **(1)**

(Welsh, June 1988, Paper 1, Q5–8)

Question 1.8

(a) Name the chemical technique which could usefully be used to separate:
   (i)   the mixture of soluble dyes used to colour 'blackcurrant' sweets;
   (ii) water from a solution of sodium chloride in water.   **(1)**
(b) A pupil decides to separate a mixture of the solids calcium hydroxide and ammonium chloride by shaking the mixture with hot water and then filtering. Will this procedure work? Explain your answer.   **(3)(OLE)**

1.8 Answers to Self-test Questions

1.1 **D**.

> Diagrams A, C and E represent molecules. Although diagram B represents atoms, the atoms are of one type only.

1.2 (a) Mercury.
   (b) Chlorine, sodium.
   (c) Carbon or hydrogen.
   (d) Sulphur.
   (e) Sodium.
   (f) Water.
   (g) Air or rock salt.

1.3 (a) Decantation.
   (b) Centrifugation.
   (c) Residue.
   (d) Filtrate.
   (e) Evaporating, condensing, distillation.

1.4 **D**.
1.5 **E**.

> Titration is the process in which dilute acid is run from a burette into a solution of alkali until it is neutral.

1.6 **A**.

> Liquid nitrogen and oxygen have different boiling points.

1.7 **C**.
1.8 (a) (i) chromatography;
      (ii) distillation.
   (b) This procedure will not work. Ammonium chloride is very soluble in hot water but calcium hydroxide is slightly soluble too. Thus, although most of the calcium hydroxide would remain on the filter paper, some would dissolve and contaminate the ammonium chloride in the filtrate.

2 ATOMS AND MOLECULES

Topic Guide

2.1 Introduction

Matter consists of tiny particles, either atoms, or groups of atoms called molecules.

An **atom** is the smallest particle of an element that can exist and still retain the ordinary chemical properties of that element.

Many elements consist of groups of atoms joined together, e.g. oxygen, O_2, sulphur, S_8. In addition, atoms of different elements may join together in groups to form particles of a compound. These groups of atoms are called molecules.

A **molecule** is the smallest particle of an element or compound that can exist naturally and still retain the ordinary chemical properties of that element or compound.

The results of many experiments can be explained in terms of the particle theory of matter and hence they provide evidence to support it, e.g. the dissolving of a solid in a liquid or the mixing of two gases may be interpreted in terms of the intermingling of the particles of the various substances. Crystals of a particular compound all have more or less the same shape. This can easily be understood if we assume that every crystal consists of layers of particles packed together in a regular pattern.

2.2 The States of Matter

Table 2.1 summarises some differences in the structure and properties of solids, liquids and gases.

Table 2.1

	Solid	Liquid	Gas
Ease of compression	Difficult to compress	Difficult to compress	Easy to compress
Molecular packing	Close	Close	Spread out
Shape	Fixed	Variable	Variable
Molecular movement	Vibrate and rotate about fixed points	Free to move	Free to move
Attractive forces	Relatively high	Relatively high	Very small
Diffusion	Very slow	Slow	Rapid

When the temperature of a solid is raised, the particles vibrate more and more violently until they are moving to such an extent that they can no longer be held in an ordered arrangement by the forces of attraction. When this happens the solid melts. Raising the temperature of a liquid increases the speed of movement of the particles until their kinetic energy is sufficient to overcome the forces of attraction between them. At this point the liquid boils. On cooling the reverse changes occur. The particles of the gas gradually slow down as the temperature falls until the forces of attraction are able to condense them together and form a liquid. Cooling the liquid causes further loss of kinetic energy until eventually the particles settle into a solid crystal where they vibrate and rotate about fixed points (see Examples 2.1, 2.2 and 2.3).

2.3 Diffusion

Gases have a tendency to spread in all directions, and this can be explained by the idea that gases are made up of moving particles.

The process of spreading is known as **diffusion**. In general, the denser the gas the slower the diffusion process (see Question 4.2).

2.4 Atomic Structure

Atoms consist of a minute nucleus, where all the positive charge and most of the mass of the atom is concentrated, surrounded by electrons. The nucleus is made up of two types of particle: protons and neutrons.

A **proton** is a positively charged particle, with mass approximately equal to that of a hydrogen atom.

A **neutron** is a neutral particle, with mass approximately equal to that of a hydrogen atom.

An **electron** is a negatively charged particle, its charge being equal but opposite to that of a proton, and its mass approximately 1/1840 of that of a proton.

Since atoms are electrically neutral, the numbers of protons and electrons in an atom must be equal.

The number of protons in the nucleus of an atom is its **atomic number** and gives its position in the periodic table.

The total number of protons and neutrons in an atom is its **mass number**.

Information about the atomic number and mass number of an element can be given with its symbol. Thus $^{12}_{6}C$ represents an atom of carbon with an atomic number of 6 and a mass number of 12.

(a) Arrangement of Electrons (see Example 2.5 and Question 2.3)

The electrons surround the nucleus and are found at varying distances from it in groups known as energy levels or 'shells'. Each shell contains electrons with similar energies and can contain up to a certain maximum number. The first shell, nearest the nucleus, can contain up to two electrons, the second up to eight and the third up to 18. For example, a potassium atom, atomic number 19, will have the electron arrangement shown in Fig. 2.1.

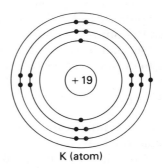

K (atom)

Fig. 2.1

There is a special stability associated with having eight electrons in a shell. Thus, in a potassium atom, there are eight electrons in the third shell and one in the fourth shell even though the third is not full.

Table 3.1 (page 24) shows the atomic structures of the most common isotopes of the first 20 elements.

(b) Isotopes (see Example 2.6)

It is the number of protons in the nucleus of an atom that identifies it. However, it is possible to have atoms of the same element with different numbers of neutrons in their nuclei. They are called **isotopes**, e.g.

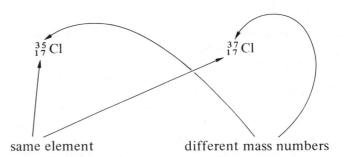

same element   different mass numbers

2.5 Radioactivity

All atoms with atomic numbers greater than 83, together with some of the lighter ones, are radioactive. This means that their nuclei are unstable and split up, emitting radiation which is of three distinct types – α, β and γ. When either an α- or a β-particle is emitted, the remaining nucleus usually has an excess amount of energy. This extra energy is given out in the form of γ-rays, which are like X-rays but with an even shorter wavelength. When the nucleus of a radioactive atom gives off an α- or a β-particle, an atom of a new element is formed. If this new atom is stable, the disintegration process stops, but if it is radioactive, then the splitting-up process continues. Some of these radioactive nuclei (radioisotopes) occur naturally but others are made in nuclear reactors.

(a) Half-life

The **half-life** of an isotope is the time taken for the number of radioactive nuclei to be reduced to half the initial value (see Example 2.7).

(b) The Uses of Radioactive Isotopes

1. Nuclear power stations generate electricity from the energy produced when isotopes like uranium-235 decay. Uranium-235 absorbs neutrons to form uranium-236 and then nuclear fission occurs according to the following equation:

$$\, ^{1}_{0}n + \, ^{235}_{92}U \rightarrow [\, ^{236}_{92}U] \rightarrow \, ^{89}_{36}Kr + \, ^{144}_{56}Ba + 3\, ^{1}_{0}n$$

   The neutrons emitted can cause the fission of more uranium atoms and so produce more and more neutrons. The controlled production of neutrons releases a considerable amount of heat energy which can be used to generate electricity (see Example 2.8).
2. In living animals and plants the percentage of the radioactive isotope $\, ^{14}_{6}C$ (carbon-14) remains constant because it is continually being replaced from the carbon dioxide in the air and from food. In dead tissue this does not happen so the percentage of $\, ^{14}_{6}C$ gradually decreases as the isotope decays. Hence by comparing the percentage of carbon-14 in a dead sample with that in living matter, the age of the sample can be found.
3. If radioactive compounds are injected into a patient, the functioning of glands and the flow of blood around the body may be checked by means of a Geiger counter or some other detecting device.
4. Cancer may be cured in some cases by killing the cancerous cells by exposing them to the penetrating power of radiation (see Example 2.6).
5. γ-radiation will completely destroy bacteria and so can be used to sterilise surgical equipment.
6. Radioactive sources also have a number of industrial uses, e.g. to test for leaks in pipelines by allowing a solution of a radioactive isotope to flow through the pipe and measuring the radioactivity of the surrounding soil.

(c) The Dangers of Radiation

Radioisotopes have some potentially harmful effects. The most penetrating radiation is γ-radiation, but all radioactive sources must be handled with care since radiation kills all living cells. One of the problems associated with radioactive material is in the disposal of waste. Some radioisotopes have long half-lives and so can emit radiation for many years after they are no longer needed. Some radioactive waste is recycled into useful material but otherwise it must be stored in lead containers until it is no longer harmful.

2.6 Worked Examples

Example 2.1

The diagram below shows a substance as a solid, liquid and gas.

(a) Complete the diagram to show how the particles are arranged in liquids and gases. The diagram for solids has been done for you.   **(2)**

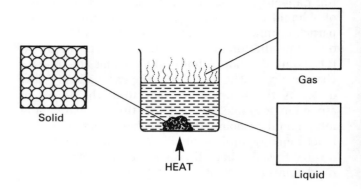

The diagram should be completed as shown:

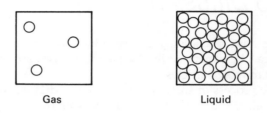

> In a gas, the particles are well separated but in a liquid they are close together although they are not arranged in a regular manner as in a solid.

(b) (i) What happens to the particles when the liquid boils?   **(2)**
The particles have sufficient energy to escape from the surface of the liquid and pass into the gas state.
    (ii) What is the change called when a solid becomes liquid?   **(1)**
Melting.

               (SEG, June 1988, Paper 1, Q2)

Example 2.2

Give TWO ways in which the ions in an ionic lattice may be made free to move.   **(2)**
Melting the ionic solid or dissolving it in water enables the ions to move.

                       (SUJB)

Example 2.3

This question is about changing naphthalene from solid to liquid. Naphthalene, $C_{10}H_8$, is a white crystalline solid. 6.4 g of naphthalene crystals were weighed and placed in a test tube together with a thermometer. The tube was placed in a beaker of boiling water and a stop-clock was started. The water was kept boiling and the naphthalene crystals were stirred continuously with the thermometer. The temperature of the naphthalene was recorded every 15 seconds. The results are shown in Fig. 2.2.

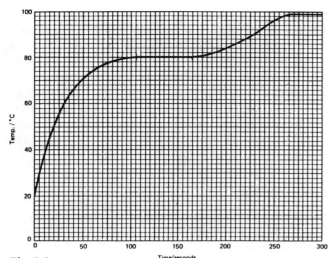

Fig. 2.2

(a) What was the boiling point of the water? **(1)**

99°C.

> The maximum constant temperature obtained
> must be the boiling point of the water.

(b) What was the melting point of the naphthalene? **(1)**

80°C.

(c) Explain why the temperature of the naphthalene
remained constant from 105 seconds to 165
seconds even though the water was kept boiling. **(2)**

*Since the water was kept boiling, heat was being supplied to
the naphthalene. This was used up in overcoming the forces
holding the particles together in the solid lattice (i.e. energy
was used up in pulling the particles apart). The temperature
remained constant until all of the solid had melted.*

(d) Describe how the movement of the naphthalene
molecules changes within the crystals during the
first 30 seconds of heating. **(2)**

*As the temperature increases, the naphthalene molecules
vibrate more vigorously about fixed points.*

(e) On Fig. 2.2, sketch the curve you would expect to
obtain if the test tube and naphthalene were

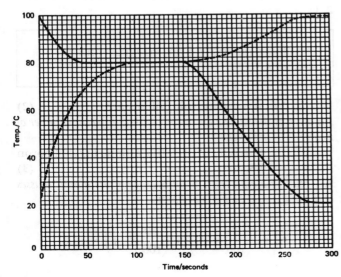

Fig. 2.3

removed from the beaker of boiling water and
placed in a beaker of water at 20°C, the temperature of the naphthalene being recorded at regular
intervals of time. Begin your graph at time = 0 s.
  (3)

The answer is given in Fig. 2.3.

(f) Calculate the number of moles of naphthalene
molecules used in the experiment. (Relative atomic masses: C = 12, H = 1) **(2)**

> See Section 5.1 if you do not understand the
> calculation which follows.

$$\text{Molar mass of naphthalene } (C_{10}H_8) = (10 \times 12) + (8 \times 1)$$
$$= 128\,g\,mol^{-1}$$
$$\text{Moles of naphthalene} = \frac{mass}{molar\ mass}$$
$$= \frac{6.4}{128}$$
$$= 0.05$$
  (L)

Example 2.4

The following table gives the atomic structures of a
number of different atoms. Which one is the structure
of an atom of mass number 12?

	Atomic Structure		
	Protons	Electrons	Neutrons
A	3	3	4
B	6	6	6
C	10	10	12
D	11	11	12
E	12	12	12

The answer is **B**.

> The mass number is found by adding together the
> numbers of neutrons and protons in the nucleus.

Example 2.5

The table gives some information concerning the
structures of four atoms, W, X, Y and Z. Work out the
missing figures (a) to (l).

	Atomic number	Mass number	Number of protons	Number of neutrons	Electronic configuration
W	19	39	(a)	(b)	(c)
X	(d)	20	10	(e)	(f)
Y	(g)	(h)	6	6	(i)
Z	(j)	(k)	(l)	8	2.4

  (1 each)

*(a) 19 (b) 20 (c) 2.8.8.1 (d) 10 (e) 10 (f) 2.8
(g) 6 (h) 12 (i) 2.4 (j) 6 (k) 14 (l) 6*

Use the letters W, X, Y, Z when answering the
following questions.

(a) Which is the atom of a noble gas? **(1)**

X.

> X has a full outer shell of 8 electrons and must be in Group 0.

(b) Which two atoms are isotopes of the same element? **(1)**
Y and Z.

> Both have the same number of protons in their nuclei.

(c) Which is a metal atom? **(1)**
W.

> W has one electron in its outermost shell and so is in Group 1 and hence is a metal.

Example 2.6

(a) Chlorine has two common isotopes with symbols $^{35}_{17}Cl$ and $^{37}_{17}Cl$.
   (i) Using chlorine as an example, explain the meaning of the term *isotope*.
Isotopes are atoms of the same element with different numbers of neutrons in their nuclei. Both $^{35}_{17}Cl$ and $^{37}_{17}Cl$ have 17 protons and 17 electrons but $^{35}_{17}Cl$ has 18 neutrons whereas $^{37}_{17}Cl$ has 20 neutrons.
   (ii) Explain why chlorine, whether as the element or in its compounds, always has a relative atomic mass of about 35.5. **(4)**
The relative atomic mass is the average mass of one of the atoms and has to take into account the relative abundances of the various isotopes. Natural chlorine always contains about 3/4 $^{35}_{17}Cl$ and 1/4 $^{37}_{17}Cl$.
Therefore, relative atomic mass = (3/4 x 35) + (1/4 x 37)
                                    = 35.5

> See Section 5.1.

(b) Some radioactive isotopes are playing increasingly important roles in medicine. Write down the name of **one** such isotope and briefly describe its use in medicine. **(2)**
Cobalt-60 gives off intense γ-radiation which can be used to destroy cancerous growths.

(OLE)

Example 2.7

(a) Explain what is meant by the term 'half-life'. **(3)**
The half-life of an isotope is the time taken for the number of radioactive nuclei to be reduced to half the initial value.
(b) The half-life of iodine-131 is 8 days. How much iodine-131 will be left after 8 days if you have an initial mass of 1 g? **(1)**
½ g.
(c) Name one naturally occurring radioactive metal which is used in nuclear power stations. **(1)**
Uranium.
(d) Name one radioactive metal which is made in a nuclear reactor and is used in nuclear power stations. **(1)**
Plutonium.
(e) Most of our electricity is obtained from nuclear power stations or by burning fuels. Give two other sources of energy which can be used to generate electricity. **(2)**
Any two of moving water, wind or sunlight.

Example 2.8

Many power stations convert heat to electrical energy. In a nuclear power station the heat comes from the fission of uranium.
(a) Complete the table by correctly adding the missing information for the uranium-238 isotope.

Isotope	$\underset{\text{atomic number}}{\overset{\text{mass number}}{\text{Symbol}}}$	Number of protons	Number of neutrons	Number of electrons
Uranium-235	$^{235}_{92}U$	92	143	92
Uranium-238		92		92

(2)
The missing information is $^{238}_{92}U$ and 146 neutrons.
(b) The uranium-235 isotope will undergo fission by bombardment with neutrons. The nuclear change can be represented by this equation.
$^{235}_{92}U + 1\ \text{neutron} \rightarrow\ ^{89}_{36}Kr\ +\ ^{144}_{56}X + 3\ \text{neutrons}$
   (i) Why is this equation called a nuclear change and not a chemical change? **(2)**
Different atoms are being formed with different nuclei; it is not just a rearrangement of atoms.
   (ii) Use the periodic table in your Data Booklet to find out which element is represented by $^{144}_{56}X$. **(1)**
Barium, $^{144}_{56}Ba$
(c) The control rods in a nuclear reactor often contain boron. Natural boron contains about 20% boron-10 ($^{10}_{5}B$) and 80% boron-11 ($^{11}_{5}B$). **(1)**
   (i) Give the electronic structure of a boron atom.
2.3

> The atomic number is 5 and so it must have 5 electrons.

   (ii) What is the meaning of *isotope*? **(2)**
An atom of the same element but with a different number of neutrons in the nucleus.
   (iii) Explain why the relative atomic mass of boron is 10.8. **(3)**
The relative atomic mass is an average of the atomic masses of the individual atoms. For boron:

$$A_r = \left(\frac{20}{100} \times 10\right) + \left(\frac{80}{100} \times 11\right) = 10.8$$

(SEG, June 1988, Paper 3, Q3)

2.7 Self-test Questions

Question 2.1

The diagrams below show two atoms and two ions.

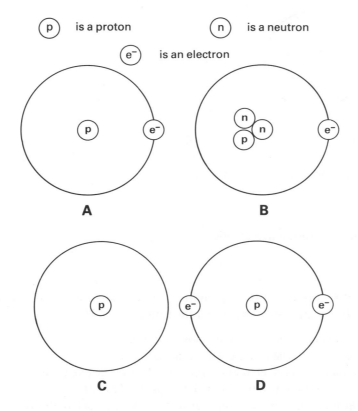

(a) Which of **A**, **B**, **C** or **D** has a mass number of 3?   **(1)**
(b) Which two diagrams show atoms?   **(2)**
(c) Which diagram shows a positive ion?   **(1)**
(d) Why are **A** and **B** diagrams of isotopes of the same element?   **(1)**

(MEG, June 1988, Paper 2, Q3)

Question 2.2

An atom contains 11 electrons, 11 protons and 12 neutrons. What is its mass number?

    A   11
    B   12
    C   22
    D   23
    E   34

Use your periodic table (p. 24) to answer **Questions 2.3–2.5.**

Question 2.3

Which atom has the electron arrangement shown in the diagram?

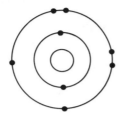

Question 2.4

How many protons are present in an atom of magnesium?

Question 2.5

How many electrons are present in a chloride ion (Cl^-)?

Question 2.6

The isotope $^{14}_{6}C$ (i) is radioactive, (ii) is a β-emitter, (iii) has a half-life of 5730 years.
  Which **one** of the following statements about the isotope is true?

    A   It is used to generate electricity in a power station.
    B   In 5730 years, 1 g of the isotope will decay to 0.25 g.
    C   The mass number of the element formed by the radioactive decay is 12.
    D   The radiation emitted will be stopped by a piece of paper.
    E   The atomic number of the element formed by the radioactive decay is 7.

(Welsh, June 1988, Paper 1, Q17)

2.8 Answers to Self-test Questions

2.1 (a) **B**.
   (b) **A** and **B**.

> The number of protons equals the number of electrons.

   (c) **C**.

> There is one proton but no electrons.

   (d) Isotopes are atoms containing the same number of protons (and electrons) but different numbers of neutrons.

2.2 **D**.
2.3 Oxygen.
2.4 12.
2.5 18.

> A chlorine atom has 17 electrons and so the extra electron present in the ion makes 18.

2.6 **E**.

> The decay process is:
> $$^{14}_{6}C \rightarrow \, ^{0}_{-1}e + \, ^{14}_{7}N$$
> β-particle.

2.9 Grading of Self-test Questions

The questions in Section 2.7 are all relatively straightforward and will be found in the compulsory part of the examination paper, although Question 2.6 on radioactivity is not covered by all syllabuses – check with your syllabus to see if you need to know about radioactivity.

The total number of marks for this section is 10 and the marks/grades will be something like:

8 or more marks ——————— at least C grade (A and B grades are obtained from marks on harder questions – see Section 4.7).
6 marks ——————— around E grade.
4 marks ——————— around G grade.

THE PERIODIC TABLE

Topic Guide

3.1 Introduction

The periodic table is obtained by arranging the elements in order of increasing atomic number and placing them in rows so that similar elements fall into vertical columns (see page 26). The horizontal rows are called *periods* and the vertical columns are called *groups*.

Table 3.1 shows that atoms of similar elements, such as sodium and potassium, have the same numbers of electrons in their outermost shells.

For the outer blocks of the periodic table the number of electrons in the outermost shells of the atoms is the same as the number of the group in which they are found.

Hydrogen and helium do not fit properly into any of the groups and are often separated from the rest of the table.

When element 21 is reached the electronic structures of the atoms become more complicated and a centre block of *transition elements* has to be added.

Several of the groups have 'family' names: group I elements are called the *alkali metals*, groups II elements are the *alkaline earths*, group VII elements are the *halogens* and group 0 (plus helium) the *noble gases*.

Table 3.1

Element	Atomic number	Number of neutrons	Mass number	Electronic arrangement
Hydrogen	1	0	1	**1**
Helium	2	2	4	**2**
Lithium	3	4	7	2.**1**
Beryllium	4	5	9	2.**2**
Boron	5	6	11	2.**3**
Carbon	6	6	12	2.**4**
Nitrogen	7	7	14	2.**5**
Oxygen	8	8	16	2.**6**
Fluorine	9	10	19	2.**7**
Neon	10	10	20	2.**8**
Sodium	11	12	23	2.8.**1**
Magnesium	12	12	24	2.8.**2**
Aluminium	13	14	27	2.8.**3**
Silicon	14	14	28	2.8.**4**
Phosphorus	15	16	31	2.8.**5**
Sulphur	16	16	32	2.8.**6**
Chlorine	17	18 or 20	35 or 37	2.8.**7**
Argon	18	22	40	2.8.**8**
Potassium	19	20	39	2.8.8.**1**
Calcium	20	20	40	2.8.8.**2**

3.2 The Noble Gases

Atoms of the noble gases (group 0 plus helium) have very stable electronic structures. For this reason they exist singly rather than being joined in pairs and form very few compounds. The attraction between the atoms is very small, giving the noble gases very low boiling points.

3.3 Trends in Properties Going Across a Period (Outer Blocks Only)

Going across a period the elements change from metals to non-metals.

The valencies (see Section 5.1) of the elements in groups I–IV are equal to the group numbers: for the elements in groups V–VII they are usually equal to 8 minus the group number (e.g. for magnesium in group II, the valency is 2; for nitrogen, in group V, the valency is $8 - 5 = 3$). In oxides, the valencies of the elements in groups V–VII can sometimes be equal to the group numbers (see Table 3.2).

3.4 Trends in Properties Going Down a Group

The changes found on going down a group are less marked than those seen in going across a period, since all members of a particular group have the same number of electrons in the outermost shells of their atoms. There are three important trends:
(1) The metallic nature of the elements increases as a group is descended. This is most noticeable in group IV, which starts with the non-metal carbon and ends with the metal lead.
(2) The reactivity of *metals* increases down a group (see Example 3.2).

(3) The reactivity of *non-metals* decreases down a group.

3.5 The Transition Elements

These are all metals but, except for the first and last members of each row, they differ from the outer block metals in a number of important ways:
(1) They have relatively high melting points and densities.
(2) They form coloured compounds (e.g. copper(II) sulphate).
(3) They can have more than one valency (e.g. iron(II) and iron(III)).
(4) Both the metals and their compounds can act as catalysts (e.g. platinum in the oxidation of ammonia and manganese(IV) oxide in the decomposition of hydrogen peroxide).

3.6 Worked Examples

Example 3.1

Consider the following information about an imaginary new element named bodium, symbol Bo, which has recently been discovered.

Bodium is a solid at room temperature but is easily cut with a knife to reveal a shiny surface which rapidly tarnishes. It reacts vigorously with water liberating a flammable gas and forming a solution with a high pH value. When bodium reacts with chlorine, it forms a white solid containing 29.5% by mass of chlorine. $A_r(Bo) = 85$.
(a) Calculate the empirical formula of bodium chloride. **(3)**

$$
\begin{array}{lcc}
 & Bo & : Cl \\
ratio\ of\ g & 70.5 & : 29.5 \\
ratio\ of\ mol & \dfrac{70.5}{85} & : \dfrac{29.5}{35.5} \\
 & = 0.829 & : 0.831 \\
 & \approx\quad 1 & : 1
\end{array}
$$

$\therefore$ *empirical formula of bodium chloride is* $BoCl$

Empirical formula calculations are explained in Example 5.3.

Table 3.2

Element	Sodium	Magnesium	Aluminium	Silicon	Phosphorus	Sulphur	Chlorine	Argon
Appearance	Silvery metal	Silvery metal	Silvery metal	Black solid	Yellow solid	Yellow solid	Greenish gas	Colourless gas
Electronic structure	2.8.1	2.8.2	2.8.3	2.8.4	2.8.5	2.8.6	2.8.7	2.8.8
Most common valency	1	2	3	4	3	2	1	0
Oxide	Na_2O	MgO	Al_2O_3	SiO_2	P_4O_{10}	SO_3	Cl_2O_7	—
Melting point of oxide/°C	1193	3075	2045	1728	563	30	−91	—
Bonding and structure of oxide	←———— Giant ionic lattice ————→			Giant atomic lattice (covalent)	←———— Covalent molecules ————→			—
Nature of oxide	←— Decreasingly basic —→ Amphoteric				←———— Increasingly acidic ————→			—

(b) To which group in the periodic table should bodium be assigned?   **(1)**

Bodium should be assigned to Group I.

(c) What type of bonding is likely to be present in bodium chloride?   **(1)**

Ionic bonding will be present in bodium chloride.

(d) If concentrated aqueous bodium chloride were electrolysed, what would be the main products discharged at carbon electrodes? Write equations for the reactions that take place.   **(4)**

At the anode the product would be chlorine.

$$2Cl^-(aq) - 2e^- \rightarrow Cl_2(g)$$

At the cathode the product would be hydrogen.

$$2H^+(aq) + 2e^- \rightarrow H_2(g)$$

(e) Write an equation and name the products for the reaction between bodium and water.   **(2)**

$$2Bo(s) + 2H_2O(l) \rightarrow 2BoOH(aq) + H_2(g)$$

The products are bodium hydroxide solution and hydrogen.

(f) Write the formula for (i) bodium nitrate and (ii) bodium carbonate. For each of these compounds, state whether it would be expected to decompose at bunsen burner temperature. Name any product(s) and write an equation for any reaction which occurs.   **(5)**

(i) $BoNO_3$ *Bodium nitrate would decompose at bunsen burner temperature into bodium nitrite and oxygen.*

$$2BoNO_3(l) \rightarrow 2BoNO_2(l) + O_2(g)$$

(ii) Bo_2CO_3 *Bodium carbonate would not decompose at bunsen burner temperatures.*

(AEB, 1983)

From the information given, bodium is similar to potassium and sodium. Answers (b)–(f) are obtained by considering what would happen in corresponding circumstances to potassium, sodium and their compounds. The two metals are in group I of the periodic table, their chlorides are ionic (Section 4.1) and electrolysis of their aqueous chlorides gives chlorine and hydrogen (Section 6.2). Their reactions with water and the effect of heat on their nitrates and carbonates are given in Sections 12.1 and 12.2.

Example 3.2

The diagram shows the first 20 elements in the periodic table. One of the elements is represented by X which is not its usual chemical symbol.

(a) (i) State the name and chemical symbol of the element represented by X.   **(1)**

Argon, Ar

(ii) Why does this element form no chemical compounds?   **(1)**

The atoms contain the stable arrangement of 8 electrons in their outermost shells.

(b) (i) Complete the following table:

Element	Atomic number	Electronic structure of atom
Magnesium	12	2.8.2
Fluorine	9	2.7

(2)

(ii) Magnesium and fluorine react to form the ionic compound, magnesium fluoride. Show, by a diagram or otherwise, the electronic changes that take place in this reaction and give the electronic structure and formulae of the ions formed.   **(3)**

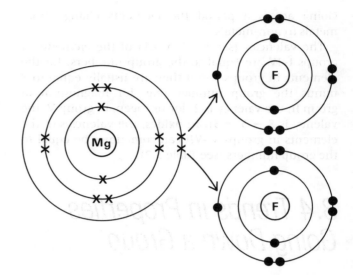

See Section 4.1 if you are unfamiliar with ionic bonding.

Name of ion formed	Electronic structure	Formula
Magnesium	2.8	Mg^{2+}
Fluoride	2.8	F^-

The magnesium atom has lost its two outer electrons and so the ion has the electron arrangement 2.8. The fluorine atom has gained an electron and so its ion also has the electron arrangement 2.8.

H																	He
Li	Be											B	C	N	O	F	Ne
Na	Mg											Al	Si	P	S	Cl	X
K	Ca																

(c) In the group of alkali metals, lithium (Li), sodium (Na), potassium (K), the element that follows potassium is rubidium (Rb).

    (i) What would you expect to see if a very small piece of rubidium was added to water? **(2)**

Very violent reaction: the rubidium melts and shoots all over the surface of the water.

    (ii) Give a word equation for the reaction occurring in (i). **(1)**

Rubidium + water → rubidium hydroxide solution + hydrogen.

    (iii) What would be the best way of storing rubidium in the laboratory? Give one reason for your answer. **(2)**

Under oil since rubidium reacts with water and air.

              (Welsh, June 1988, Paper 1, Q35)

Example 3.3

Three elements X, Y and Z, are in the same period of the periodic table. The accompanying table gives some data concerning the elements and their oxides. One of the elements forms another oxide in addition to that listed.

Element	X	Y	Z
Appearance	Shiny black solid	Silvery solid	Yellow crystals
Oxide	White solid, XO_2	White solid, YO	White solid, ZO_3

Use the letters X, Y and Z in answering the following questions. Do not try to identify the elements.

(a) What is the valency of each element in its oxide? **(3)**

Valencies are: X=4, Y=2, Z=6.

(b) Write the letters X, Y and Z in the order in which the elements appear in the period. **(1)**

Y, X, Z.

> Because valency = group number (Section 3.3).

(c) To which groups do the elements belong? **(3)**

Y *is in group II, X is in group IV, Z is in group VI.*

(d) Write the formulae of the compounds which the elements would form with hydrogen. **(3)**

YH_2, XH_4, ZH_2

(e) Which element would be the best conductor of electricity? **(1)**

Y.

> Because it is in group II and therefore is a metal.

(f) Which oxide is most likely to be ionic? **(1)**

The oxide of Y.

> Because Y is a metal.

Example 3.4

The group in the periodic table which contains the element with eleven protons in its nucleus is

A 1
B 2
C 3
D 5
E 7

The answer is **A**.

              (AEB, 1982)

> Because the atoms have eleven electrons, arranged 2. 8. 1 and the number of electrons in the outermost shell gives the group number for the outer block elements.

3.7 Self-test Questions

Question 3.1

Which of the following contains three elements in the same group of the periodic table?

  A   lithium, sodium, magnesium
  B   fluorine, oxygen, nitrogen
  C   chlorine, bromine, iodine
  D   sodium, magnesium, aluminium
  E   oxygen, sulphur, chlorine

Question 3.2

Elements which are in the same group of the periodic table:

  A   are found in the same state at room temperature
  B   have the same number of neutrons in the nucleus
  C   have the same number of electron shells
  D   have the same physical properties
  E   have the same outer shell electron arrangement

Question 3.3

Zirconium is a transition metal. It is therefore likely to:

  A   react with cold water
  B   form a coloured chloride
  C   float on water
  D   have only one valency
  E   be stored under oil because it reacts with air

3.8 Answers to Self-test Questions

3.1 **C.**
3.2 **E.**
3.3 **B.**

Forming coloured compounds is a typical property of transition metals. Try to think of the other typical properties – Section 3.5 should help you if you get stuck.

The Periodic Table of the Elements

						H Hydrogen 1											**He** Helium 2
Li Lithium 3	**Be** Beryllium 4											**B** Boron 5	**C** Carbon 6	**N** Nitrogen 7	**O** Oxygen 8	**F** Fluorine 9	**Ne** Neon 10
Na Sodium 11	**Mg** Magnesium 12											**AL** Aluminium 13	**Si** Silicon 14	**P** Phosphorus 15	**S** Sulphur 16	**Cl** Chlorine 17	**Ar** Argon 18
K Potassium 19	**Ca** Calcium 20	**Sc** Scandium 21	**Ti** Titanium 22	**V** Vanadium 23	**Cr** Chromium 24	**Mn** Manganese 25	**Fe** Iron 26	**Co** Cobalt 27	**Ni** Nickel 28	**Cu** Copper 29	**Zn** Zinc 30	**Ga** Gallium 31	**Ge** Germanium 32	**As** Arsenic 33	**Se** Selenium 34	**Br** Bromine 35	**Kr** Krypton 36
Rb Rubidium 37	**Sr** Strontium 38	**Y** Yttrium 39	**Zr** Zirconium 40	**Nb** Niobium 41	**Mo** Molybdenum 42	**Tc** Technetium 43	**Ru** Ruthenium 44	**Rh** Rhodium 45	**Pd** Palladium 46	**Ag** Silver 47	**Cd** Cadmium 48	**In** Indium 49	**Sn** Tin 50	**Sb** Antimony 51	**Te** Tellurium 52	**I** Iodine 53	**Xe** Xenon 54
Cs Caesium 55	**Ba** Barium 56	**La** Lanthanum 57	**Hf** Hafnium 72	**Ta** Tantalum 73	**W** Tungsten 74	**Re** Rhenium 75	**Os** Osmium 76	**Ir** Iridium 77	**Pt** Platinum 78	**Au** Gold 79	**Hg** Mercury 80	**Tl** Thallium 81	**Pb** Lead 82	**Bi** Bismuth 83	**Po** Polonium 84	**At** Astatine 85	**Rn** Radon 86
Fr Francium 87	**Ra** Radium 88	**Ac** Actinium 89															

BONDING AND STRUCTURE

Topic Guide

4.1 Introduction

Bonds are formed between atoms when electrons are redistributed among those atoms to give each one the stable electronic configuration of the nearest noble gas in the periodic table. Usually this results in the formation of an octet of electrons.

An **ionic (electrovalent) bond** is formed when one or more electrons are transferred from an atom of an element on the left-hand side of the periodic table (i.e. a metal) to an atom of one on the right-hand side (i.e. a non-metal). Ionic compounds are made up of ions (see Example 4.1).

An **ion** is an electrically charged particle formed from an atom or group of atoms by the loss or gain of one or more electrons.

The number of electrons lost or gained by an atom in forming an ion is its **valency**. For metals outside the centre block of the periodic table, the number of electrons lost per atom is equal to the group number; for non-metals, the number of electrons gained by each atom is equal to (8 minus group number).

A **covalent bond** is formed when a pair of electrons is shared between two atoms which both need to gain electrons (i.e. non-metals).

Covalent compounds are made up of molecules (see Example 4.1).

The number of electron pairs shared by an atom is often called its valency.

4.2 Crystal Structure

The ways in which the particles are arranged in a solid can be determined by X-ray diffraction. A crystal consists of particles arranged in a repeating pattern extending in three dimensions. Such three-dimensional arrangements are called lattices.

(a) Giant Ionic Lattices

The sodium chloride lattice is shown in Fig. 4.1.

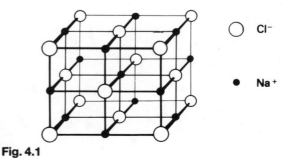

○ Cl⁻

● Na⁺

Fig. 4.1

This arrangement extends throughout the crystal, involving millions of ions. Each cube is joined to its neighbours and the whole crystal is thus a continuous giant structure of ions or a giant ionic lattice.

(b) Giant Metallic Lattices

Metals consist of an array of positively charged ions embedded in a 'sea' of electrons. It is the forces of attraction between the positive ions and these electrons which hold the lattice together.

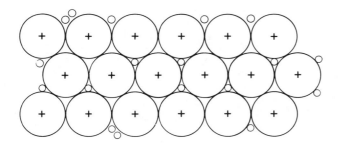

+ nucleus
◌ electron

Fig. 4.2

(c) Molecular Lattices

Most covalent compounds are gases, liquids or solids which crystallise with a molecular lattice. The particles are molecules, linked by very weak attractive forces. It must be emphasised that the individual atoms *within* the molecule are joined together by strong covalent bonds. For example, in solid carbon dioxide, there are only weak forces acting between separate molecules but each carbon dioxide molecule contains a carbon atom linked by strong covalent bonds to two oxygen atoms.

(d) Giant Atomic Lattices (Sometimes Called Giant Molecular Lattices)

There are a number of substances such as silicon(IV) oxide, diamond and graphite which have very high melting points. They consist of giant atomic lattices with strong covalent bonds acting throughout the whole crystal. The particles in these cases are atoms so they must be held together by covalent bonds, but there can be no separate molecules or the melting points would be much lower (see Example 13.1).

The properties shown by the main structural types are summarised in Table 4.1 (see Example 4.1).

(e) Macromolecules

Some substances such as plastics, fibres and proteins are made up of molecules containing thousands of atoms. They do not have giant structures but their molecules are much bigger than the simple ones dealt with earlier. They are called macromolecules and are discussed in Section 18.3.

Table 4.1

Property	Giant structures			Molecular structures
	Metallic	Ionic	Atomic	
m.p. & b.p.	← High →			Low
Solubility in organic solvents	← Generally insoluble →			Generally soluble
Solubility in water	Insoluble	Generally soluble	Insoluble	Generally insoluble
Conductors of electricity (molten)	← Yes →		← No →	
Conductors of electricity (solid)	Yes	← No →		
Conduction of heat	Good	← Bad →		

4.3 Oxidation and Reduction

Oxidation is:
1. the addition of oxygen to a substance;
2. the removal of hydrogen from a substance;
3. any change in which there is a loss of one or more electrons.

Reduction is the opposite of oxidation (see Example 4.7). It is:

1. the removal of oxygen from a substance;
2. the addition of hydrogen to a substance;
3. any change in which there is a gain of one or more electrons.

Electrons cannot simply disappear, and hence if one particle loses electrons (i.e. is oxidised), another must gain them (i.e. be reduced). In other words, oxidation cannot occur without reduction. Reactions involving changes of this type are often known as **redox** (**red**uction-**ox**idation) reactions.

Common oxidising agents include oxygen, chlorine, nitric acid, acidified potassium manganate(VII) and acidified potassium dichromate(VI). Common reducing agents include hydrogen, carbon and carbon monoxide.

4.4 Worked Examples

Example 4.1

(a) Name an ionic and a covalent compound and explain how each structure is formed from its elements. **(6)**

Sodium chloride, NaCl, is an ionic compound. Each sodium atom (electron configuration 2.8.1) has one electron in its outermost shell while each chlorine atom (2.8.7) has seven. If the outer electron is transferred from an atom of sodium to one of chlorine, then both will have a stable octet of electrons in their outermost shells (see Fig. 4.3).

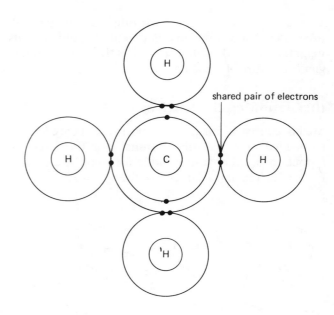

shared pair of electrons

Fig. 4.4

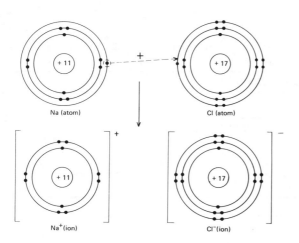

Fig. 4.3

When the sodium atom has lost its electron, it is left with a net positive charge of 1 unit since it has 11 protons (i.e. 11 positive charges) but now has only 10 electrons (i.e. 10 negative charges). Similarly, the chlorine atom acquires a unit negative charge since it contains the original 17 protons but now has 18 electrons. These charged particles, called ions, strongly attract one another, the Na^+ and Cl^- ions being arranged in a repeating pattern in three dimensions (see Section 4.2).

Methane, CH_4, is an example of a covalent compound. Carbon (electron configuration 2.4) has 4 electrons in its outermost shell and would have to form the C^{4+} ion in order to attain the stable electronic configuration of helium. So much energy is required to form the C^{4+} ion that the carbon and hydrogen atoms combine by an easier method: they share pairs of electrons. Each atom contributes one electron to a shared pair and in this way the carbon achieves a stable octet (Fig. 4.4) and the hydrogen, a stable pair of electrons. The atoms are held together by the attraction of the two nuclei for the shared pair of electrons. The particles formed are molecules which are free to move in all directions.

(b) Show how each type of bonding influences the properties of the compound in terms of physical appearance, melting point and electrical conductivity. **(9)**

Sodium chloride is a solid with a high melting point because a large amount of energy has to be provided to overcome the strong forces of electrostatic attraction holding the oppositely charged ions together. On the other hand, the forces of attraction between neighbouring methane molecules are weak and so the melting point is low – methane is a gas at room temperature.

Sodium chloride does not conduct an electric current when solid because the ions are only able to vibrate about fixed positions in the crystal lattice and cannot migrate towards the electrodes. When sodium chloride is melted or dissolved in water, the ions are free to move and hence carry an electric current. Covalent compounds cannot conduct an electric current because they do not contain ions.

(SUJB)

Example 4.2

Element X has an atomic number of 12. The formula of its chloride will be:

A X_2Cl
B XCl
C XCl_2
D XCl_3
E XCl_4

The answer is **C**.   (AEB, 1982)

The electron configuration of X must be 2.8.2. This means that X must lose two electrons in order to attain a stable octet, but each atom of chlorine (2.8.7) can only accept one. Hence the X atom must give its two electrons to two chlorine atoms as illustrated in Fig. 4.5.

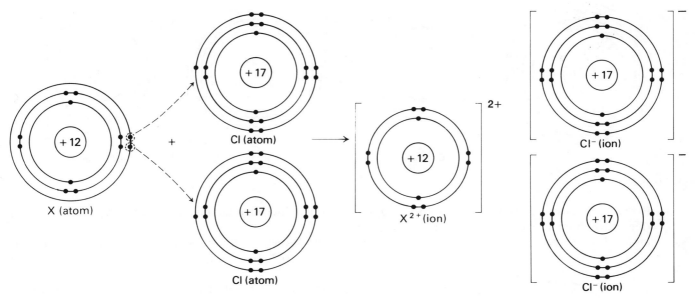

Fig. 4.5

Examples 4.3 and 4.4.

The diagrams below show the structures of some common elements or compounds.

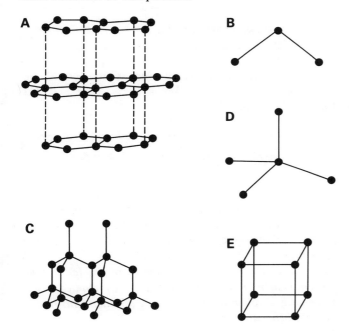

Example 4.3

Which structure shows the arrangement of atoms in a diamond?
The answer is **C.**

Example 4.4

Which structure shows the arrangement of ions in a crystal of sodium chloride?
The answer is **E.**

Example 4.5

(a) Name two types of particle, other than electrons, which can be found in an atom. **(2)**

Protons and neutrons.

(b) Where are these particles usually found in the atom? **(1)**

Nucleus.

(c) Calcium has an atomic number of 20 and a mass number of 40. State how many of each type of particle are present in an atom of calcium. **(3)**
Protons 20
Neutrons 20
Electrons 20

(d) By means of a diagram (Fig. 4.6) show how the electrons are arranged in a calcium atom. **(2)**

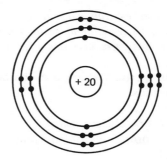

Fig. 4.6

(e) Calcium combines with oxygen (atomic number = 8) to form calcium oxide. How are the electrons arranged in an oxygen atom? **(2)**
There are 2 electrons in the first shell and 6 electrons in the second shell.

(f) How many electrons does calcium need to lose in order to possess a stable octet in its outer shell? **(1)**
2.

(g) How many electrons does oxygen need to gain in order to possess a stable octet in its outer shell? **(1)**
2.

(h) By means of a diagram (Fig. 4.7) show how calcium oxide is formed from its elements. **(2)**

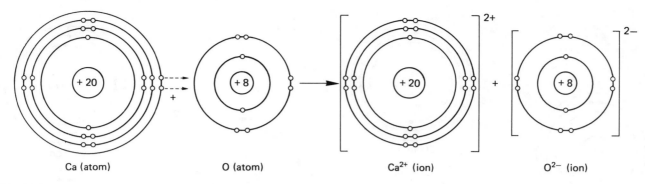

Fig. 4.7

(i) Explain, either in words or by means of a diagram (Fig. 4.8), how the electrons are arranged in a molecule of water. **(2)**

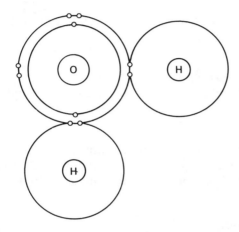

Fig. 4.8

Each atom donates one electron to a shared pair of electrons, and in this way the oxygen atom gains a stable octet of electrons and each hydrogen atom has a full outer shell of two electrons.

(j) Give two properties which are characteristic of ionic compounds. **(2)**
High melting point.
Conduct an electric current when molten.

(k) How do the properties of covalent compounds differ from this? **(2)**
Covalent compounds generally have low melting points and will not conduct an electric current.

Example 4.6

The following table gives some data for elements A to E. These letters are **not** the chemical symbols for the elements.

Element	Melting point (°C)	Boiling point (°C)
A	− 219	− 183
B	650	1117
C	− 7	58
D	232	2687
E	1540	2887

(a) Which element is a gas at room temperature? **(1)**
A.

(b) Which element is a liquid at room temperature? **(1)**
C.

(c) Will element E be a solid, a liquid or a gas at 1000°C? **(1)**
Solid.

(d) Which of these elements do you think are composed of simple molecules? **(1)**
A and C.

> They have low melting points.

(e) Give TWO of the elements which could be metals. **(1)**
Any two of B, D and E.

> They have high melting points and boiling points.

(f) Explain why copper is a good conductor of electricity. Suggest two reasons for using aluminium instead of copper for high-voltage overhead power cables. **(3)**
The 'sea' of electrons normally moves in the lattice with random motion but if a potential difference is applied, it will move easily through the metal in one direction, this flow of electrons being an electric current.
Aluminium is much cheaper than copper. It is also of lower density.

Example 4.7

On heating, hydrogen changes copper(II) oxide to copper.

(a) Which substance is reduced?
Copper(II) oxide.

(b) What would you see when the reaction takes place? **(3)**
The mixture glows and the black copper(II) oxide changes to reddish-brown copper.

> $$CuO(s) + H_2(g) \rightarrow Cu(s) + H_2O(g)$$

4.5 Self-test Questions

Question 4.1

An atom of X has two electrons in its outer shell and an atom of Y has six electrons in its outer shell. The formula for a compound formed between X and Y would be:

    A XY
    B X_2Y
    C XY_2
    D XY_3
    E X_2Y_3

(Welsh, June 1988, Paper 1, Q13)

*Question 4.2

Use your periodic table to help you to answer the following questions:
(a) For one atom of fluorine (atomic number 9), write down:
    (i) the number of protons,
    (ii) the electronic structure. **(2)**
(b) For one atom of gallium (atomic number 31), write down the number of neutrons. **(1)**
(c) Suggest the formula of the compound formed between gallium and fluorine. **(1)**
(d) Draw a diagram, showing the outer energy level electrons only, to show the covalent bonding in F_2O. **(2)**
(e) Explain why the relative atomic mass of chlorine (atomic number 17) is not a whole number. **(2)**

(f) Sulphur dichloride (SCl_2), bromomethane (CH_3Br) and krypton (Kr) are all gases at 300 K.
    (i) Which one will diffuse at the greatest rate at 300 K?
    (ii) Explain your answer to (i). **(2)**

(MEG, June 1988, Paper 3, Q4)

Question 4.3

The reaction between aluminium and iron oxide is exothermic.
$$Fe_2O_3(s) + 2Al(s) \rightarrow Al_2O_3(s) + 2Fe(s)$$
(a) What do you understand by the term 'exothermic'? **(1)**
(b) Name the reducing agent in this reaction. **(1)**

4.6 Answers to Self-test Questions

4.1 **A.**

> The compound is ionic; X gives its two outer electrons to Y so that both X and Y will have outer shells of eight electrons.

4.2 (a) (i) 9.
   (ii) 2.7.
   (b) 70 − 31 = 39 neutrons.

> The mass number is 70.

   (c) GaF_3.

> Gallium is in Group III and so it will have a valency of 3.

(d)

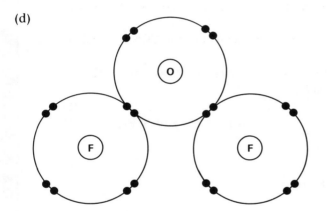

(e) Chlorine contains two isotopes, $^{35}_{17}Cl$ and $^{37}_{17}Cl$. The relative atomic mass is the average of the masses of the two isotopes, taking into account the fact that there is 75% $^{35}_{17}Cl$ and 25% $^{37}_{17}Cl$.

$$\text{Relative atomic mass} = \left(\frac{75}{100} \times 35\right) + \left(\frac{25}{100} \times 37\right) = 35.5$$

   (f) (i) Krypton.
      (ii) Molar masses in g mol^{-1} are: SCl_2 103, CH_3Br 95, Kr 84.
         Krypton diffuses the fastest because it has the lowest molar mass.

4.3 (a) The reaction gives out heat.
   (b) Aluminium.

4.7 Grading of Self-test Questions

Question 4.2 is part of an extension paper designed to award the A and B grades. It is worth 10 marks and you will need at least 7 to be considered for an A grade and at least 5 to be in line for a B grade.

5

MOLES, FORMULAE AND EQUATIONS

Topic Guide

5.1 Introduction

The **relative atomic mass**, A_r, of an element is the number of times that the average mass of one of its atoms is greater than 1/12 of the mass of an atom of $^{12}_6C$. (For an explanation of the figures in $^{12}_6C$, see page 17.) The relative atomic mass is approximately equal to the mass number of the atom. Since it is a ratio, relative atomic mass has no units. Values of relative atomic masses are given on page 24.

A **mole** of any substance is the amount of it which contains 6×10^{23} particles. The number of particles per mole is called the **Avogadro Constant.**

The **molar mass** of a substance, M, is the mass of one mole of it. The units are $g\,mol^{-1}$ (or g/mol).

For practical purposes, particularly in calculations, remember that one mole of *atoms* of any element:
(a) contains 6×10^{23} atoms;
(b) has a mass in grams which is numerically equal to the relative atomic mass of the element.

From (b), conversion of a mass in grams to an amount in moles involves dividing by the molar mass,
  i.e. **mol = mass/molar mass** – see Examples 5.1 and 5.2.

Conversion of an amount in moles to a mass in grams involves multiplying the amount in moles by the molar mass,
  i.e. **mass = mol × molar mass** – see Example 5.2.

The **empirical formula** of a compound shows the simplest ratio of the numbers of atoms of the different elements in it.

A **radical** is a group of atoms which occurs in compounds but which cannot exist on its own. For example, the sulphate radical, SO_4, is found in all sulphates but there is no substance which is just called 'sulphate'.

Empirical formulae can be calculated from experimental results (see Example 5.3), or worked out using valencies (see Example 5.5). The **valency** of an ion (Section 4.1) shows its combining power, and combination between ions takes place in such proportions that the sum of the valencies of the positive ions or hydrogen atoms in a formula equals the sum of the valencies of the negative ions or non-metal atoms (see Example 5.5). For example, in aluminium nitrate the ratio of aluminium ions (valency 3) to nitrate ions (valency 1) is 1:3, making the empirical formula $Al(NO_3)_3$.

$$Al(NO_3)_3$$
valencies: 3 (3 × 1)

Notice that if a radical appears more than once in a formula it must be enclosed in a bracket.

Table 5.1 shows the valencies of the commonly encountered ions.

Table 5.1

Metal or other positive ion		Valency	Non-metal or other negative ion	
Ammonium	NH_4^+		Br^-	Bromide
Hydrogen	H^+		Cl^-	Chloride
Potassium	K^+	1	OH^-	Hydroxide
Silver	Ag^+		I^-	Iodide
Sodium	Na^+		NO_3^-	Nitrate
Barium	Ba^{2+}			
Calcium	Ca^{2+}			
Copper	Cu^{2+}			
(in copper(II) compounds)			CO_3^{2-}	Carbonate
Iron	Fe^{2+}		O^{2-}	Oxide
(in iron(II) compounds)		2	SO_4^{2-}	Sulphate
Lead	Pb^{2+}			
(in lead(II) compounds)				
Magnesium	Mg^{2+}			
Zinc	Zn^{2+}			
Aluminium	Al^{3+}			
Iron	Fe^{3+}	3	PO_4^{3-}	Phosphate(V)
(in iron(III) compounds)				

The **relative molecular mass**, M_r, of an element or compound is the number of times that the average mass of one of its molecules is greater than 1/12 of the mass of an atom of $^{12}_6C$. Like relative atomic mass, this is a ratio and has no units.

The relative molecular mass of a substance may be calculated by adding together the relative atomic masses of the individual atoms in one molecule of it, e.g. the relative molecular mass of carbon dioxide, CO_2, is (12 + 16 + 16) = 44.

For compounds with giant structures of atoms or ions (see Section 4.2) the term 'relative molecular mass' applies to a *formula unit* of the substance. Thus for potassium chloride, empirical formula KCl, the relative molecular mass is (39 + 35.5) = 74.5.

The **molecular formula** of a compound shows the actual numbers of atoms of the different elements in one molecule of it. For example, a molecule of hydrogen peroxide consists of two hydrogen atoms and two oxygen atoms and so its molecular formula is H_2O_2. (Note that its *empirical* formula is HO.) Unlike relative molecular mass, the term 'molecular formula' must be applied *only* to substances that consist of separate molecules.

The definition of the mole given on page 37 applies to molecules and formula units, as well as to atoms. Thus, just as a mole of atoms of an element contains 6×10^{23} atoms and has a mass in grams which is numerically equal to its relative atomic mass, so a mole of a *compound* contains 6×10^{23} *molecules* (or formula units) and its mass in grams is numerically equal to its relative *molecular* mass.

It is usual to quote the concentration of a solution in moles of solute per dm^3 of solution. This can be abbreviated to 'M'. Thus a 1 M solution of sodium chloride contains 1 mol (58.5 g) of NaCl per dm^3 of solution.

Percentage Composition (see Example 14.1 and Question 5.3)

The percentage by mass of an element in a compound may be calculated using the following steps:
1. Work out the relative molecular mass of the compound.
2. Write down the fraction by mass of each element and convert to a percentage.
3. Check that the percentages add up to 100.

5.2 Gas Volumes

Avogadro's principle states that equal volumes of all gases at the same temperature and pressure contain the same number of molecules.

Thus if two *volumes* of gas A combine with one *volume* of gas B (measured at the same temperature and pressure), then two *molecules* of gas A must combine with one *molecule* of gas B (see Example 5.7).

The **molar volume** of a gas is the volume of one mole of it. Since one mole of *any* gas contains the same number of molecules (6×10^{23}), all gases must have the same molar volume, at the same temperature and pressure. At room temperature and pressure the value is usually taken to be $24 \ dm^3 \ mol^{-1}$.

Just as dividing the *mass* of a substance by its molar *mass* gives the amount of the substance in moles (Section 5.1), so dividing the *volume* of a gas by its molar *volume* also gives an amount in moles.

Multiplying an amount of gas in moles by its molar volume gives the volume of the gas.

5.3 Chemical Equations

A chemical equation shows the relative numbers of atoms and molecules taking part in a chemical reaction. It can also show whether the various substances involved are in the solid (s), liquid (1) or gaseous (g) state, or are dissolved in water (aq). To write an equation you should:
1. Know what the reactants and products are.
2. Write down the formulae and states of the reactants and products, leaving space in front of each formula for balancing.
3. Work through the equation from left to right, checking that the same numbers of atoms of the various elements appear on both sides.

For example, when magnesium burns in oxygen it forms magnesium oxide. Applying step (2) we have:
$$Mg(s) + O_2(g) \rightarrow MgO(s)$$

The magnesium atoms balance but there are two oxygen atoms on the left and only one on the right. Therefore we try a 2 in front of the MgO(s):
$$Mg(s) + O_2(g) \rightarrow 2MgO(s)$$

The 2 in front of the MgO(s) doubles the number of magnesium atoms as well as the number of oxygen atoms so, in order to balance the whole equation, we need a 2 in front of the Mg(s), giving:

$2Mg(s) + O_2(g) \rightarrow 2MgO(s)$

5.4 Ionic Equations

These include only those ions that change in some way during a reaction. For example, when two solutions react together to form a precipitate, an ionic equation is sometimes used to represent the reaction that takes place. To write the ionic equation you simply write the formula of the precipitate on the right-hand side and then the formulae of the ions which go to make it up on the left-hand side. When aqueous solutions of magnesium sulphate and barium chloride are mixed, a white precipitate of barium sulphate is formed. The ionic equation is therefore

$$Ba^{2+}(aq) + SO_4{}^{2-}(aq) \rightarrow BaSO_4(s)$$

Another example of an ionic equation is a metal displacement reaction, e.g. when iron is placed in copper(II) sulphate solution, copper and iron(II) sulphate solution are formed. The ionic equation is

$$Fe(s) + Cu^{2+}(aq) \rightarrow Cu(s) + Fe^{2+}(aq)$$

You can see that two electrons are transferred from each iron atom to each copper ion. The sulphate ions do not appear because they do not affect the reaction.

5.5 Calculating Reacting Masses from Equations

The steps in this type of calculation are shown in Examples 5.2 and 5.6.

5.6 Worked Examples

Example 5.1

(a) 0.5 mol of a hydrated salt contains 63 g of water. How many grams of water of crystallisation are contained in 1 mol of salt?
   ($M_r (H_2O) = 18$.)   **(1)**

0.5 mol of hydrated salt contains 63 g H_2O.
∴. 1 mol of hydrated salt contains 126 g H_2O.

(b) How many moles of water is this?   **(1)**
Molar mass of water = 18 g mol^{-1}.

$$\therefore Mol\ H_2O = \frac{126}{18} = 7$$

Example 5.2

The action of heat on sodium hydrogencarbonate is represented by the following equation:

$$2NaHCO_3 \rightarrow Na_2CO_3 + H_2O + CO_2$$

($A_r(H) = 1$, $A_r(C) = 12$, $A_r(O) = 16$, $A_r(Na) = 23$.)

(a) (i) Calculate the mass in grams of one mole of carbon dioxide, CO_2 **(1)**
12 + (2 x 16) = 44 g.

   (ii) Calculate the mass in grams of one mole of sodium hydrogencarbonate, $NaHCO_3$.   **(1)**
23 + 1 + 12 + (3 × 16) = 84 g.

   (iii) Calculate the number of moles of sodium hydrogencarbonate in 4.2 g.   **(1)**
4.2 ÷ 84 = 0.05 mol.

   (iv) How many moles of carbon dioxide are formed from 4.2 g of sodium hydrogencarbonate?   **(1)**
0.025 mol.

> Since 2 mol $NaHCO_3 \rightarrow$ 1 mol CO_2

   (v) What mass of carbon dioxide is formed from 4.2 g of sodium hydrogencarbonate?   **(1)**
Mass = 0.025 × 44 = 1.1 g.

(b) What use does the above reaction have in baking?   **(1)**
It produces carbon dioxide and makes the dough rise.

(c) Sodium hydrogencarbonate is used in the pharmaceutical industry as a component of anti-acid medicines. Explain why it is used in this way.   **(2)**
Acid in the stomach causes indigestion. Sodium hydrogencarbonate, being alkaline, neutralises the acid and stops the discomfort.

(Welsh, 1988, Paper 1, Q34)

Example 5.3

2.38 g of tin was converted to 3.02 g of tin oxide. What is the formula of the oxide?
($A_r (Sn) = 119$, $A_r(O) = 16$.)

A Sn_4O
B Sn_2O
C SnO
D SnO_2
E SnO_4

The answer is **D**.   (AEB, 1983)

Mass of oxygen combined with 2.38 g of tin = (3.02 − 2.38) = 0.64 g

            Sn : O

ratio of g   2.38 : 0.64

ratio of mol $\dfrac{2.38}{119} : \dfrac{0.64}{16}$ (No. of mol = mass/molar mass)

     = 0.02 : 0.04 (Divide by smallest to convert to whole numbers)

     = 1 : 2

∴ Empirical formula is SnO_2

Example 5.4

(a) A hydrocarbon contains 82.8% carbon. Determine the empirical (i.e. simplest) formula for this compound. **(5)**

> A hydrocarbon is made up of hydrogen and carbon only, so if the percentage of carbon is 82.8, the rest (17.2%) must be hydrogen.

$$\begin{array}{ccc} & C: & H \\ \textit{ratio of mol} & \dfrac{82.8}{12} : & \dfrac{17.2}{1} \\ = & 6.90: & 17.2 \\ = 1 & : & 2.49 \\ \approx 2 & : & 5 \end{array}$$ $\therefore$ *Empirical formula is* C_2H_5.

(b) A rough estimate puts the relative molecular mass of this hydrocarbon between 50 and 60. What is the actual value? Explain your answer. **(3)**

Relative mass of $C_2H_5 = (24 + 5) = 29$
Molecular formula must be a whole number $\times$ C_2H_5, *i.e.* C_2H_5, C_4H_{10}, *etc.*
$\therefore$ M_r *must be a whole number* $\times$ 29. *In this case it must be 58.* **(OLE)**

Example 5.5

Metal M, with atomic number 3, has an oxide with formula:
A M_3O_2
B M_2O
C M_2O_3
D MO_2
E MO_3
The answer is **B**.

Valency bonds

> M has the electronic configuration 2,1 and therefore is in group I of the periodic table with valency I. Oxygen has valency 2, so 2 M atoms are needed for each O atom.

Example 5.6

2.8 g of iron reacted completely with chlorine according to the equation:
$2Fe(s) + 3Cl_2(g) \rightarrow 2FeCl_3(s)$ (Fe=56, FeCl$_3$=162.5)
The mass of iron (III) chloride formed would be about:
A 2.8 g
B 4.0 g
C 5.6 g
D 8.1 g
E 16.2 g
The answer is **D**. **(L)**

A_r = Weight in grams.

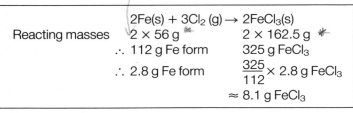

Reacting masses
$2Fe(s) + 3Cl_2(g) \rightarrow 2FeCl_3(s)$
2×56 g 2×162.5 g
$\therefore$ 112 g Fe form   325 g FeCl$_3$
$\therefore$ 2.8 g Fe form $\dfrac{325}{112} \times 2.8$ g FeCl$_3$
               ≈ 8.1 g FeCl$_3$

Example 5.7

100 cm³ of nitrogen oxide gas (NO) combine with 50 cm³ of oxygen to form 100 cm³ of a single gaseous compound, all volumes being measured at the same temperature and pressure. Which of the following equations fits these facts?
A $NO(g) + O_2(g) \rightarrow NO_3(g)$
B $NO(g) + 2O_2(g) \rightarrow NO_5(g)$
C $2NO(g) + O_2(g) \rightarrow 2NO_2(g)$
D $2NO(g) + O_2(g) \rightarrow N_2O_4(g)$
E $2NO(g) + 2O_2(g) \rightarrow N_2O_6(g)$
The answer is **C**. **(L)**

> From Avogadro's principle, the ratio of reacting molecules is the same as that of reacting volumes, i.e. 2 : 1 : 2

*Example 5.8

A rack of test tubes is set up each containing 10 cm³ of aqueous iron(III) chloride. Varying volumes of aqueous sodium hydroxide are added. The heights of the precipitates are measured after settling.
(a) (i) Name the precipitate.
Iron(III) hydroxide.
    (ii) What colour is the precipitate? **(2)**
Red/brown.
The results are given in the table:

Volume of aqueous sodium hydroxide /cm³	4	8	12	16	20
Height of precipitate /mm	6	12	15	15	15

(b) Plot the results on the grid: **(2)**

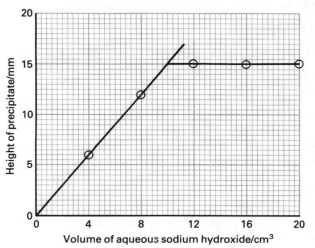

(c) Use your graph to determine the minimum volume of aqueous sodium hydroxide needed to give a precipitate of height 15 mm. **(1)**
Minimum volume = 10 cm³.
(d) (i) Write the chemical equation for the reaction between iron(III) chloride and sodium hydroxide. **(1)**
$FeCl_3(aq) + 3NaOH(aq) \rightarrow Fe(OH)_3(s) + 3NaCl(aq)$

(ii) The concentration of the aqueous iron(III) chloride is 1.00 mol/dm³. Calculate the concentration, in mol/dm³, of the aqueous sodium hydroxide. **(1)**

10 cm³ FeCl₃ react with 10 cm³ NaOH. The reaction needs 3 times as much NaOH as FeCl₃.

∴ the NaOH solution contains 3 mol/dm³.

(Total 7)

(MEG, June 1988, Paper 3, Q3)

Example 5.9

What volume of hydrogen is produced at room temperature and pressure, when 0.6 g of magnesium reacts with excess 1 M sulphuric acid?

$Mg(s) + 2H^+(aq) \rightarrow Mg^{2+}(aq) + H_2(g)$

(Relative atomic mass: Mg = 24; 1 mole of any gas occupies 24000 cm³ at room temperature and pressure.) **(3)**

1 mol Mg *gives 1 mol* H_2

24 g Mg *gives 24000 cm³* H_2

0.6 g Mg *gives* $\dfrac{24000}{24} \times 0.6$ *cm³* H_2

= 600 cm³ H_2

Example 5.10

(a) Use the periodic table to answer the following questions.

(i) Give the symbol of one element in Group 2.

One of Be, Mg, Ca, Sr, Ba, Ra.

(ii) Give the symbol of one element in Group 6.

One of O, S, Se, Te, Po.

(iii) Give the symbol for the most reactive element in Group 7.

F.

(iv) Find the relative atomic mass of copper and oxygen. **(5)**

Copper 64, oxygen 16.

(b) Copper(II) oxide was heated in a stream of hydrogen. The following results were obtained:

Mass of container + copper(II) oxide	= 4.80 g
Mass of container	= 4.00 g
Mass of copper(II) oxide	= 0.80 g
Mass of container + copper	= 4.64 g
Mass of container	= 4.00 g
Mass of copper	= 0.64 g
Mass of oxygen in copper(II) oxide	= 0.16 g

(i) Complete the table above.

(ii) What is the mass of 1 mole of copper(II) oxide (CuO)?

64 + 16 = 80 g

(iii) How many moles of copper(II) oxide were used in the experiment?

0.80 ÷ 80 = 0.01 mol.

(iv) How many moles of copper were formed?

0.64 ÷ 64 = 0.01 mol.

(v) Give the word and chemical equations for the reaction between copper(II) oxide and hydrogen. **(10)**

Word equation: Copper(II) oxide + hydrogen → Copper + water.

Chemical equation: $CuO(s) + H_2(g) \rightarrow Cu(s) + H_2O(g)$

(MEG, June 1988, Paper 2, Q10)

5.7 Self-test Questions

Question 5.1

Which one of the following is the mass of 2 moles of hydrated copper(II) sulphate, $CuSO_4.5H_2O$?

    A   178
    B   186
    C   250
    D   372
    E   500

Question 5.2

A compound of relative molecular mass 180 and empirical formula CH_2O has the molecular formula:

    A CH_2O
    B $C_2H_4O_2$
    C $C_3H_6O_3$
    D $C_4H_8O_4$
    E $C_6H_{12}O_6$

Question 5.3

The percentage by mass of water of crystallisation in hydrated sodium sulphate, $Na_2SO_4.10H_2O$, is about:

    A   10
    B   20
    C   28
    D   56
    E   70

Question 5.4

Which one of the following is incorrectly balanced?

    A $2Fe + 3Cl_2 \rightarrow 2FeCl_3$
    B $2H_2 + O_2 \rightarrow 2H_2O$
    C $Zn + CuSO_4 \rightarrow ZnSO_4 + Cu$
    D $Fe_2O_3 + 2CO \rightarrow 2Fe + 3CO_2$
    E $CuSO_4 + 2NaOH \rightarrow Cu(OH)_2 + Na_2SO_4$

(Welsh, June 1988, Paper 1, Q18)

Question 5.5

A sample of gas, mass 0.39 g, was enclosed in a gas syringe and the volume of the gas was recorded at various temperatures but at a constant pressure of 1 atmosphere.

The results are shown in the table below:

Temperature (°C)	0	40	60	80	100
Volume (cm³)	224	258	274	291	308

(a) Plot the data on a grid, with temperature (°C) as your y-axis and volume (cm^3) as your x-axis, and draw the best straight line through the points. **(3)**

(b) Read from the graph the volume of the gas at 20°C. **(2)**

(c) Calculate the mass of gas which would have a volume of 24,100 cm^3 at 20°C. **(2)**

(d) What is the relative molecular mass of the gas to the nearest whole number? **(1)**

5.8 Answers to Self-test Questions

5.1 . E

> 2 mol $CuSO_4.5H_2O$ has a mass of $2 \times (64 + 32 + (4 \times 16) + (5 \times 18))$ g = 2 x 250 g = 500 g.

5.2 E.

> Relative empirical formula mass of CH_2O is $(12 + 2 + 16) = 30$
> Relative molecular mass is 180, which is 6×30
> $\therefore$ Molecular formula is $6 \times$ empirical formula.

5.3 D.

> M_r $(Na_2SO_4.10H_2O)=(2 \times 23) + 32 + (4 \times 16) + (10 \times 18) = 322$
>
> Percentage of water $= \dfrac{10 \times 18}{322} \times 100 = 55.9 \approx 56$

5.4 D.

> There are two carbon atoms on the left-hand side but three on the right-hand side.

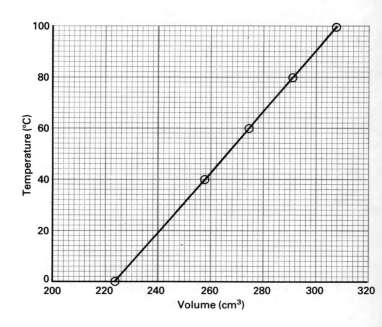

5.5 (a)

(b) 241 cm^3.

(c) 241 cm^3 of gas at 20°C and 1 atm has a mass of 0.39 g.
     $\therefore$ 24,100 cm^3 of gas at 20°C and 1 atm has a mass of 39 g.

(d) 39

> 24,000 cm^3 of gas at r.t.p.is 1 mol of the gas.

ELECTRO-CHEMISTRY

Topic Guide

6.1 Introduction

Substances that allow electricity to pass through them are known as **conductors**; those that do not are called **insulators**.

Metallic elements conduct electricity when solid or molten but are not decomposed by it (compare with electrolytes below). The current is carried by loosely held electrons, which move from one atom to the next.

Non-metallic elements do not conduct electricity because their electrons cannot move from one atom to the next (graphite is an exception).

An **electrolyte** is a compound which, when molten and/or in solution, conducts an electric current and is decomposed by it (compare with metals above). The current is carried by ions, which are free to move through the liquid to the oppositely charged electrodes, where they are discharged. Acids, alkalis and salts are examples of electrolytes.

A **non-electrolyte** is a compound which does not conduct an electric current, either when molten or in solution, because no ions are present. Sugar and ethanol are non-electrolytes. Most metal compounds, particularly salts, have giant ionic lattices (see Section 4.2). When they are dissolved in water the ions separate and diffuse throughout the liquid, thus providing a solution which is a good conductor of electricity. Such substances are examples of *strong electrolytes*.

Covalent substances are generally non-electrolytes. However, when the covalent gas, hydrogen chloride, dissolves in water it forms hydrochloric acid, which is a strong electrolyte. The water reacts with the gas molecules, changing them into ions:

$$HCl(g) + H_2O(l) \rightarrow H_3O^+(aq) + Cl^-(aq)$$

Sulphuric acid and nitric acid molecules also react with water in this way.

Some other covalent substances, such as ammonia and ethanoic acid, have similar reactions with water but form far fewer ions. They are examples of *weak electrolytes*, their solutions being poor conductors of electricity, e.g.

$$NH_3(aq) + H_2O(l) \rightleftharpoons NH_4^+(aq) + OH^-(aq)$$

6.2 Electrolysis

Electrolysis is the decomposition of an electrolyte by the passage of an electric current through it.

During electrolysis negatively charged ions are attracted to the **anode** (positive electrode) and so are called **anions**; positively charged ions are attracted to the **cathode** (negative electrode) and are called **cations**.

Since electrons are removed at the anode, the process taking place is oxidation; at the cathode, electrons are added and so reduction is occurring (see Section 4.3).

(a) The Electrolysis of Lead(II) Bromide

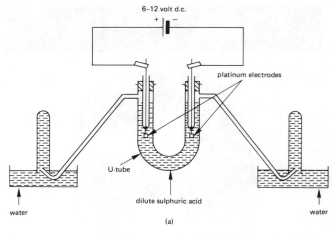

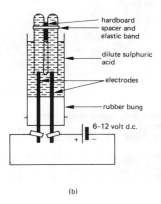

Fig. 6.2

Consider the electrolysis of dilute sulphuric acid in the apparatus shown in Fig. 6.2. The following ions are present:

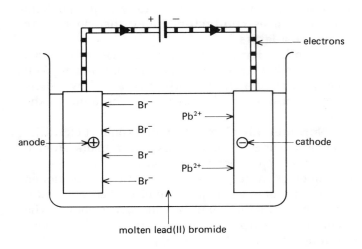

Fig. 6.1

Solid lead(II) bromide does not conduct electricity because its ions are fixed in the crystal lattice. When the solid is melted the ions are free to move and travel to the oppositely charged electrodes. At the anode, electrons are removed from the bromide ions giving bromine atoms, which combine in pairs to form molecules; reddish brown bromine gas is given off. At the cathode, electrons are added to the lead ions, forming lead atoms, and a bead of molten lead collects at the bottom of the cell.

	Ions attracted to anode	Ions attracted to cathode
From sulphuric acid	SO_4^{2-} (aq)	$2H^+$ (aq)
From water (very few)	OH^- (aq)	H^+ (aq)

At the anode, hydroxide ions are discharged in preference to sulphate ions, forming water and oxygen; hydrogen ions are discharged at the cathode, giving hydrogen gas.

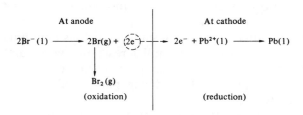

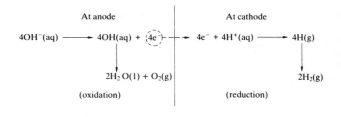

(b) The Electrolysis of Aqueous Solutions

Water is a very weak electrolyte; one molecule in about 550 million ionises as shown:

$$H_2O(l) \rightleftharpoons H^+(aq) + OH^-(aq)$$

(c) Predicting the Products of the Electrolysis of Aqueous Solutions

First, all of the ions in the solution should be listed under the electrodes to which they are attracted, as in the above example. The ions that will be discharged may, in most cases, be predicted from two simple rules:

1. At the anode, hydroxide ions will be discharged and the products will be oxygen and water, unless:
   (a) chloride, bromide or iodide ions are present (see Example 6.5); or
   (b) the anode dissolves or reacts with the oxygen formed from the hydroxide ions (see Examples 6.3 and 17.3).
2. At the cathode, the ions of the element which is lowest in the reactivity series (see Section 12.1) will be discharged.

(d) Applications of Electrolysis

1. The manufacture of elements. Examples include sodium, aluminium and chlorine (see Section 17.2).
2. The manufacture of compounds, e.g. sodium hydroxide (see Section 17.3).
3. Purification of metals. Copper is purified by electrolysing aqueous copper(II) sulphate solution with blocks of impure copper as anodes and thin sheets of the pure metal as cathodes. Pure copper is transferred from the anode to the cathode (see Example 6.3).
4. Electroplating. The article to be plated is made the cathode in the electrolysis cell, the anode is made of the plating metal, and the electrolyte is a solution containing its ions. When a current passes, the plating metal is transferred from the anode to the cathode, as in the purification of copper.
5. Anodising. Aluminium is coated with a layer of aluminium oxide which protects the metal from corrosion. This oxide coating can be thickened by making the aluminium the anode during the electrolysis of sulphuric acid. The oxide layer will absorb dyes and so is often coloured.

6.3 Worked Examples

Example 6.1

(a) From the following list of substances: copper(II) chloride, hydrogen chloride, copper, potassium chloride and iodine, name those that:
   (i) conduct electricity in the solid state,
Copper.
   (ii) conduct electricity when molten,
Copper(II) chloride, copper, potassium chloride.
   (iii) conduct electricity in aqueous solution,
Copper(II) chloride, hydrogen chloride, potassium chloride.

> Hydrogen chloride dissolves in water to give hydrochloric acid.

   (iv) do not readily conduct under any conditions. **(4)**

Iodine.

> Check with Section 6.1 if you are uncertain about these answers.

(b) Draw a simple circuit (Fig. 6.3) to show that the substance you chose in (a) (i) will conduct an electric current. **(2)**

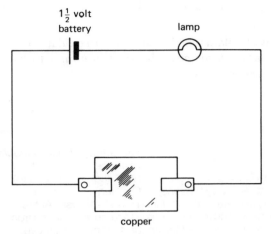

Fig. 6.3

Example 6.2

(a) Potassium iodide will conduct an electric current when molten. Name the product formed at
   (i) the negative electrode. **(1)**
Potassium.

> $$2K^+(l) + 2e^- \rightarrow 2K(l)$$

   (ii) the positive electrode. **(1)**
Iodine.

> $$2I^-(l) - 2e^- \rightarrow 2I(g) \rightarrow I_2(g)$$

(b) Why does potassium iodide not conduct electricity in the solid state? **(1)**
In the solid state, the ions are not free to move.

Example 6.3

Copper may be purified by electrolysis of aqueous copper(II) sulphate solution.
(i)   Give the name, charge and material of each electrode. **(3)**

Name:	*Anode*	Name:	*Cathode*
Charge:	*Positive*	Charge:	*Negative*
Material:	*Impure copper*	Material:	*Thin sheet of pure copper*

(ii)   Describe briefly how the copper is purified. **(2)**

At the anode, electrons are removed from copper atoms, forming Cu^{2+} ions which go into solution. Impurities dissolve or sink to the bottom of the container. At the cathode, Cu^{2+} ions gain electrons, forming copper atoms, and so the cathode becomes coated with pure copper.

(iii) Write ion–electron half equations for the reactions that take place at each electrode.

(2)

At anode   At cathode

$$Cu(s) \longrightarrow Cu^{2+}(aq) + (2e^-) \dashv \vdash \longrightarrow 2e^- + Cu^{2+}(aq) \longrightarrow Cu(s)$$

(iv) Explain which reaction is an oxidation.   **(1)**

The reaction at the anode is oxidation because each copper atom loses two electrons here.

	Ions attracted to anode	Ions attracted to cathode
From $CuSO_4$	SO_4^{2-} (aq)	Cu^{2+} (aq)
From H_2O (very few ions)	OH^- (aq)	H^+ (aq)

No gases are given off during this electrolysis. At the anode, it requires less energy to remove electrons from the copper atoms of the anode itself than to remove them from the OH^- or SO_4^{2-} ions. At the cathode, Cu^{2+} ions are discharged in preference to H^+ ions because copper is below hydrogen in the reactivity series.

Example 6.4

The table gives information about 5 substances:

Substance	Melting point (°C)	Does it conduct electricity when solid?	Does it conduct electricity when molten?
A	800	No	Yes
B	3700	Yes	Yes
C	−39	Yes	Yes
D	0	No	No
E	−117	No	No

Which letter in the table corresponds to each substance given below?
(a) ethanol **E**
(b) mercury **C**
(c) graphite **B**
(d) sodium chloride **A**
(e) water **D**

(5)

Only mercury and graphite will conduct electricity in the solid state, and the melting point suggests that **C** is mercury. Sodium chloride, being the only ionic solid, will conduct electricity when molten but not when solid, and so **A** must be sodium chloride. Water and ethanol are covalent and non-conductors of electricity, and the melting point suggests that **D** is water rather than ethanol.

*Example 6.5

(a) Consider the substances sodium chloride and magnesium metal. For **EACH** substance
   (i) name the type of bonding and give the formula of the species present,
In sodium chloride, there is ionic bonding with Na^+ and Cl^- ions present. Magnesium consists of an array of Mg^{2+} ions in a sea of electrons. The bonding is metallic.
   (ii) draw a diagram of the structure of the solid,

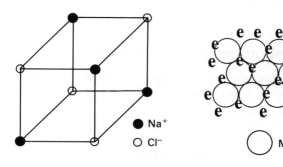

(iii) explain how, and under what conditions, each will conduct electricity.   **(6)**
Sodium chloride conducts electricity only when molten or in aqueous solution. Under these conditions, the ions are free to move to the oppositely charged electrodes. Magnesium will conduct electricity either in the solid state or when molten. The electrons are free to move through the solid or liquid metal and can carry the current.

(b) The Salt Tech Company manufactures chemicals by the electrolysis of sodium chloride. The company is researching into the use of lithium iodide (a similar compound to sodium chloride). Predict the names of three chemicals that could be produced by the electrolysis of lithium iodide, either molten or in aqueous solution. Suggest uses for two of these products.   **(4)**
The electrolysis of molten lithium iodide produces lithium and iodine, whereas in aqueous solution electrolysis gives hydrogen and iodine.

When molten:

    At anode   At cathode

$$2I^-(l) \rightarrow 2I(g) + 2e^- \qquad 2e^- + 2Li^+(l) \rightarrow 2Li(l)$$
$$\downarrow$$
$$I_2(g)$$

In aqueous solution,

$$2I^-(aq) \rightarrow 2I(aq) + 2e^- \qquad 2e^- + 2H^+(aq) \rightarrow 2H(g)$$
$$\downarrow \qquad\qquad\qquad\qquad\qquad \downarrow$$
$$I_2(aq) \qquad\qquad\qquad\qquad\qquad H_2(g)$$

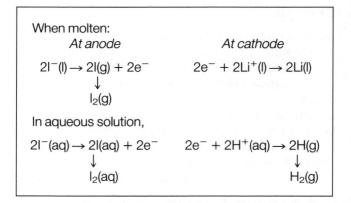

Hydrogen has a variety of uses (see Section 10.4), e.g. in the hardening of oils to make margarine. Iodine can be converted to silver iodide which is used in the manufacture of photographic film.   **(Total 10)**

(MEG, June 1989, Paper 3, QB3)

This question is part of an extension paper designed to award the A and B grades. It is one of 3 questions, of which you must answer 2. The examination paper advises you to spend about 15 minutes on this question, which you answer on lined paper at the end of the examination paper. This question is quite difficult, and so marks gained here could be lower than for other questions yet still give you an A grade – something like 6 marks for an A grade and 4 for a B grade.

6.4 Self-test Questions

Question 6.1

A student used the apparatus shown to get hydrogen from hydrochloric acid:

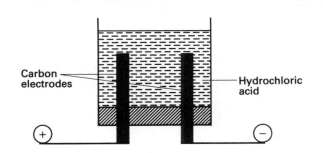

(a) Hydrogen forms at one electrode. Name the substance that forms at the other electrode. **(1)**

(b) On the diagram show how the hydrogen gas can be collected. **(2)**

(c) Give a simple test for hydrogen gas. **(2)**

Test	Result

(SEG, June 1988, Paper 1, Q8)

Questions 6.2 and 6.3

Directions. These two questions deal with laboratory situations. Each situation is followed by a set of questions. Select the best answer for each question.

The apparatus below was used to investigate the electrolysis of sodium chloride, NaCl. The crucible contained molten sodium chloride. The U-tube contained an aqueous solution of sodium chloride. The bulb lit when the switch was closed.

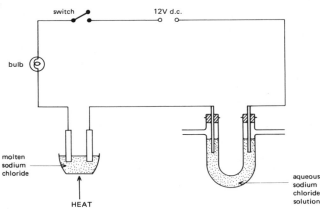

Question 6.2

What were the products at the two cathodes in this experiment?

	At the cathode in molten sodium chloride	*At the cathode in aqueous sodium chloride solution*
A	Sodium	Hydrogen
B	Chlorine	Oxygen
C	Hydrogen	Hydrogen
D	Sodium	Sodium
E	Chlorine	Chlorine

(L)

Question 6.3

What would happen in the experiment if the heat supply under the crucible were to be removed and the contents allowed to cool to room temperature?

	Bulb	*Electrolysis in the crucible*	*Electrolysis in the U-tube*
A	Stays alight	Continues	Continues
B	Stays alight	Stops	Continues
C	Stays alight	Continues	Stops
D	Goes out	Stops	Continues
E	Goes out	Stops	Stops

(L)

Question 6.4

(a) Chlorine is a member of a family of elements called the Halogens. Some of the properties of the Halogens are given below.

Name	Symbol	Colour at room temperature	Reaction with hydrogen
Fluorine	F	almost colourless	
Chlorine	Cl	greenish yellow	explodes in direct sunlight
Bromine	Br	reddish brown	a slow reaction
Iodine	I	dark grey	some reaction on heating
Astatine	At		no reaction

Using the information given in the table, suggest the
  (i)   least reactive of the Halogens   (1)
  (ii) reaction of fluorine with hydrogen   (1)
  (iii) colour of astatine at room temperature   (1)
(b) Write a balanced equation for the reaction between hydrogen and chlorine.   (1)
(c) Chlorine is produced at the anode in the industrial electrolysis of brine.
  (i)   Name a solution produced in large quantities during this electrolysis.   (1)
  (ii) Why do you think that the anodes are made from carbon rather than from iron?   (1)
  (iii) Give one major industrial use of chlorine.   (1)
(d) The electrolysis of some salts was carried out using carbon electrodes. The results are as follows:

Electrolyte	Product at the cathode	Product at the anode
Molten lead(II) bromide	lead	bromine
Aqueous copper(II) nitrate	copper	oxygen

Using only the information in the table above, complete the table below. **(4)**

Electrolyte	Product at the cathode	Product at the anode
Molten copper(II) bromide Aqueous copper(II) sulphate		

(e) The melting point of pure aluminium oxide is 2050°C. The melting point of a mixture of aluminium oxide and cryolite is 1000°C.

    (i) Why do you think that electrolysing pure molten aluminium oxide to make aluminium is uneconomic compared with using a molten mixture of aluminium oxide and cryolite? **(1)**

    (ii) Why do you think that making iron in the blast furnace is a cheaper process than the one used to produce aluminium? **(1)**

(f) Scrap iron is sometimes added to solutions of copper salts to recover copper metal.

    (i) Give a reason why this method works. **(1)**

    (ii) Suggest a method which could be used to separate the copper formed from this solution. **(1)**

(g) It has been suggested that the world supply of copper ore will have been used up by the middle of the next century. Suggest two ways of extending the time for which copper is available to man. **(2)**

(Total 17)

(MEG, Nov. 1988, Paper 2, Q8)

6.5 Answers to Self-test Questions

6.1 (a) Chlorine.

(b)

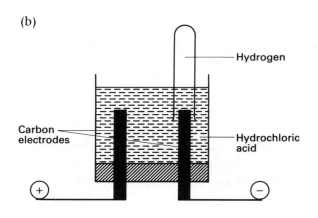

Hydrogen

Carbon electrodes

Hydrochloric acid

+   −

(c) Test: apply a flame to the gas.
Result: a 'pop' should be heard.

6.2 **A.**

| Since hydrogen is below sodium in the reactivity series. |

6.3 **E.**

| Sodium chloride solidifies; ions can no longer travel to the electrodes, no current flows. |

6.4 (a) (i) Astatine.
(ii) Explodes even in the dark and at a low temperature.
(iii) Black.

(b) $H_2(g) + Cl_2(g) \rightarrow 2HCl(g)$

(c) (i) Sodium hydroxide solution.

(ii) Chlorine reacts with iron but it has no reaction with carbon.

(iii) Chlorine is used in the manufacture of plastics (e.g. PVC) but any of the uses given in Section 16.3 could have been given here.

| The ions present in brine (sodium chloride solution) are $Cl^-(aq)$, $OH^-(aq)$, $Na^+(aq)$ and $H^+(aq)$. Chlorine is produced at the anode and at the cathode, hydrogen ions are discharged in preference to sodium ions since hydrogen is much lower in the reactivity series than sodium. This leaves Na^+ and OH^- ions in solution, i.e. sodium hydroxide solution. The relevant electrode equations are:

$2Cl^-(aq) \rightarrow 2Cl(g) + 2e^-$ $\qquad$ $2e^- + 2H^+(aq) \rightarrow 2H(g)$
$\qquad\qquad\downarrow$ $\qquad\qquad\qquad\qquad\qquad\downarrow$
$\qquad\quad Cl_2(g)$ $\qquad\qquad\qquad\qquad\qquad H_2(g)$ |

(d)

Product at the cathode	Product at the anode
Copper	Bromine
Copper	Oxygen

| The relevant equations are:

$Cu^{2+}(l) + 2e^- \rightarrow Cu(s)$ $\qquad$ $2Br^-(l) \rightarrow 2Br(g) + 2e^-$
$\qquad\qquad\qquad\qquad\qquad\qquad\qquad\qquad\qquad\downarrow$
$\qquad\qquad\qquad\qquad\qquad\qquad\qquad\qquad Br_2(g)$

$2Cu^{2+}(aq) + 4e^- \rightarrow 2Cu(s)$ $\quad$ $4OH^-(aq) \rightarrow 4OH(aq) + 4e^-$
$\qquad\qquad\qquad\qquad\qquad\qquad\qquad\qquad\qquad\downarrow$
$\qquad\qquad\qquad\qquad\qquad\qquad\qquad 2H_2O(l) + O_2(g)$ |

(e) (i) It is uneconomic because a lot more electricity has to be used to keep the aluminium oxide molten and this is costly.

(ii) Because it does not involve the use of electricity.

(f) (i) Iron is above copper in the reactivity series and will displace copper from solutions of its salts.

(ii) Filtration.

(g) Recycle the copper.
Alloy the copper with other metals.

6.6 Grading of Self-test Questions

These questions are all relatively straightforward and will be found in the compulsory part of the examination paper. The questions test various different skills – factual recall skills and the ability to use information given in the question and reason out an answer. The total mark for these four questions is 24 and the marks/grades will be something like:

20 or more marks _____ at least C grade
15 marks _____ around E grade
10 marks _____ around G grade

ENERGY CHANGES IN CHEMISTRY

Topic Guide

7.1 Introduction

Energy can be neither created nor destroyed, but it can be converted from one form to another. For example, the chemical energy stored up in petrol can be converted to heat energy and kinetic energy (energy associated with movement) in a car engine. Another important energy conversion is the changing of solar energy (energy from the sun) into chemical energy in photosynthesis (see Section 9.4).

Most of the energy which we use today is obtained from 'fossil fuels' – gas, oil and coal. Supplies of these fuels will not last forever, and they must not be wasted. They can be supplemented by nuclear energy (see Section 2.5), and energy from wind, flowing water and from the sun, but these last three energy sources do not contribute very greatly to world supplies at the moment. They are, however, renewable: they can be used again and again, unlike fossil and nuclear fuels (see Question 18.8). Also, they do not cause pollution. Combustion of fossil fuels causes air pollution (see Section 9.1), and nuclear reactors give rise to radioactive waste. Choice of fuel depends largely upon availability, convenience and cost. Only fairly recently has large-scale concern about pollution had any bearing on the matter.

During almost all chemical changes energy is exchanged with the surroundings: if it is given out by the reaction, the change is said to be *exothermic*; if it is absorbed, the reaction is *endothermic*. The reason that the energy changes occur is that bonds between atoms or ions in the reactants have to be broken and new ones formed in the products. Bond breaking absorbs energy, but bond making releases it. The overall energy change that occurs results from the difference between the energy supplied for the breaking of the reactant bonds and that evolved in the making of the product bonds (see Question 7.2).

7.2 Electrical Cells

Electrical cells enable electrical energy to be obtained from chemical reactions. This is the reverse of what happens during electrolysis, where chemical reactions are brought about by the use of electrical energy. The simplest type of cell consists of two metals dipping into an electrolyte (see Section 6.1) and connected to one another by a wire.

Suppose that the metals are zinc and copper and the electrolyte is dilute sulphuric acid (Fig. 7.1). Zinc, being more reactive than copper, forms ions more readily and so its atoms each give up two electrons and go into solution as Zn^{2+} ions. The electrons flow through the wire to the copper rod where H^+ ions from the acid take them to become H atoms, which join in pairs to form H_2 molecules.

At zinc: $\quad Zn(s) \rightarrow Zn^{2+}(aq) + 2e^-$
At copper: $\quad 2H^+(aq) + 2e^- \rightarrow H_2(g)$

Adding: $\quad 2H^+(aq) + Zn(s) \rightarrow Zn^{2+}(aq) + H_2(g)$

Clearly, the overall chemical change taking place is the same as that which occurs when zinc is dipped into dilute sulphuric acid, i.e. displacement, but the cell enables us to obtain electrical energy from the reaction.

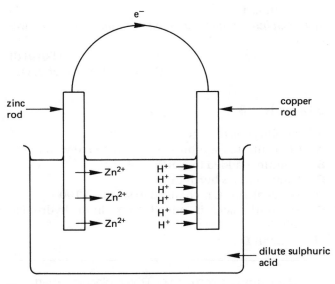

Fig. 7.1

7.3 Light Energy in Chemistry

Light energy can be produced by a chemical reaction (e.g. in a flame) or can be absorbed (e.g. in the reaction between hydrogen and chlorine, in photography and, very importantly, in photosynthesis (see Section 9.4)).

7.4 Worked Examples

Example 7.1

100 cm³ of water, at room temperature, was placed in a beaker and then heated with a burner supplying heat at a constant rate. The temperature of the water was recorded at regular intervals until 10 cm³ of it had boiled away.

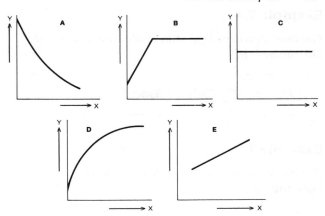

Fig. 7.2

Select from **A** to **E** in Fig. 7.2 the graph that best represents the way Y changes with X.
(Y = Temperature of water, X = Time.)
The answer is **B**.

(L)

> The temperature rises steadily until the liquid boils and then remains constant. Energy is being supplied but it is being used up in pulling the water molecules apart to form steam.

Examples 7.2–7.6 concern the following energy conversions:
A Solar energy → chemical energy
B Electrical energy → chemical energy
C Chemical energy → electrical energy
D Chemical energy → heat energy
E Heat energy → chemical energy
Choose, from **A** to **E**, the type of energy conversion represented by each of the following:
(LEAG, June 1988, Paper 1, Q11–15)

Example 7.2

The manufacture of aluminium from bauxite.
The answer is **B**.

> This is electrolysis, where electrical energy produces chemical changes. More details are given in Example 17.3.

Example 7.3

The formation of sugar in sugar cane.
The answer is **A**.

> This is photosynthesis – light is needed to produce the chemical change. See Section 9.4.

Example 7.4

The manufacture of calcium oxide from limestone.
The answer is **E**.

$$CaCO_3(s) \xrightarrow{heat} CaO(s) + CO_2(g)$$

Example 7.5

The operation of a battery powered radio.
The answer is **C**.

Example 7.6

The production of a flame by a decorator's blow torch.
The answer is **D**.

Example 7.7

The pie chart shows our main sources of energy.

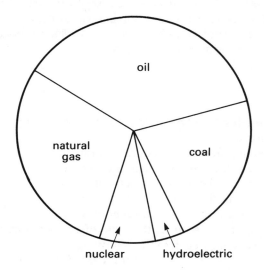

(a) (i) Name a fuel which burns to produce carbon
dioxide and water.   **(1)**
Natural gas or oil.
(ii) Which one of the sources of energy produces
no pollution?   **(1)**
Hydroelectric.

Running water drives a turbine which produces
electricity.

(b) (i) Which one of the sources of energy is most
likely to replace the three fossil fuels (coal, oil
and natural gas) when they run out?   **(1)**
Nuclear.
(ii) Give a reason for your answer.   **(1)**

*There are large supplies of nuclear fuel. A small quantity of
nuclear fuel provides a large amount of energy.*
(c) The coal which is used in a power station contains
sulphur as an impurity. The water in a lake near
the power station was found to be acidic. Name
the gas likely to have caused this problem.   **(1)**
Sulphur dioxide.
(d) Powdered limestone (calcium carbonate) was
added to this lake to neutralise the acidity of the
water. During this operation bubbles of gas were
given off.
(i) Name the gas given off.   **(1)**
Carbon dioxide.

Carbonate + acid → salt + water + carbon dioxide.

(ii) Why should the limestone be powdered?   **(1)**
To speed up the reaction. (See Section 8.1.)
(iii) Suggest why the acidity of the water in the
lake increased during the cold winter
months.   **(1)**
*More sulphur dioxide was produced since more coal was
burnt.*

(Total 8)
(MEG, Nov. 1988, Paper 2, Q2)

Example 7.8

An endothermic change takes place when
A   Concentrated sulphuric acid is added to water
B   Sodium is added to water
C   Magnesium is burnt in air
D   Water at 100°C is changed to steam at 100°C
E   Sulphuric acid is added to sodium hydroxide
solution.
The answer is **D**.

In **D**, energy is taken in to pull the molecules apart.
All the other changes are exothermic.

Example 7.9

In the cell shown in Fig. 7.3 there is a flow of electrons
from metal P to metal Q through the meter.

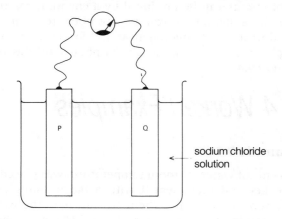

Fig. 7.3

Which of the following produce this result?

	P	Q
A	silver	copper
B	zinc	copper
C	copper	zinc
D	silver	zinc
E	copper	magnesium

The answer is **B**.

Atoms of the more reactive of the two metals give up electrons and go into solution as positive ions. The electrons flow to the less reactive metal (see Section 7.2).

7.5 Self-test Questions

Question 7.1

The equation for the production of sulphur trioxide in the Contact Process from sulphur dioxide and oxygen is given below:

$2SO_2 + O_2 \rightleftharpoons 2SO_3$

(a) What does the sign $\rightleftharpoons$ indicate?   (1)

(b) What effect does each of the following have on the reaction?
   (i)   a catalyst,
   (ii) increasing the temperature.   (2)

(c)

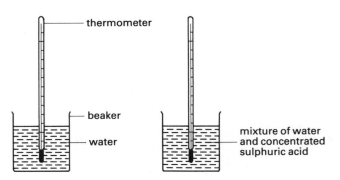

Concentrated sulphuric acid was diluted by carefully adding it to water. The temperature of the water was recorded before the acid was added and the final temperature of the mixture was also recorded. The results are given below.

Final temperature of the mixture	=	54°C
Temperature of the water	=	21°C
Difference in temperature	=	____

Complete the table of results.
   (i)   What kind of heat change has occurred?
   (ii)   What do you think would happen to the temperature if more concentrated sulphuric acid was added?
   (iii) Give one major industrial use of sulphuric acid.   (4)

(d) The diagram below shows part of the pictorial hazard sign on a tanker used to carry sulphuric acid.

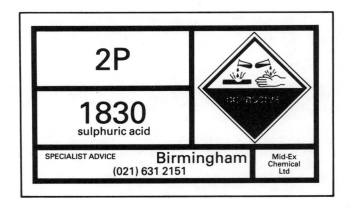

(i) Give one property of the material used to make the container which holds the acid.

(ii) Give one advantage of using pictorial hazard warnings on chemical containers.

(iii) The word underneath the 'picture' has been covered by dirt from the road. What does this picture symbol indicate? **(3)**

(MEG, June 1988, Paper 2, Q9)

*Question 7.2

(a) When a chemical bond is broken heat is taken in. When a bond is formed, heat is given out.

For example, when 1 mole of nitrogen molecules are converted into nitrogen atoms, 945 kJ are taken in. This can be represented by the equation:

$$N_2 \rightarrow 2N$$

Similarly, when N atoms and H atoms combine to form 1 mole of N–H bonds, 389 kJ are given out.

This energy change is called the bond energy. Bond energy is measured in kilojoules (kJ). Given the following values for bond energy.

$$
\begin{array}{ll}
N\equiv N & 945 \text{ kJ} \\
H-H & 436 \text{ kJ} \\
N-H & 389 \text{ kJ}
\end{array}
$$

calculate the total energy change for the reaction in the Haber process.

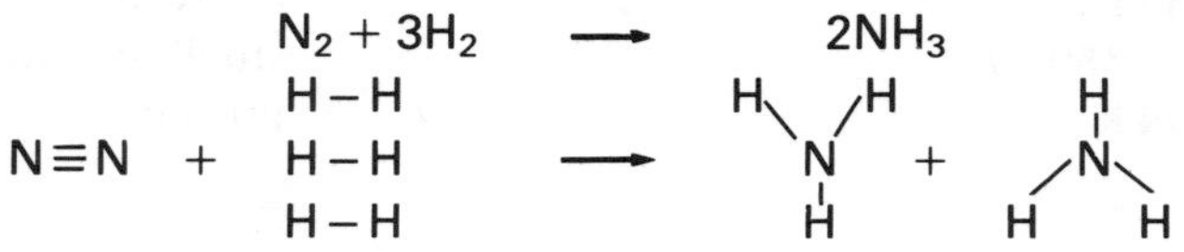

State clearly whether the energy is given out or taken in. **(3)**

(b) State the conditions used for the Haber process. Comment on the temperature used with reference to your calculation in (a). **(3)**

(c) (i) Ammonium nitrate is used as a fertiliser. Indicate the problems caused by the application of too much ammonium nitrate in farming.

(ii) Describe how you would show the presence of NH_4^+ ions in a sample of this fertiliser. **(4)**

(Total 10)

(MEG, June 1989, Paper 3, QB2)

7.6 Answers to Self-test Questions

7.1 (a) The reaction is reversible.
   (b) (i)   Increases the rate of the reaction.
       (ii) Increases the rate of production of sulphur trioxide.

> Increasing the temperature decreases the yield of sulphur trioxide for reasons which are beyond the scope of this book.

   (c) The difference in temperature is 33°C.
        (i)   An exothermic change.
        (ii) More heat would be given out and the temperature would rise still further.
        (iii) To manufacture fertilisers such as ammonium sulphate and 'superphosphate'.
   (d) (i)   It must be acid resistant.
       (ii) It can be understood by foreigners or non-readers.
       (iii) Corrosive.

7.2 (a) Energy taken in = 945 + (3 × 436) kJ
                        = 2253 kJ
        Energy given out = 6 × 389 kJ
                         = 2334 kJ

> There are 6 N–H bonds made.

        Energy change = 2334 − 2253 kJ
                      = 81 kJ given out.
   (b) The conditions used are 500°C, 250 atm pressure and an iron catalyst. Exothermic reactions are favoured by low temperatures. This temperature has been chosen so that the rate of the reaction is acceptable, as well as the yield of ammonia.
   (c) (i)   If excess ammonium nitrate is used, it will be washed into rivers, causing water pollution. The addition of fertilisers to a river leads to the too rapid growth of lower plant life, resulting in the decay of other plants and the death of animals.

> See Section 10.3 and Example 10.6 if you need more help with this answer.

       (ii) Sodium hydroxide solution is added to a solution of ammonium nitrate (the fertiliser) and the mixture heated. Ammonia is evolved – this gas has a characteristic smell and turns universal indicator paper purple.

RATE OF REACTION

Topic Guide

8.1 Introduction

If dilute hydrochloric acid is added to excess marble chips, carbon dioxide is given off and the mass of reactants decreases. A graph of decrease in mass against time is shown in Fig. 8.1:

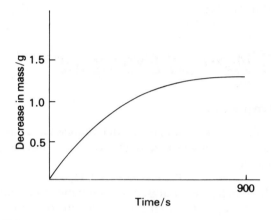

Fig. 8.1

The slope of the graph is steepest at the beginning, showing that the mass is decreasing at the greatest rate (i.e. the rate of evolution of carbon dioxide is greatest) when the acid is at its most concentrated. As the reaction proceeds the slope becomes less steep, indicating that the reaction is slowing down. This is because the acid is being used up and becoming more dilute. Where the graph becomes a horizontal straight line the reaction has ceased: no further change in mass occurs because all of the acid has been used up.

A **catalyst** is a substance which alters the rate of a chemical reaction but may be recovered unchanged in mass at the end. Positive catalysts speed up chemical reactions; negative catalysts (inhibitors) slow them down. Examples of positive catalysts include manganese(IV) oxide in the decomposition of hydrogen peroxide solution into water and oxygen (see Example 8.1), iron in the manufacture of ammonia by the Haber process (see Section 17.5), and vanadium(V) oxide in the manufacture of sulphuric acid by the Contact process (see Section 17.4). Many biological processes involve natural catalysts, called **enzymes** (see Section 18.5 and Example 8.1).

The rate of a chemical reaction may be increased by:
1. Making the reactants more finely divided.
2. Increasing the concentration of the reactants, or increasing the pressure if they are gases.

3. Increasing the temperature.
4. Adding a (positive) catalyst.
5. Increasing the light intensity (applies to a few reactions only).

8.2 Reversible Reactions

A **reversible reaction** is one that can proceed in either direction depending on the conditions under which it is carried out.

For example, if blue copper(II) sulphate crystals are heated, water is given off and white anhydrous copper(II) sulphate remains. When water is added to this solid, blue hydrated copper(II) sulphate is formed once more.

$$CuSO_4.5H_2O(s) \rightleftharpoons CuSO_4(s) + 5H_2O(l)$$

(The $\rightleftharpoons$ sign shows that the reaction can proceed in both directions.)

8.3 Worked Examples

*Example 8.1

(a) Hydrogen peroxide, H_2O_2, decomposes in aqueous solution to give oxygen gas. The equation for the reaction is

$$2H_2O_2 \rightarrow 2H_2O + O_2$$

The reaction is catalysed by manganese(IV) oxide. In two separate experiments 100 cm^3 of a solution of hydrogen peroxide was stirred with the same quantity of manganese(IV) oxide at 20°C. In the first experiment coarse particles of the catalyst were used, whilst in the second experiment a finely powdered form of the catalyst was used. The volume of oxygen produced was measured at 1 minute intervals. The results obtained are shown on graphs labelled A and B below.

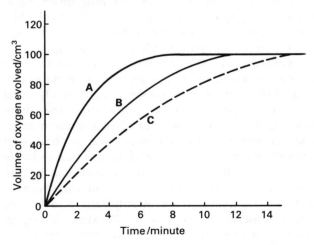

(i) State which graph corresponds to the coarse particles of catalyst. Give one reason for your answer.   **(2)**

B – because the particles are larger, the total surface area is less for B compared to A.

> Reaction rate decreases with decrease in surface area.

(ii) In both experiments, the volume of oxygen evolved per minute decreases with time. Give an explanation of this.   **(2)**

The hydrogen peroxide is becoming more dilute.

> Reaction rate decreases with decrease in concentration.

(iii) If experiment B were carried out at 10°C instead of 20°C, sketch on the graph the type of curve you would expect to obtain (label it C) and give an explanation.   **(2)**

Explanation: Reaction rate decreases with drop in temperature.

> Note that the final volume of oxygen is the same in each case since the same quantity of hydrogen peroxide is used each time.

(b) The decomposition of hydrogen peroxide in living cells is catalysed by an enzyme called catalase, which protects cells from the toxic effects of hydrogen peroxide.

(i) Explain what is meant by an *enzyme*.   **(1)**

A biological catalyst.

(ii) State whether you would expect catalase to be a more efficient catalyst than manganese(IV) oxide or a less efficient one.   **(1)**

A more efficient catalyst.

> The catalase is in solution.

(c) An oxide of potassium of formula KO_2 reacts with carbon dioxide, CO_2, to give potassium carbonate, K_2CO_3, and oxygen O_2.

(i) Write down a balanced equation for the reaction that takes place.   **(1)**

$4KO_2 + 2CO_2 \rightarrow 2K_2CO_3 + 3O_2$

> You are not expected to know this reaction but you should be able to balance the equation from the data given.

(ii) How could this reaction be made use of in space travel?   **(1)**

In the reaction, carbon dioxide is absorbed and oxygen regenerated for breathing.

(Welsh, June 1988, Paper 2, Q3)

Example 8.2

When magnesium ribbon reacted with excess dilute hydrochloric acid at room temperature, the total volume of hydrogen produced was noted every 20 seconds.

The results obtained are given in the graph labelled C drawn below.

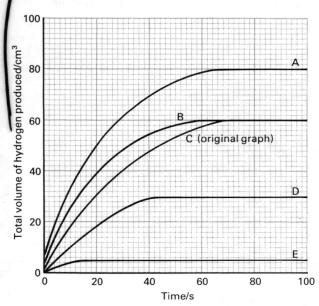

(a) Which of the graphs, A, B, D or E would have been obtained if
   (i) a leakage of gas occurred during the experiment? **(1)**

E.

   (ii) only half the magnesium ribbon had been used as compared with the original amount used in C? **(1)**

D.

   (iii) slightly warmer excess acid had been used? **(1)**

B.

   (iv) a greater mass of powdered magnesium had been used? **(1)**

A.

(b) What was the final volume of hydrogen obtained in Experiment C? **(1)**

60 cm³.

(c) Give a word equation for the reaction between magnesium and dilute hydrochloric acid. **(1)**

Magnesium + hydrochloric → magnesium + hydrogen
acid   chloride solution

(Total 6)

(MEG, Nov. 1988, Paper 2, Q 11)

The equation for the reaction is:
$$Mg(s) + 2\,HCl(aq) \rightarrow MgCl_2(aq) + H_2(g)$$
Therefore, 1 mole of magnesium gives 1 mole of hydrogen. If the mass of magnesium is halved, then the quantity of hydrogen is halved also. If more magnesium is used, then more hydrogen is obtained. Increasing the temperature of the acid increases the rate at which the hydrogen is formed but does not increase the yield.

Example 8.3

The formation of carbon monoxide and hydrogen from methane and steam at 750°C can be represented by the equation:
$$CH_4(g) + H_2O(g) \rightleftharpoons CO(g) + 3H_2(g); \Delta H = -206\,kJ$$

(a) What mass of methane would have to react in order to produce 206 kJ of energy? **(1)**

1 mole of methane is needed, i.e. (12 + 4) = 16 g.

(b) What will happen to the rate of reaction if the pressure is increased? Explain. **(2)**

The rate of reaction will become greater because an increase in pressure will increase the concentration of a gas.

$\Delta H = -206\,kJ$ indicates that 206 kJ are given out when the number of moles of substances shown in the equation react together.

8.4 Self-test Questions

Question 8.1

The graph below shows the volume of oxygen formed during the decomposition of 50 cm^3 of hydrogen peroxide solution using 1 g of manganese(IV) oxide as the catalyst.

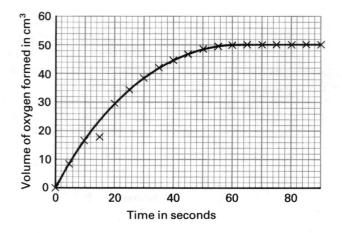

(a) Give **one** possible reason why the point ($\times$) at 15 seconds is **not** on the graph line. **(1)**
(b) What volume of oxygen is collected after 20 seconds? **(1)**
(c) How long does it take to collect 40 cm^3 of oxygen? **(1)**
(d) When the reaction stopped, the 1 g of manganese(IV) oxide was still left. What caused the reaction to stop? **(1)**
(e) In another experiment the same amount of hydrogen peroxide is used but with twice as much manganese(IV) oxide. Sketch, on the same grid above, a graph line of the expected results. **(2)**

(SEG, Winter 1988, Paper 1, Q8)

Question 8.2

The rate of production of hydrogen by the reaction of magnesium with 0.5 M hydrochloric acid (containing 0.5 mole of HCl per dm^3) was investigated using the apparatus shown.

The following results were obtained with a laboratory temperature of 15°C and 1 atmosphere pressure, using 0.0669 g of magnesium ribbon.

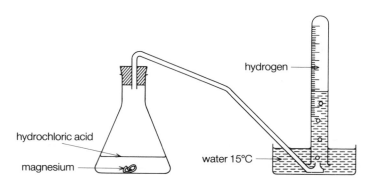

Time in minutes	0	½	1	1½	2	2½	3	3½	4	4½	5	5½
Total volume of H$_2$ in cm^3 (at 15°C and 1 atm.)	0	9.5	18.0	26.5	33.5	41.4	48.0	54.0	59.0	62.0	63.0	63.0

(a) (i) On squared paper, plot a graph of volume of hydrogen (vertical axis) against time (horizontal axis). **(4)**

(ii) On the same graph paper, sketch and label the curve you would have expected if the hydrochloric acid had been heated to 25°C before the experiment. **(2)**

(iii) What is the total volume of hydrogen obtained from 0.0669 g of magnesium at 15°C according to this experiment? **(2)**

(iv) Calculate the volume that would have been obtained at this temperature from 1 mole of magnesium. **(4)**

(v) How does your answer compare with the 24 dm^3 normally accepted for the molar volume of a gas? Give one possible reason for the discrepancy you have found. **(2)**

(b) When a similar experiment was conducted with pieces of calcium carbonate instead of magnesium, a value of 16.8 dm^3 for the molar volume of carbon dioxide was found.

(i) Why do you think the value was so low? **(2)**

(ii) State and explain two ways in which the rate of reaction of calcium carbonate with hydrochloric acid could be increased, other than by heating. **(4)** (OLE)

8.5 Answers to Self-test Questions

8.1 (a) The volume of oxygen was read incorrectly.
  (b) 30 cm³.
  (c) 32 seconds.
  (d) The hydrogen peroxide was used up.
  (e)

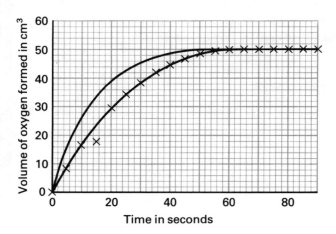

The oxygen is produced more quickly since there are more collisions between hydrogen peroxide molecules and the manganese(IV) oxide.

8.2 (a) (i) and (ii), see graph below.

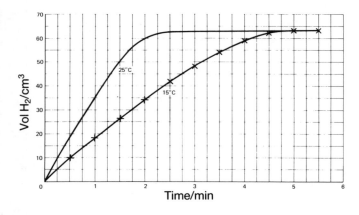

The reaction would be faster at 25°C because the particles in the acid would be speeded up and would collide more frequently and more violently with the magnesium. However, the final volume of hydrogen would be the same as before because the same amounts of magnesium and hydrochloric acid are used and the hydrogen is collected at the same temperature.

(iii) 63.0 cm³.
(iv) Moles of Mg used = mass/molar mass (see Section 5.1)

$$= \frac{0.0669}{24}$$

$\frac{0.0669}{24}$ mol of Mg gives 63.0 cm³ of H_2

$\therefore$ 1 mol of Mg gives $63.0 \div \dfrac{0.0669}{24}$

$$= 22{,}600 \text{ cm}^3 \text{ of } H_2$$

(v) The value is lower than expected. Possibly the magnesium had an oxide coating so that the actual mass of *metal* was less than 0.0669 g.

(b) (i) Carbon dioxide is slightly soluble in water and could dissolve in both the dilute acid and the water in the trough.

(ii) The rate could be increased by using more concentrated acid so that more $H^+(aq)$ ions would be colliding with the surface of the calcium carbonate.
  If the calcium carbonate were broken up into smaller pieces, there would be a greater surface area in contact with the acid and the reaction would be speeded up.

THE ATMOSPHERE AND COMBUSTION

Topic Guide

9.1 Introduction

Air consists of a mixture of gases, the percentages being as shown in Fig. 9.1.

Water vapour will also be present (cobalt(II) chloride paper turns pink in the air), the exact proportion depending on conditions.

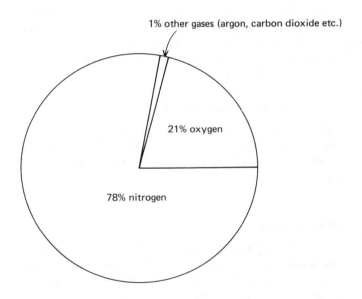

Fig. 9.1

Air in built-up areas will be polluted by fumes from cars, fires, factories, etc. (see Examples 9.5 and 9.7). Substances present may include dust, soot, lead compounds from car exhaust gases (although this is much reduced with the introduction of lead-free petrol), carbon monoxide (see Section 13.5), unburnt hydrocarbons from petrol and other fuels, nitrogen dioxide (see Section 14.2) and sulphur dioxide (see Section 15.5). Most of these are corrosive and/or poisonous. Finally, there are usually bacteria and viruses which may or may not be harmful. Pollution must be controlled, and this can be achieved by means of, for example, smokeless zones, lead-free petrol and control of exhaust emissions.

N.B. Hydrogen is not generally found in the atmosphere.

9.2 Separating the Gases in the Air

Since air is a mixture of gases, it can be separated into its components by physical means: fractional distillation of liquid air. The air is cooled from room temperature to about $-200°C$, ice being removed at $0°C$ and solid carbon dioxide at $-78°C$. Fractional distillation then takes place to yield nitrogen (b.p. $-196°C$), argon (b.p. $-186°C$) and finally oxygen (b.p. $-183°C$).

9.3 Processes which use up Oxygen

There are three main ways in which oxygen is used up – burning, corrosion and respiration. If a piece of iron is allowed to rust or a substance is allowed to burn in a closed container, then the percentage of oxygen in the air can be found, as Examples 9.2 and 9.6 show.

(a) Burning (Combustion)

When a substance burns in air it combines with oxygen (i.e. oxidation occurs). Combustion continues until all of the substance or all of the oxygen is used up.

(b) Rusting

Iron will only rust if both air and water are present; dissolved salt is found to speed up the process (see Example 9.6 and Question 9.3). The gas in the air which is responsible for rusting is oxygen. Rusting, like combustion, is an example of oxidation, but in this case the temperature is much lower and the reaction occurs much more slowly.

Many metals tarnish in air but the coating formed on the surface often prevents further corrosion, e.g. zinc, copper and aluminium. However, rust does not prevent air and water from reaching the iron underneath.

(c) Respiration

When we and other animals breathe, the air we breathe out is warmer and contains more water vapour and carbon dioxide than it did when we inhaled it. We are 'burning' food inside us to provide energy for movement and warmth. The overall change may be summed up as:

sugar + oxygen → carbon dioxide + water + energy.

9.4 Photosynthesis

Combustion, rusting and respiration remove oxygen from the atmosphere. Photosynthesis replaces the oxygen.

Photosynthesis is the process by which green plants synthesise carbohydrates from carbon dioxide and water, using sunlight as the source of energy and chlorophyll as a catalyst, oxygen being liberated into the air. The overall change may be written:

carbon dioxide + water + energy → sugar + oxygen,

which is the reverse of the equation summarising respiration.

9.5 Worked Examples

Example 9.1

If air is bubbled through pure water (pH 7), the pH gradually changes to 5.7. The gas in air which is responsible for this change is:

A   carbon dioxide
B   nitrogen
C   hydrogen
D   argon
E   oxygen.

The answer is **A**.

> Air contains carbon dioxide and this is an acidic oxide, dissolving in water to give carbonic acid.

Example 9.2

In order to find the proportion by volume of one of the main constituents of air, a sample of air was passed through two wash bottles, the first containing aqueous sodium hydroxide and the second containing concentrated sulphuric acid, and was then collected in a gas syringe.

(a) Suggest a reason for passing the air through:
   (i) aqueous sodium hydroxide.
To remove carbon dioxide.
   (ii) concentrated sulphuric acid.   **(2)**
To dry the gas.

(b) The volume of gas collected in the syringe was 80 cm^3. This was passed several times over hot copper powder until no further contraction of volume took place. After cooling to the original temperature the volume was found to be reduced to 63.2 cm^3.
   (i) How would the copper change in appearance?
It would turn black.
   (ii) Which gas had been removed by the copper?
Oxygen.
   (iii) Calculate the volume of this gas present in the sample of air.
$80 - 63.2 \ cm^3 = 16.8 \ cm^3$.
   (iv) Calculate the percentage of this gas present in the sample of air.   **(4)**

$$\% \, Oxygen = \frac{Volume \, of \, oxygen}{Original \, volume \, of \, air} \times 100$$

$$\% \, Oxygen = \frac{16.8}{80} \times 100 = 21$$

(c) (i) What is the main gas remaining in the syringe?
Nitrogen.
   (ii) There will be small amounts of other gases remaining in the syringe. Name one of these gases. **(2)**
Argon.

> In addition to nitrogen there are traces of the noble gases, e.g. argon, neon, helium.

   (iii) Give one use of argon. **(1)**
In electric light bulbs.
(d) How would you treat the solid remaining to obtain copper for re-use? **(1)**
The solid remaining is copper(II) oxide. It needs to be reduced to copper, e.g. by heating it in a stream of hydrogen.
(L)

Example 9.3

Explain why magnesium gains in mass but coal loses mass when each is burned in air. **(2)**
Both substances combine with oxygen when they burn but the magnesium forms a solid product which can be weighed. The coal forms some gaseous products which go into the atmosphere and are not weighed.

Example 9.4

Fig. 9.2

(a) What is the remaining part of the fire triangle (Fig. 9.2)? **(1)**
Air or oxygen.

> For combustion to occur, the three components of the fire triangle are needed. The three requirements of fire fighting are exclusion of air, removal of fuel and temperature reduction.

(b) A small child has been playing with matches and its clothes have caught fire. Explain how you would put out the flames. **(2)**

Air must be excluded as quickly as possible so that burning will cease. Therefore the child must be wrapped in something like a rug or a blanket or turned over so that the flames are between its body and the floor.

Example 9.5

The table shows the composition of the air in an industrial town in 1959 and 1989.

Year	Oxygen %	Nitrogen %	Sulphur dioxide %	Carbon dioxide %	Carbon monoxide and lead %
1959	20.0	79.0	0.2	0.3	0.5
1989	20.6	79.0	0.0	0.1	0.3

(a) Suggest **one** reason for the decrease in sulphur dioxide. **(1)**
Fewer coal fires.
(b) Suggest **two** reasons why the amount of carbon monoxide and lead have decreased. **(2)**
1. More efficient car engines.
2. The use of lead-free petrol.
(c) From the figures, give **one** feature of the town in 1959. **(1)**
The town was heavily industrialised.
(d) In 1959 the water in the local reservoir was found to be slightly acidic but in 1989 the acidity had decreased. Study the table and then suggest a reason for this change. **(1)**
Both sulphur dioxide and carbon dioxide levels have decreased.
(e) It was reported in a newspaper that since the sulphur dioxide had been removed from the atmosphere in the town, blackspot and other diseases had started to attack roses in the area. Suggest a reason for this fact. **(1)**
Sulphur dioxide attacks bacteria and fungi. **(Total 6)**
(MEG, June 1989, Paper 2, Q6)

Example 9.6

(a) Name the two substances which are essential if iron is to rust. **(2)**
(i) Water. (ii) Oxygen.
(b) Name one other substance which will accelerate the rusting process. **(1)**
Salt.
(c) Why is the use of this substance of particular importance to motorists? **(1)**
Salt is put on the roads in winter to melt the ice: an ice/salt mixture has a lower melting point than pure ice. The salt must be washed off to prevent rapid rusting of the car.
(d) Give three methods which can be used to prevent rusting. **(3)**
(i) Painting.
(ii) Coating with grease or oil.
(iii) Coating with metal, e.g. tin plating or galvanising.

> In order to prevent rusting, air and water must be kept away from the iron.

(e) Draw labelled diagrams to show three experiments you could do to show that the substances mentioned in (a) (i) and (ii) are needed for iron nails to rust, and that if either of the substances are absent, no rusting occurs. **(3)**

See Fig. 9.3.

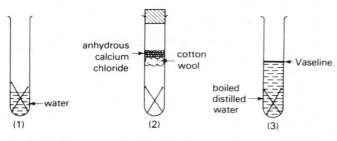

Experiment 1
(a) (i) and (ii) present
– rusting occurs

Experiment 2
Water absent
– no rusting

Experiment 3
air absent
– no rusting

Fig. 9.3

Some moist iron wool was placed in a test tube and the tube was inverted and placed in a beaker of water (Fig. 9.4). The apparatus was inspected each day for one week. The iron rusted and the level of the water in the tube rose during the first few days. After this, no further change took place, even though some air remained and not all of the iron was rusty. The air left in the tube was found to put out a burning splint.

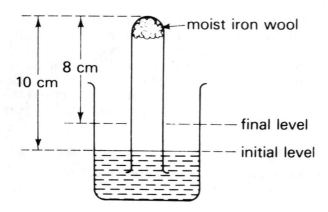

Fig. 9.4

(f) What fraction of the air, approximately, has been used up? **(1)**

The water has moved 2 cm up the tube.

$$Fraction\ of\ air\ used = \frac{2}{10} = \frac{1}{5}$$

(g) Does this experiment show that the air is made up of (i) one, (ii) two, (iii) at least two, gases? Explain your answer. **(2)**

At least two gases. One gas has been used up but we have no means of knowing in this experiment how many gases remain in the tube.

(h) Which gas has been used up during rusting? How can you tell? **(2)**

Oxygen. Oxygen is needed for a splint to burn; since the splint went out, the air must no longer contain oxygen.

(i) What would be the effect on the level of the water if a larger piece of iron wool were used? How did you reach your conclusion? **(2)**

No effect. Not all the iron had rusted and so a larger piece of iron would make no further change.

Example 9.7

In America cars are fitted with catalytic converters in their exhaust systems so that nitrogen monoxide and carbon monoxide are converted into relatively harmless substances.

$$2CO(g) + 2NO(g) \rightarrow 2\ CO_2(g) + N_2(g)$$

(a) How is nitrogen monoxide formed in the engine? **(1)**

Nitrogen and oxygen combine at the high temperature inside the engine to give nitrogen monoxide.

(b) What happens if nitrogen monoxide is released into the atmosphere? **(2)**

It combines with oxygen to produce nitrogen dioxide. This is a respiratory irritant and also dissolves in water to produce acid rain.

(c) Where does the carbon monoxide come from? **(1)**

It is formed by the partial combustion of petrol.

(d) Why is carbon monoxide considered to be harmful? **(2)**

It is poisonous but it is also odourless.

(e) Carbon dioxide could also be considered to be a pollutant. Explain why. **(2)**

The carbon dioxide layer in the atmosphere results in the 'greenhouse effect'. The sun's rays pass through the carbon dioxide layer. The heat carried by these rays is absorbed by objects on the ground which then re-radiate it at longer wavelengths. This new radiation cannot pass back through the carbon dioxide layer and thus the atmosphere slowly heats up.

(f) Name one other pollutant that could be found in the exhaust gases from British cars. **(1)**

Lead compounds from petrol additives.

(g) How could this pollutant be eliminated? **(1)**

The use of lead-free petrol.

9.6 Self-test Questions

Question 9.1

The diagram shows the pollution caused by burning petrol in car engines. Some of this pollution comes from impurities in petrol or from lead compounds that are added to make the engine work better.

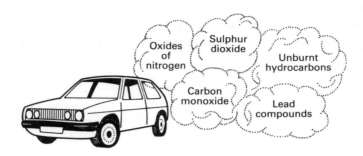

(a) Use your Data Booklet to name one fraction of crude oil that has a higher boiling point than petrol. **(1)**

(b) Petrol consists mainly of a hydrocarbon that has the chemical formula C_8H_{18}.

  (i) What is the meaning of the word *hydrocarbon*? **(2)**

  (ii) Name two products, which are not shown in the diagram, that form when C_8H_{18} completely burns in air. **(2)**

  (iii) Name the poisonous product, which is shown in the diagram, that is formed when C_8H_{18} does not completely burn in air. **(1)**

(c) Sulphur dioxide is formed when any sulphur in petrol burns in air. Write equations for the burning of sulphur in air. **(1)**

  (i) Word equation;

  (ii) Balanced chemical equation. **(2)**

(d) Why do the car exhaust gases contain oxides of nitrogen? **(2)**

(e) Give one way by which the amount of harmful lead compounds from car exhausts could be reduced. **(1)**

(SEG, June 1988, Paper 1, Q10)

Question 9.2

(a) Which two substances are necessary for iron to rust? **(2)**

(b) Why does tin plating prevent iron from rusting? **(1)**

(c) If the tin surface is scratched then the iron will rust. Why does this not happen with zinc plating (galvanising)? **(2)**

Question 9.3

The table below shows how certain substances affect the rusting of steel. A tick ($\checkmark$) indicates that the substance is present. A cross ($\times$) indicates that the substance is absent.

Speed of Rusting	Substances present			
	Water	Air	Salt	Mud
Nil	$\checkmark$	$\times$	$\times$	$\times$
Nil	$\times$	$\checkmark$	$\times$	$\times$
Slow	$\checkmark$	$\checkmark$	$\times$	$\times$
Fast	$\checkmark$	$\checkmark$	$\checkmark$	$\times$
Very fast	$\checkmark$	$\checkmark$	$\checkmark$	$\checkmark$

(a) Using the table, answer the following questions.
   (i)   Which two substances are needed for rusting to occur?
   (ii) Which substances together produce very fast rusting?
   (iii) Mr and Mrs Thomas, who live on a farm by the seaside, said that there was no point in
         washing their car during the winter because it became muddy as soon as it was taken out
         again. Say whether or not you agree with the statement, giving a reason for your answer.
   (iv) The door of the Thomas's car became dented and some of the paint covering the door was
         scraped off. The exposed metal rusted very quickly. Give a reason.   **(6)**
(b) Why do you think that the exhaust system of a car rusts more rapidly than the body?   **(2)**
(c) In view of the fact that iron and steel rust, suggest suitable alternative materials for each of the
     following:
   (i)   A household bath
   (ii) A Coca-Cola can   **(2)**

(MEG, June 1988, Paper 2, Q7)

Question 9.4

Complete the following sentences.
(a) The most abundant gas in the air is ＿＿＿＿＿＿ .
(b) Liquid air is separated into its components by ＿＿＿＿＿＿ ＿＿＿＿＿＿ .
(c) ＿＿＿＿＿＿ is the process by which green plants synthesise carbohydrates from carbon
     dioxide and water, using sunlight as the source of energy, and chlorophyll as a catalyst.
(d) A pollutant in the air which leads to the production of acid rain is ＿＿＿＿＿＿ ＿＿＿＿＿＿ .
(e) The incomplete combustion of diesel fuel produces a poisonous gas called ＿＿＿＿＿＿ .   **(5)**

9.7 Answers to Self-test Questions

9.1 (a) Kerosene.
   (b) (i) A compound containing hydrogen and carbon *only*.
     (ii) Carbon dioxide and water.
     (iii) Carbon monoxide.
   (c) (i) Sulphur + oxygen $\rightarrow$ Sulphur dioxide
     (ii) $S(s) + O_2(g) \rightarrow SO_2(g)$
   (d) Nitrogen and oxygen from the air combine at high temperature in the engine.
   (e) Use unleaded petrol.
9.2 (a) Water and oxygen.
   (b) It covers the iron and stops the air and water reaching the iron.
   (c) Zinc is above iron in the reactivity series and so will tend to pass into solution rather than the iron, which remains intact. Tin is below iron and so will not corrode in preference to the iron.
9.3 (a) (i) Water and air.
     (ii) All four substances.
     (iii) No, I do not agree. The car would rust very quickly if it were scratched and not washed since both salt and mud would be present.
     (iv) The metal was exposed to both air and water and possibly salt and mud, and hence rusted quickly.
   (b) Heat accelerates rusting and there are corrosive gases in contact with the exhaust.
   (c) (i) Either plastic or fibreglass.
     (ii) Aluminium or plastic.
9.4 (a) Nitrogen.
   (b) Fractional distillation.
   (c) Photosynthesis.
   (d) Sulphur dioxide.
   (e) Carbon monoxide.

WATER AND HYDROGEN

Topic Guide

10.1 Introduction

Pure water, formula H_2O, is a colourless, odourless, tasteless liquid which freezes at 0°C and boils at 100°C at 1 atm pressure (see Question 10.1). Water is unusual in that it expands on freezing whereas most liquids contract. Thus ice is less dense than water and forms on the surface rather than at the bottom of the liquid.

Water reacts with reactive metals, non-metals and various compounds (see Example 10.5), e.g.
$$2Na(s) + 2H_2O(l) \rightarrow 2NaOH(aq) + H_2(g)$$
(see Section 12.2)
$$SO_2(aq) + H_2O(l) \rightleftharpoons H_2SO_3(aq) \text{ (see Section 15.5)}$$

(a) Tests for Water (see Example 10.1)

White anhydrous copper(II) sulphate turns blue and blue cobalt(II) chloride turns pink when water is added.

$$CuSO_4(s) + 5H_2O(l) \rightleftharpoons CuSO_4.5H_2O \text{ (s)}$$
white   blue
$$CoCl_2(s) + 6H_2O(l) \rightleftharpoons CoCl_2.6H_2O(s)$$
blue   pink

These two reactions simply prove that a liquid *contains* water. To prove that a liquid is *pure* water, a boiling point determination must be carried out as well (see Question 10.1).

(b) Uses of Water

Water is essential for all life: over two-thirds of your own body mass is water. Water is extensively used in industry for heating and cooling, for producing steam to drive turbines and as a solvent. It is a raw material in the manufacture of ammonia (see Example 17.7) and ethanol (see Section 18.5). In addition, vast amounts are used in the home.

10.2 Water as a Solvent

A **solution** consists of a **solute** dissolved in a **solvent**; if the solvent is water, then an aqueous solution is obtained.

A **saturated solution** is one that contains as much solute as can be dissolved at the temperature concerned, in the presence of undissolved solute.

The **solubility** of a solute in a solvent at a particular temperature is the mass of solute required to saturate 100 g of solvent at that temperature (see Example 10.2).

For most solids, the solubility in a given solvent increases as the temperature is raised, but the reverse is true for gases: the solubility decreases with rise in temperature. The gases which are most soluble in water are those that react with it in some way, e.g. ammonia or hydrogen chloride.

A graph showing the variation of solubility with temperature is known as a solubility curve (see Example 10.2).

Many crystals contain water chemically combined within them. This water is referred to as water of crystallisation, and salts containing it are called hydrated salts. Water of crystallisation can often be driven off by gentle heating, and when this is done it is found that there are a definite number of water molecules associated with every formula unit of the compound concerned.

Water of crystallisation is that definite quantity of water with which some substances are associated on crystallising from an aqueous solution.

10.3 Water Supplies

Our water supplies come from rivers, lakes and underground sources. These are replenished by the rain by means of the water cycle (Fig. 10.1, see also Example 10.3).

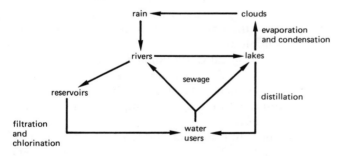

Fig. 10.1

When water evaporates from a sea or lake, the vapour rises and condenses to form many very small droplets (a cloud). If these droplets come together, they fall as rain which eventually returns to a sea or lake so that the cycle can begin again.

In recent years, water pollution has become a serious problem. Water contains dissolved oxygen which is used by fish and other aquatic creatures and also by bacteria which feed on animal and vegetable remains and keep our rivers healthy. Too much untreated sewage causes the bacteria to multiply and they may use up so much oxygen that there is insufficient left for fish to survive. Fertilisers, insecticides, detergents and industrial waste all help to upset the delicate balance of life in the water (see Examples 10.4 and 10.6).

Our drinking water must contain none of the pollutants mentioned above. The water is filtered and chlorine added to kill bacteria. In some areas, a trace of sodium fluoride is added to reduce dental decay. Tap water contains other dissolved solids, particularly calcium and magnesium salts (see Section 12.3 and Example 12.4).

10.4 Hydrogen, H₂

Hydrogen is generally prepared in the laboratory by the action of dilute sulphuric acid on zinc in the apparatus shown in Question 10.4.

$$Zn(s) + H_2SO_4(aq) \rightarrow ZnSO_4(aq) + H_2(g)$$

It is also a product in the electrolysis of acidified water (see Section 6.2) and of the reaction of metals with water and/or steam (see Section 12.3 and Example 10.5).

(a) Test for Hydrogen

A mixture of hydrogen with air or oxygen explodes when a flame is applied.

$$2H_2(g) + O_2(g) \rightarrow 2H_2O(g)$$

(b) Properties of Hydrogen

1. Hydrogen is a colourless, odourless gas.
2. It is almost insoluble in water.
3. It is less dense than air.
4. Pure hydrogen burns quietly in air with a faint, blue flame to give water (see Question 10.1).
5. On heating, hydrogen reduces the oxides of metals low in the reactivity series (see Example 10.7), e.g.
$$CuO(s) + H_2(g) \rightarrow Cu(s) + H_2O(g)$$
6. Hydrogen reacts with some metals and non-metals, e.g.
$$N_2(g) + 3H_2(g) \rightleftharpoons 2NH_3(g)$$
(see Example 17.7)

(c) Uses of Hydrogen

1. In the large-scale syntheses of ammonia and hydrogen chloride (see Example 17.7 and Section 16.1).
2. In the hardening of oils to make margarine and cooking fats (see Example 10.7).
3. As a fuel. There are no pollutant products but there is always the risk of explosion.

(d) Manufacture of Hydrogen

Hydrogen is produced on a large scale:
1. in the cracking of oils (see Section 18.4);
2. in the electrolysis of brine (see Example 17.5); and
3. by the action of steam on hydrocarbons such as methane (North Sea Gas).

10.5 Worked Examples

Example 10.1

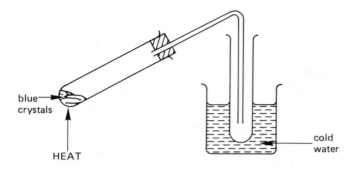

Fig. 10.2

The apparatus is set up as shown in Fig. 10.2, and the left-hand tube is gently heated.

(a) Why is the right-hand tube placed in a beaker of water? **(2)**

To condense the vapour that is given off when the crystals are heated.

(b) What colour changes are seen when the crystals are heated? **(2)**

The crystals change from blue to white.

(c) Draw a diagram (Fig. 10.3) to show how you can measure the boiling point of the product. **(2)**

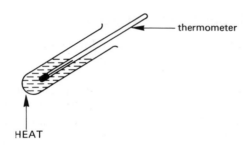

Fig. 10.3

(d) The boiling point of the liquid is 100°C. Suggest what the liquid might be. **(1)**

Water.

(e) Name the original crystals. **(1)**

Copper(II) sulphate crystals.

(f) What would happen if a piece of cobalt(II) chloride paper were placed in the liquid? **(2)**

The cobalt(II) chloride paper would change from blue to pink.

> This test shows the presence of water in a liquid.

Example 10.2

(a) Complete the passage below by putting words from the following list into the gaps. Each word may be used once, more than once or not at all.

saturated solution   **solute**

solution   **solvent**

At the dry cleaners an organic *solvent* is used to dissolve grease from clothes. The *solution* containing the dissolved grease is distilled to get back pure *solvent* and separate it from the grease. If this is not done, more and more grease becomes dissolved until a *saturated solution* is formed. **(5)**

(b) Water does not dissolve grease but it will dissolve many compounds. The graph shows how many grams (g) of three different compounds dissolve in 100 g of water at different temperatures.

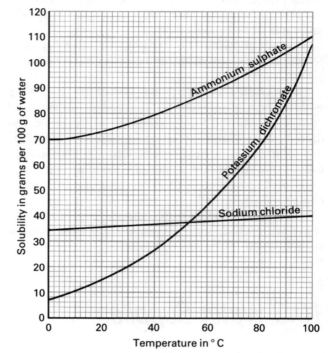

Fig. 10.4

(i) Give the name of the substance which is *most* soluble at

20°C. *Ammonium sulphate.*

70°C. *Ammonium sulphate.*

(ii) Give the name of the substance which is *least* soluble at

20°C. *Potassium dichromate.*

70°C. *Sodium chloride.*

(iii) For which substance is the solubility *least* affected by changes in temperature? **(5)**

Sodium chloride.

(c) Why do you think that the temperature axis only goes up to 100°C? **(1)**

Water boils at this temperature.

(d) A student wanted to purify some potassium dichromate. The student added the compound to 100 cm³ of water and heated gently while stirring. The compound *just* dissolved at 90°C. The solution was then allowed to cool to 50°C.

(i) What mass of potassium dichromate was added (ignore impurities)?

84 g.

> Since the compound just dissolves, the mass of potassium dichromate must equal the solubility at this temperature.

(ii) What mass of potassium dichromate would still be dissolved when the solution had cooled to 50°C?

34 g.

(iii) What mass of crystals would be produced after the solution had stopped crystallising at 50°C?

84 − 34 = 50 g.

(iv) How could the student obtain a sample of dry crystals of potassium dichromate from this experiment? **(5)**

Filter off the crystals, wash them with a little distilled water and dry them between sheets of filter paper.

(e) Two of the three substances named on the graph are used in large amounts in many countries. Name these substances and give an important use for each. **(3)**

Ammonium sulphate; fertiliser.

Sodium chloride; used to make sodium hydroxide, hydrogen and chlorine.

(Total 19)

(LEAG, June 1988, Paper 2, Q5)

Example 10.3

(a) The water we drink has been around for a long time. The same water molecules are used over and over again because of the water cycle.

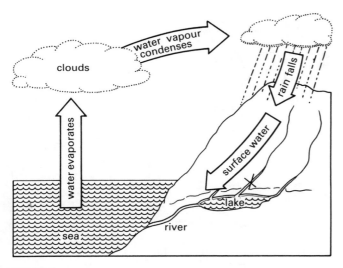

Fig 10.5

(i) Mark a cross (X) on the diagram to show a place from which water for household use could be taken. **(1)**

(ii) Give a reason for your chosen position in (i). **(2)**

This water has flowed off the hillside and so should be unpolluted.

(iii) Chlorine is a poisonous gas. Why are small amounts of chlorine added to household water? **(1)**

To sterilise it.

(iv) Air and water are often polluted. Complete the table below, using a **different** pollutant for the air and the river. **(4)**

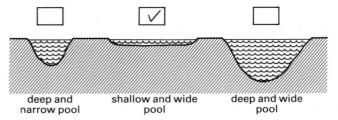

	Found in the air (atmosphere)	Found in a river
Name of a chemical pollutant	*Carbon monoxide*	*Ammonium sulphate*
Where does the chemical pollutant come from?	*Car exhaust fumes*	*Fertilisers*

(b) Sodium chloride (common salt) can be obtained by the evaporation of sea water.

(i) Put a tick (√) in the box above the diagram of the pool where sodium chloride crystals form the fastest. **(1)**

Pools containing sea-water

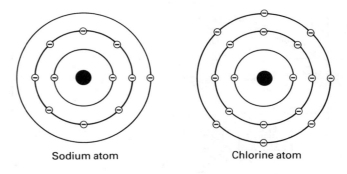

deep and narrow pool   shallow and wide pool   deep and wide pool

Fig. 10.6

(ii) Explain your choice for part (i). **(2)**

Evaporation depends on surface area to volume ratio – a small volume spread over a large area evaporates more quickly.

(c) Sodium and chlorine react, when heated, to form sodium chloride.

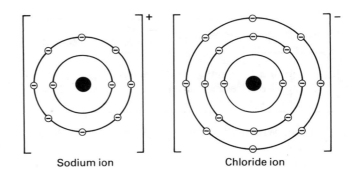

Sodium atom   Chlorine atom

(i) What is shown by the following on the diagrams above? **(2)**

● *Represents a nucleus.*

⊖ *Represents an electron.*

(ii) Use the space below to draw the electronic arrangement of the ions formed when sodium has reacted with chlorine. **(4)**

Sodium ion   Chloride ion

(iii) Write equations for the reaction between sodium and chlorine.

Word equation: sodium + chlorine → sodium chloride. **(1)**
Balanced chemical equation: 2Na(s) + Cl₂(g) → 2NaCl(s) **(2)**

> See Section 4.1 – sodium gives its outer electron to chlorine so that each has a stable arrangement of eight outer electrons.

(SEG, Winter 1988, Paper 1, Q11)

Example 10.4

The drawing below shows the paths of various streams and rivers flowing from hills to the sea.

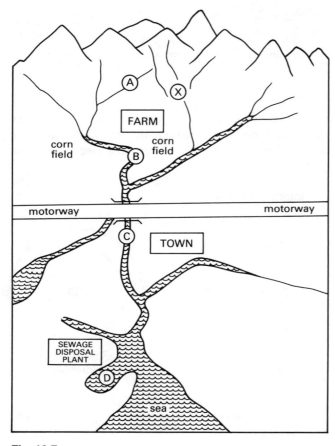

Fig. 10.7

Samples of water were taken at the points labelled A, B, C, D and tested. The results of the tests are given below.

Sample	pH	Appearance	Oxygen content	Lead content
1	6.5	very dirty	0.2%	0.0%
2	7.4	clean	4.0%	0.0%
3	7.8	slightly dirty	2.0%	4.0%
4	6.2	fairly dirty	2.5%	0.4%

(a) From which of the points A, B, C or D do you think
  (i) sample 1 was taken? **(1)**

D.
  (ii) sample 2 was taken? **(1)**
A.
  (iii) sample 3 was taken? **(1)**
C.
In each case give a reason for your answer.   **(1 each)**
  (i) Sample 1 has no lead and so must be a long way from the motorway. It is dirty and contains little oxygen – it is downstream from the town and the sewage works.
  (ii) Sample 2 is clean, with no lead and a lot of oxygen. The water is unpolluted and is from the hills.
  (iii) Sample 3 contains 4.0% lead and must be near the motorway.
(b) The sample from B was found to contain traces of nitrate, phosphate and potassium ions. Give a reason for this. **(1)**
It contains fertilisers from the land.
(c) The local water board decided to site a reservoir at point X. Why do you think this was a good choice? **(1)**
The water draining into it will be similar to sample A, i.e. unpolluted. **(Total 8)**

(MEG, Nov. 1988, Paper 2, Q3)

Example 10.5

Steam is passed over heated magnesium in the apparatus shown in Fig. 10.8.

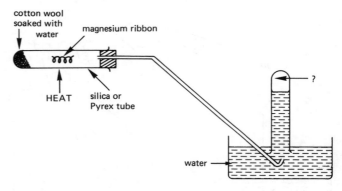

Fig. 10.8

(a) Name the gas produced. **(1)**
Hydrogen.
(b) How could you test for this gas? **(2)**
If a flame is applied to a tube of the gas, a 'pop' is heard.
(c) What is the other product of the reaction between magnesium and steam? **(1)**
Magnesium oxide.
(d) Write a word equation for the reaction. **(2)**
Magnesium + steam → magnesium oxide + hydrogen.
(e) Write a symbol equation for the reaction. **(2)**
  $Mg(s) + H_2O(g) → MgO(s) + H_2(g)$
(f) Would you pass steam over sodium in a similar way? Explain your answer. **(2)**
No, since the reaction is too violent.

Example 10.6

Excess nitrates or excess heat in a river can be regarded as pollution. In each case, describe **one** possible source of this pollution and the effect on the river and its environment.

(a) Various nitrates.

Source: *Fertilisers, e.g. ammonium nitrate or sodium nitrate. Fertilisers are added to soil, but heavy rain washes them into rivers.* **(1)**

Effect: *The addition of fertilisers to a river upsets the ecological balance of the river by promoting the too rapid growth of lower plant life. For example, vast amounts of algae could grow on the surface of the river, thus reducing the amount of light to plants on the bottom of the river. These plants decay, no longer generate oxygen and thus the animals in the river die.* **(2)**

(b) Excess heat.

Source: *Industrial effluent. Many industrial processes use water as a coolant. If this hot water is discharged into a river, then the temperature increases.* **(1)**

Effect: *As long as the temperature increase is moderate, the effect is generally beneficial since the growth of all forms of aquatic life is promoted.* **(2)**

(c) (i) Name one other pollutant of river water. **(1)**
Phosphates.

(ii) What is the source and what is the effect of this pollutant? **(3)**

Source: *Washing powders.*

Effect: *Like nitrates, phosphates are plant nutrients and encourage the growth of algae.*

(d) (i) How is reservoir water filtered? **(1)**
The water is passed through gravel or sand.

(ii) Why is this process carried out? **(2)**
To remove solids and to enable oxygen from the air to kill some bacteria.

(iii) Explain why the water is treated with chlorine. **(2)**
Chlorine kills bacteria.

Household tap water contains neither dirt nor harmful bacteria.

Example 10.7

(a) Hydrogen can be prepared in the laboratory by the electrolysis of dilute sulphuric acid.

(i) At which electrode is hydrogen obtained? **(1)**
The cathode.

(ii) Give the electrode equation. **(1)**

$$2e^- + 2H^+ (aq) \rightarrow 2H(g)$$
$$\downarrow$$
$$H_2(g)$$

(b) A current of dry hydrogen was passed over 4.78 g of heated lead oxide, the excess hydrogen being burnt in the air. 4.14 g of lead was obtained.

(i) Calculate the empirical formula of the oxide. **(3)**

$$(A_r(O) = 16, \quad A_r(Pb) = 207)$$

Mass of oxygen combined with 4.14 g of lead $= 4.78 - 4.14$
$$= 0.64\,g$$

$$
\begin{array}{ccc}
& Pb & : O \\
\textit{ratio of g} & 4.14 & : 0.64 \\
\textit{ratio of mol} & \dfrac{4.14}{207} & : \dfrac{0.64}{16} \\
& = 0.02 & : 0.04 \\
& = 1 & : 2
\end{array}
$$

Empirical formula is PbO_2 *(see Section 5.1).*

(ii) Name one other oxide which can be reduced to the metal by hydrogen. **(1)**
Copper(II) oxide.

(iii) Name one oxide which cannot be reduced to the metal by hydrogen. **(1)**
Sodium oxide.

Hydrogen will reduce only the oxides of those metals which are low in the reactivity series (see Section 12.1).

(c) (i) Write an equation for the reaction between hydrogen and ethene. Name the product and give the necessary conditions. **(2)**

$$H_2(g) + C_2H_4(g) \rightarrow C_2H_6(g)$$
$$\textit{ethane}$$

Hydrogen adds on to ethene in the presence of a finely divided nickel catalyst at about 200°C.

(ii) In the margarine industry, this type of reaction is used to convert animal and vegetable oils into solid fats. What does this tell you about the bonding in natural oil molecules? **(1)**

This tells us that natural oil molecules must contain $C=C$ *bonds, i.e. they are unsaturated.*

(d) There are vast reserves of hydrogen in sea water, and its use as a fuel carries no pollution risk. Suggest one reason in each case why

(i) we have not obtained hydrogen on a large scale from water. **(1)**
Hydrogen can be obtained from sea water by electrolysis but the cost of electricity makes this method too expensive.

(ii) its use as a fuel carries no pollution risk. **(1)**
When hydrogen is burnt, the only product is water, which is not a pollutant.

$$2H_2(g) + O_2(g) \rightarrow 2H_2O(g)$$

10.6 Self-test Questions

Question 10.1

A pupil set up the apparatus shown in the figure.
(a) Name the substance labelled A in the figure, and state **one** physical test which would help to identify it.   **(3)**
(b) Explain the significance of the tube filled with anhydrous calcium chloride granules.   **(2)**

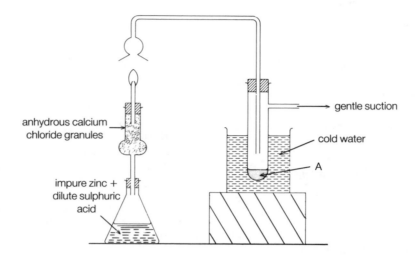

Fig. 10.9

(c) For each of the following substances, name an alternative reagent which could be used successfully in its place:
  (i) impure zinc;   **(1)**
 (ii) dilute sulphuric acid;   **(1)**
(iii) anhydrous calcium chloride granules.   **(1)**
(d) Write down a balanced equation to represent the reaction between the substances named in your answers to (c) (i) and (c) (ii) above.   **(1)**
(e) Write down an aspect of chemistry which the pupil could demonstrate with this equipment.   **(2)**
                                                    (OLE)

Question 10.2

Fill in the blanks in the following sentences:
(a) The element used to sterilise water in swimming pools is _____ .
(b) _____ is the element in drinking water which is good for the growth of healthy teeth.
(c) _____ is an element which can be extracted from sea water.
(d) _____ _____ is a solid used as a drying agent for gases.
(e) An ion which causes hardness in water (see Section 12.3) is _____ .
(f) When hydrochloric acid reacts with magnesium, the gas evolved is _____ .
(g) Pure water can be obtained from sea water by _____ .   **(1 each)**

Question 10.3

A desert survival kit contains a plastic sheet and a cup. A hole is dug in the ground and the sheet is stretched over the hole whilst a stone in the middle forms the sheet into a cone. In the heat of the sun, moisture from the ground collects on the underside of the sheet, runs down to the point of the cone and drips into the cup. The overall process that takes place is an example of

    A   distillation
    B   evaporation
    C   filtration
    D   solution
    E   solvent extraction.

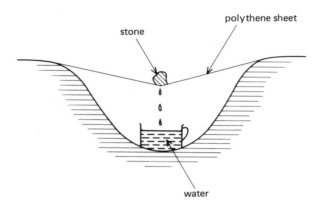

(AEB, 1981)

* Question 10.4

(a) Indicate **one** method in each case by which you could make:
    (i) hydrogen from a **named** compound of hydrogen;
    (ii) a compound of hydrogen from hydrogen.

    In each example your answer should be limited to the starting materials, conditions for reaction and the method of isolation of the product. **(6)**

(b) When hydrogen is added to helium in a container they mix very quickly. When ethanol is added to water the two do not mix properly in a reasonable time unless stirred. Explain this difference. **(2)**

(c) Give one advantage and one disadvantage of hydrogen as a fuel for cars. **(2) (Total 10)**

(LEAG, June 1988, Paper 3, Q10)

10.7 Answers to Self-test Questions

10.1 (a) Water. The boiling point of the liquid could be found – water boils at 100°C at 1 atm pressure.

(b) Anhydrous calcium chloride is used to dry the hydrogen. It is no use trying to prove that water is produced if water is present already.

(c) (i) magnesium;
   (ii) dilute hydrochloric acid;
   (iii) potassium hydroxide pellets or calcium oxide.

(d) $Mg(s) + 2HCl(aq) \rightarrow MgCl_2(aq) + H_2(g)$

(e) Water is obtained by burning hydrogen in air.

10.2 (a) Chlorine.
   (b) Calcium.
   (c) Either sodium or chlorine.
   (d) Either anhydrous calcium chloride or calcium oxide.
   (e) Calcium.
   (f) Hydrogen.
   (g) Distillation.

The apparatus used in Fig. 1.6 may be used. The flask contains impure water; pure water will distil over.

10.3 **A**.

10.4 (a) (i) Hydrogen is generally prepared by the action of cold dilute sulphuric acid on zinc in the apparatus shown in Fig. 10.10. The addition of a little copper(II) sulphate will speed up the reaction. The hydrogen is collected over water.

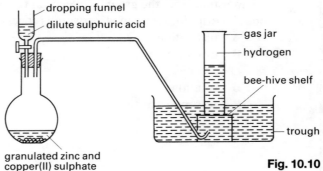

granulated zinc and copper(II) sulphate

dropping funnel
dilute sulphuric acid
gas jar
hydrogen
bee-hive shelf
trough

Fig. 10.10

$$Zn(s) + H_2SO_4(aq) \rightarrow ZnSO_4(aq) + H_2(g)$$

(ii) When hydrogen is burnt in air, water is the product. The hydrogen can be burnt at a jet and the water collected in a cooled tube as shown in Fig. 10.9.

(b) This is explained by the fact that matter is made up of moving particles. The molecules in a liquid move more slowly than those in a gas; they are much closer together and collide more frequently so that mixing is slower with liquids than with gases.

(c) Using hydrogen as a fuel produces no pollution but there is always the risk of explosion.

ACIDS, BASES AND SALTS

Topic Guide

11.1 Introduction

Acidity is measured on the **pH scale**, a scale of numbers normally ranging from 0 to 14. A pH value of 7 is neutral, less than 7 is acidic and more than 7 is alkaline. A *universal indicator* gives different colours corresponding to different pH values, typical results being red for pH = 1, purple for pH = 14.

11.2 Acids

An **acid** is a substance giving hydrated hydrogen ions, $H^+(aq)$, in aqueous solution. Acids show their normal properties only if water is present because these properties are due to $H^+(aq)$ ions, not to the molecules of the acids.

(a) Properties of Acids

1. Acids taste sour.
2. Acids have pH values less than 7 and turn blue litmus red.
3. With reactive metals (e.g. magnesium, zinc, iron) they give hydrogen.

$$\text{acid} + \text{metal} \rightarrow \text{salt} + \text{hydrogen}$$
$$2HCl(aq) + Mg(s) \rightarrow MgCl_2(aq) + H_2(g)$$

N.B. (i) Metals below iron in the reactivity series (see Section 12.1) do not give hydrogen with dilute acids.

(ii) Dilute nitric acid gives one or more of the oxides of nitrogen, not hydrogen, when reacted with metals.

4. With bases, neutralisation occurs to give a salt and water *only* (see Section 11.5).

$$\text{acid} + \text{base} \rightarrow \text{salt} + \text{water.}$$
$$2HNO_3(aq) + CuO(s) \rightarrow Cu(NO_3)_2(aq) + H_2O(l)$$

5. With carbonates (and hydrogencarbonates) effervescence occurs.

$$\text{acid} + \text{carbonate} \rightarrow \text{salt} + \text{water} + \text{carbon dioxide.}$$
$$H_2SO_4(aq) + ZnCO_3(s) \rightarrow ZnSO_4(aq) + H_2O(l) + CO_2(g)$$

11.3 Bases and Alkalis

Bases are substances containing oxide ions, O^{2-}, or hydroxide ions, OH^-. They are usually oxides or hydroxides of metals.

Alkalis are soluble bases: they give hydrated hydroxide ions on dissolving in water. The common alkalis are potassium hydroxide, sodium hydroxide, calcium hydroxide and ammonia solution (previously called ammonium hydroxide).

(a) Properties of Bases

1. Bases evolve ammonia (choking alkaline gas) from ammonium salts, especially on warming.

$$CaO(s) + (NH_4)_2SO_4 \ (s) \rightarrow CaSO_4(s) + H_2O(l) + 2NH_3(g)$$

2. With acids, bases give a salt and water *only* (see properties of acids).

(b) Properties of Alkalis

Since alkalis are bases, they have the two properties given above. Their solutions have the following additional properties:
1. They feel soapy.
2. They have pH values greater than 7 and turn red litmus blue.

11.4 Strengths of Acids and Alkalis

Acids with low pH values, such as hydrochloric, nitric and sulphuric acids, are called *strong acids*. Similarly, alkalis with high pH values, such as solutions of potassium hydroxide and sodium hydroxide, are called *strong alkalis*. These substances are completely ionised in aqueous solution. *Weak* acids and alkalis have pH values nearer to 7: they are incompletely ionised in aqueous solution. Examples include ethanoic acid and ammonia solution (see Section 6.1).

11.5 Salts

A **salt** is the product formed when the hydrogen ions of an acid are replaced by metal or ammonium ions, e.g. zinc chloride, $ZnCl_2$, is a salt of hydrochloric acid and ammonium sulphate, $(NH_4)_2SO_4$, is a salt of sulphuric acid.

Neutralisation is the reaction between the hydrated hydrogen ions of an acid and the oxide or hydroxide ions of a base to form water, a salt being formed at the same time. The ionic equation is

$$\underset{\substack{\text{from the} \\ \text{acid}}}{H^+(aq)} + \underset{\substack{\text{from the} \\ \text{alkali}}}{OH^-(aq)} \rightarrow H_2O(l)$$

(a) Methods of Preparing Salts

There are three main methods of making salts, and it is necessary to know whether a salt is soluble in water before the correct method can be chosen. Table 11.1 shows the solubilities of common salts and should be memorized.

Table 11.1

Carbonates	All *insoluble* except potassium, sodium and ammonium carbonates.
Chlorides	All *soluble* except silver and lead chlorides. Lead chloride is soluble in hot water.
Nitrates	All *soluble*.
Sulphates	All *soluble* except barium and lead sulphates. Calcium sulphate is only slightly soluble.

Note: all common potassium, sodium and ammonium salts are soluble.

1. Insoluble salts are prepared by the *precipitation method*.
2. Potassium, sodium and ammonium salts are prepared by the *titration method*.
3. All other soluble salts are made by the *insoluble base method*.
4. In addition to the above methods, *direct synthesis* from the elements is sometimes used, especially for anhydrous chlorides.

(See Example 12.2 and Question 11.5.)

11.6 Worked Examples

*Example 11.1

The colours of some indicators in solutions at various pH values are shown in the table below.

Indicator	pH									
	2	3	4	5	6	7	8	9	10	11
Methyl yellow	R		Y							
Litmus						R		B		
Bromothymol blue						Y	G	B		
Phenolphthalein								C		R

Key B = blue   G = green   Y = yellow
     C = colourless   R = red

(a) Predict the colour shown by litmus in a solution of pH 7.   **(1)**
Purple.

(b) A solution of ethanoic acid has pH 5. What colour would be shown by the following indicators in the acid solution?
(i) Methyl yellow;
Yellow.
(ii) Bromothymol blue.   **(2)**
Yellow.

(c) (i) A solution of sodium carbonate turns litmus blue and phenolphthalein red.
Suggest the pH value of this solution.

10.

(ii) What is the formula of the ion that causes this pH? **(2)**

OH⁻.

(d) Some of the ethanoic acid solution is put into a flask with five drops of bromothymol blue. Sodium carbonate solution is added slowly, whilst stirring, until present in excess. Write down what you would expect to see and construct the chemical equation for the reaction.
Observation(s): *The indicator would be yellow, then turn green and finally blue. Bubbles of gas (carbon dioxide) would be seen.* **(3)**
Equation (The formula for ethanoic acid is CH_3COOH)
$$2CH_3COOH(aq) + Na_2CO_3(aq) \rightarrow$$
$$2CH_3COONa(aq) + H_2O(l) + CO_2(g)$$
(2)
(Total 10)
(MEG, June 1989, Paper 3, Q5)

Example 11.2

Hydrogen is produced from:
A   Copper and aqueous sulphuric acid.
B   Lead and aqueous nitric acid.
C   Magnesium and aqueous sulphuric acid.
D   Silver and aqueous hydrochloric acid.
E   Zinc and aqueous nitric acid.
The answer is **C.**

See Sections 11.2 and 12.1 – nitric acid does not give hydrogen with metals; copper and silver are below hydrogen in the reactivity series and so will not displace it from acids.

Example 11.3

On warming with aqueous sodium hydroxide, compound X produced a gas which turned moist red litmus paper blue. The compound X could be
A   aluminium nitrate
B   ammonium nitrate
C   calcium nitrate
D   potassium nitrate
E   zinc nitrate.
The answer is **B.**   (AEB, 1982)

See Properties of Bases, Section 11.3. The gas must be ammonia, which is produced when ammonium salts react with sodium hydroxide solution.

Example 11.4

(a) A pupil shook a sample of soil with water and filtered the mixture.
The pupil measured the pH of the filtrate using Universal indicator paper, then added aqueous ammonia to the filtrate, measuring and recording the pH during the addition of the aqueous ammonia. The pupil drew the following graph.

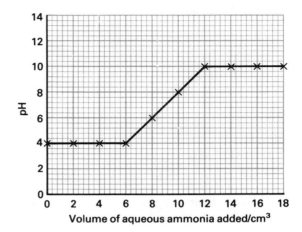

Using the graph, answer the following questions.
(i) What was the pH of the filtrate at the beginning of the experiment? **(1)**

4.

(ii) What does your answer to (i) tell you about the soil. **(1)**

It is acidic.

(iii) Suggest a value for the pH of aqueous ammonia. **(1)**

10.

(iv) How much aqueous ammonia was added to the filtrate to make it neutral? **(1)**

9 cm³.

The neutral point is at pH 7.

(b) Ammonia is used to make fertilisers.
(i) Suggest why the demand for fertilisers is increasing.
The demand for food is increasing, and fertilisers give more food from the land.
(ii) Sometimes fertilisers are washed from fields into rivers and streams. Give one reason why this kind of pollution can cause a problem. **(2)**
The fertilisers promote the too rapid growth of lower plant life and the river dies.

See Example 10.6.

(MEG, June 1988, Paper 2, Q6)

11.7 Self-test Questions

Question 11.1

Acidity in soil can be neutralised by adding:

    A   ammonium nitrate
    B   calcium hydroxide
    C   magnesium sulphate
    D   sodium chloride
    E   potassium sulphate

(LEAG, June 1988, Paper 1, Q28)

Question 11.2

A solution of hydrogen chloride in water is acidic because:

    A   hydrogen chloride is a compound of non-metals
    B   all chlorides are acidic in aqueous solution
    C   hydrogen is present in all acids
    D   hydrogen ions are formed
    E   the solution has a high pH

(LEAG, June 1988, Paper 1, Q29)

Question 11.3

To get a salt from its solution, you should:

    1   cool the solution slowly to crystallise it
    2   concentrate the solution by boiling (evaporation)
    3   wash the crystals with a little distilled water and then dry them
    4   filter off the crystals

    The ORDER in which you should do this is

    A   1, 2, 3, 4
    B   2, 1, 3, 4
    C   1, 4, 3, 2
    D   2, 1, 4, 3
    E   4, 3, 2, 1

(LEAG, June 1988, Paper 1, Q30)

Question 11.4

Which of the following compounds is a salt?

    A   Calcium oxide
    B   Lead(II) carbonate
    C   Sodium hydroxide
    D   Hydrogen chloride
    E   Carbon dioxide

Question 11.5

This question is about different methods of making nickel(II) nitrate, $Ni(NO_3)_2$.

Method I 25 cm^3 of 2M nitric acid, HNO_3, was placed in a beaker and green nickel(II) carbonate, $NiCO_3$, was added until it was in excess. After filtration green nickel(II) nitrate solution was obtained.

(a) Why was *excess* nickel(II) carbonate used?   **(1)**

(b) Why must the beaker be much larger than the volume of acid used?   **(1)**

(c) Write a word equation for the reaction.   **(2)**

Method II Nickel(II) oxide was dissolved in nitric acid according to the equation

$NiO(s) + 2HNO_3(aq) \rightarrow Ni(NO_3)_2(aq) + H_2O(l)$.

(d) What mass of nitric acid would be required to neutralise 7.5 g of nickel(II) oxide?
(Relative atomic masses: O = 16, Ni = 59.)   **(3)**

Method III Nickel(II) chloride solution was added to lead(II) nitrate solution

$NiCl_2(aq) + Pb(NO_3)_2(aq) \rightarrow PbCl_2(s) + Ni(NO_3)_2(aq)$.

(e) Outline the main operation required to obtain nickel(II) nitrate crystals from 1.0 M nickel(II) chloride solution and 1.0 M lead(II) nitrate solution.   **(2)**

    (L)

Question 11.6

Below is a table giving information about various indicators.

Indicator	Colour in acid solution	Colour in alkali solution
litmus paper	red	blue
pH indicator paper	red	blue
phenolphthalein paper	colourless	red

In a television advertisement for Deft washing powder, it was said that "most washing powders when tested with pH paper turned it red, showing the presence of alkalis".

By reference to the table say

(i) why this statement is incorrect.   **(1)**

(ii) which indicator in the table is the advertisement referring to?   **(1)**

(MEG, June 1989, Paper 2, Q2)

11.8 Answers to Self-test Questions

11.1 **B**.

> Calcium hydroxide is alkaline.

11.2 **D**.

> Water splits the hydrogen chloride molecules into $H^+(aq)$ and $Cl^-(aq)$ ions. $H^+(aq)$ ions are needed for acidic properties to be shown.

11.3 **D**.
11.4 **B**.

> **A** and **C** are bases, **D** is an acid in solution and **E** is an acidic oxide.

11.5(a) To make sure that all of the dilute nitric acid had been used up.

(b) The mixture will fizz and froth up, owing to the evolution of carbon dioxide.

(c) Nickel(II) + nitric → nickel(II) + water + carbon
     carbonate   acid   nitrate   dioxide

(d) From the equation,
    1 mol nickel(II) oxide reacts with 2 mol nitric acid.
    75 g nickel(II) oxide reacts with 2 × 63 g nitric acid.
    7.5 g nickel(II) oxide reacts with 12.6 g nitric acid.
    ∴ mass of nitric acid = 12.6 g.

(e) Mix equal volumes of the two solutions, filter off the precipitate of lead(II) chloride and obtain crystals of nickel(II) nitrate by the usual method. This involves heating the solution to the point of crystallisation and then allowing it to cool in a stoppered flask. The crystals can then be filtered off, washed with a little distilled water and dried.

11.6 (i) pH paper and litmus paper would turn blue in the presence of alkalis.

(ii) Phenolphthalein.

THE METALS

Topic Guide

12.1 Introduction

When metals are arranged in order of decreasing chemical reactivity, the *reactivity series* is obtained. The chemical properties of a metal and its compounds are related to the position of the metal in the reactivity series as shown in Table 12.1.

(a) Displacement Reactions

Any metal will displace one lower in the reactivity series from aqueous solutions containing its ions. For example, if a piece of iron is placed in copper(II) sulphate solution, a reddish brown deposit of copper forms on the iron, and the blue colour of the solution fades. This is a redox reaction (see Section 4.3) in which the iron atoms are oxidised by each losing two electrons and going into solution as Fe^{2+} ions: Cu^{2+} ions are reduced by each gaining two electrons and forming a solid deposit of copper atoms (see Example 12.2).

$$Fe(s) + Cu^{2+}(aq) \rightarrow Fe^{2+}(aq) + Cu(s)$$

A metal cannot displace another one above it in the reactivity series. Thus if a piece of copper were placed in iron(II) sulphate solution, no reaction would occur.

Hydrogen fits into the series between lead and copper. Magnesium ribbon will therefore displace hydrogen from aqueous solutions containing its ions (i.e. acids).

Since copper is below hydrogen in the series, it does not liberate the gas from dilute acids. In practice, lead does not do so either.

(b) Reduction of Metallic Oxides

A metallic oxide can be reduced to the metal by heating it with another metal which is higher in the reactivity series (see Example 12.1).

$$\text{e.g. } Zn(s) + PbO(s) \rightarrow ZnO(s) + Pb(s)$$

Carbon fits into the series between aluminium and zinc. On heating, it will reduce the oxide of zinc and those metals below it, being itself oxidised to carbon monoxide or carbon dioxide.

Table 12.1

	Action of cold air	Action of water	Action of dilute hydrochloric and sulphuric acids	Reduction of oxides	Nature of hydroxides	Effect of heat on carbonates	Effect of heat on nitrates	
K	rapidly attacked	violent in cold	explode	not reduced by carbon or hydrogen	strongly basic: stable to heat	stable	give nitrite and oxygen	K
Na								Na
Ca	attacked	attacked in cold			weakly basic or amphoteric: on heating give oxide and water with increasing ease as series is descended	give oxide and carbon dioxide with increasing ease as series is descended	give oxide, nitrogen dioxide and oxygen with increasing ease as series is descended	Ca
Mg	little action: protective oxide coating formed	react with steam	give hydrogen with decreasing vigour as series is descended	reduced by hot carbon				Mg
Al								Al
Zn								Zn
Fe	rusts in moist air			reduced by hot carbon or hydrogen				Fe
Pb	little action	no reaction	no reaction					Pb
Cu								Cu

Metals above zinc can reduce carbon dioxide on heating. For example, magnesium burns with a bright white light in carbon dioxide, being oxidised to a white ash of magnesium oxide. The carbon dioxide is reduced to black specks of carbon.

$$2Mg(s) + CO_2(g) \rightarrow 2MgO(s) + C(s)$$

Hydrogen behaves in this type of reaction as if it were *level* with iron. (Note that this is higher than its position for displacement reactions.) It will reduce the oxides of iron and metals below it, being itself oxidised to water. Iron and the metals above it reduce water to hydrogen and are themselves oxidised (see Table 12.1 and Example 12.3).

(c) Thermal Stability of Metallic Compounds

In general, the higher a metal is in the reactivity series, the less likely are its compounds to decompose on heating (see Table 12.1).

12.2 Potassium, Sodium and Lithium – the Alkali Metals

These are soft, silvery metals which are stored under oil because they rapidly tarnish in air. Lithium comes between sodium and calcium in the reactivity series.

In water, potassium melts and rushes around the surface as a silvery ball. Hydrogen is formed, and burns with a lilac flame owing to the presence of the potassium. The other product is potassium hydroxide solution.

$$2K(s) + 2H_2O(l) \rightarrow 2KOH(aq) + H_2(g)$$

Sodium reacts slightly less vigorously (the hydrogen does not inflame) and lithium less vigorously still.

The hydroxides of these metals are all strong alkalis.

Potassium nitrate and potassium sulphate are important fertilisers. Sodium hydroxide is an important industrial alkali and sodium carbonate is a water softener (see Section 12.3) and is used in glass-making, while sodium hydrogencarbonate is an ingredient of baking powder and health salts. Sodium chloride is used in preparing food and in the manufacture of chlorine and sodium hydroxide.

12.3 Calcium and Magnesium – the Alkaline Earth Metals

These are fairly reactive metals. Calcium reacts quite vigorously with cold water, producing hydrogen and a milky suspension of slightly soluble calcium hydroxide (see Example 12.3).

$$Ca(s) + 2H_2O(l) \rightarrow Ca(OH)_2(aq) + H_2(g)$$

Magnesium reacts very slowly with cold water but burns when heated in steam to give magnesium oxide and hydrogen (see Example 10.5).

$$Mg(s) + H_2O(g) \rightarrow MgO(s) + H_2(g)$$

Calcium oxide (quicklime) is an important industrial base, made by heating calcium carbonate (chalk or limestone). It reacts violently with water to form calcium hydroxide, which is a cheap industrial alkali and can be used to neutralise soil acidity (see Question 11.1).

Magnesium metal is used in lightweight alloys, while magnesium hydroxide (Milk of Magnesia) reduces stomach acidity.

(a) Hardness of Water (see Example 12.4 and Questions 12.6 and 12.7)

Hard water is water which does not readily form a lather with soap. Hardness is mostly caused by dissolved calcium or magnesium ions which react with soap to form an insoluble precipitate (scum) – see

Section 18.6. Soapless detergents do not have insoluble calcium and magnesium salts, and therefore do not form scum.

Hardness which can be removed simply by boiling is called **temporary hardness**. It is due to dissolved magnesium hydrogencarbonate or calcium hydrogencarbonate, which decomposes on heating to give a precipitate of the corresponding carbonate. How water becomes temporarily hard is described in Example 12.4.

Hardness which cannot be removed by boiling is called **permanent hardness** and is often due to dissolved sulphates of calcium and magnesium.

Methods of removing hardness ('softening' water) include:

1. Boiling – temporary hardness only.
2. Distillation – effective but expensive.
3. Adding sodium carbonate (washing soda) to precipitate insoluble magnesium carbonate or calcium carbonate.
4. Ion exchange. Some substances, called ion exchange resins, remove dissolved ions from hard water and replace them with ions of their own. If the cations (positive ions) are replaced with $H^+(aq)$ ions and the anions (negative ions) with $OH^-(aq)$ ions, these combine to form water molecules and the resulting product is very pure *deionised water*.

12.4 Aluminium

Aluminium is a silvery metal which, in spite of its high position in the reactivity series, is stable in air and water. This is because it is coated with a thin layer of oxide, which protects it from further attack. (See 'Anodising', Section 6.2 (d).) It dissolves in dilute hydrochloric acid, liberating hydrogen.

Aluminium oxide and aluminium hydroxide are amphoteric (see Example 15.2).

The metal is used to make milk-bottle tops and food containers; it is also used in overhead electric cables and in light alloys. Its manufacture is described in Example 17.3.

12.5 Iron

Iron is a member of the centre block of the periodic table (the transition metals). These metals have more than one valency, form coloured ions in solution and can act as catalysts. The rusting of iron is dealt with in Section 9.3 and Example 9.6.

Iron(II) hydroxide (dirty green) and iron(III) hydroxide (reddish brown) are formed by precipitation when sodium hydroxide solution is added to a solution of an iron(II) salt or an iron(III) salt.

Iron(II) salts are generally pale green and less stable than the corresponding iron(III) salts, which are yellow or brown.

Cast iron is cheap but impure, hard and brittle; wrought iron is almost pure iron and is softer and more flexible. Steels are alloys of iron with carbon and other elements such as chromium and manganese (see Example 17.2).

The manufacture of iron and steel is described in Section 17.2 and Example 17.4.

12.6 Differences between Metals and Non-Metals

See Example 12.3 and Table 4.1.

12.7 Worked Examples

Example 12.1

The four metals below are written in order of decreasing reactivity.

magnesium, aluminium, iron, copper.

Below is a worksheet used by a pupil to check the order of reactivity of the metals. Each metal oxide was reacted with the other metals. A cross (×) shows that no reaction took place; a tick (√) shows that a reaction took place.

Some of the results have been done for you.

CHEMISTRY WORKSHEET NO.3

The Reactivity of Metals

metal oxide \ metal	aluminium	copper	iron	magnesium
aluminium oxide	////////	×		√
copper(II) oxide		////////	√	√
iron(III) oxide	√		////////	
magnesium oxide	×	×		////////

(a) Complete the table. **(5)**

CHEMISTRY WORKSHEET NO.3

The Reactivity of Metals

metal oxide \ metal	aluminium	copper	iron	magnesium
aluminium oxide	////////	×	×	√
copper(II) oxide	√	////////	√	√
iron(III) oxide	√	×	////////	√
magnesium oxide	×	×	×	////////

A metal reacts with the oxides of metals below it in the reactivity series.

(b) Suggest which of these metals would be most suitable for making:
  (i)   car bodies   **(1)**
Iron.

It is cheap.

  (ii) fireworks.   **(1)**
Magnesium

It burns brightly.

  (iii) window frames and double glazing units.   **(1)**
Aluminium.

  Give a reason for your answer to (iii).   **(1)**
Aluminium becomes coated with a layer of aluminium oxide which protects it.

(c) Copper is widely used for water pipes and hot water tanks. Suggest a reason for this.   **(1)**
Copper does not react with hot water.

(d) To produce aluminium economically, large quantities of electricity are needed. Bearing this fact in mind, suggest a reason for siting plants for the extraction of aluminium in mountainous regions.
                                                    (1)
The water flowing down the mountains is used to generate hydroelectric power.

                                         (Total 11)
                          (MEG, June 1989, Paper 2, Q7)

*Example 12.2

The following chemicals, together with water, are available in a laboratory:
copper(II) oxide; copper(II) sulphate-5-water; magnesium metal; magnesium oxide; sodium carbonate solution; dilute sulphuric acid.
  Describe how the following experiments could be carried out choosing chemicals from the list above. *Each chemical may be used once, more than once, or not at all.*
(a) To show that magnesium lies above copper in the activity series.   **(3)**
Copper(II) sulphate-5-water is dissolved in water and magnesium metal added to the solution. A pink/brown deposit of copper is seen since magnesium is above copper in the activity series.

$$Mg(s) + CuSO_4(aq) \rightarrow Cu(s) + MgSO_4(aq)$$

OR *Heat magnesium with copper(II) oxide. A violent reaction occurs, giving white magnesium oxide and reddish brown copper.*

$$Mg(s) + CuO(s) \rightarrow MgO(s) + Cu(s)$$

(b) The preparation of a reasonably pure sample of magnesium carbonate (which is insoluble in water). **Note:** A two-stage reaction is required.
Either magnesium metal or magnesium oxide is added to warm diluted sulphuric acid until excess solid remains unreacted. The solid is filtered off and the solution added to sodium carbonate solution. The precipitate of magnesium carbonate is filtered off, washed with a little distilled water and dried.

The relevant equations are:
$Mg(s) + H_2SO_4(aq) \rightarrow MgSO_4(aq) + H_2(g)$
$MgO(s) + H_2SO_4(aq) \rightarrow MgSO_4(aq) + H_2O(l)$
$MgSO_4(aq) + Na_2CO_3(aq) \rightarrow MgCO_3(s) + Na_2SO_4(aq)$
See Section 11.5.

                          (Welsh, June 1988, Paper 2, Q4)

Example 12.3

This question concerns the properties of metals and non-metals. Shiny; flexible; do not conduct electricity; dull; form basic or amphoteric oxides; conduct electricity well when solid or molten; brittle; form covalent, acidic oxides.
(a) Underline those properties which are the properties of metals.   **(3)**
The properties to be underlined are:
Shiny, flexible, form basic or amphoteric oxides and conduct electricity well when solid or molten.

The other properties are typical of non-metals.

(b) Compare the reactions, if any, of the metals calcium, copper and iron with (i) water or steam, (ii) dilute hydrochloric acid, and place the metals in order of decreasing reactivity.   **(7)**
  (i)   *Calcium reacts fairly vigorously with cold water.*

See Section 12.3.
$Ca(s) + 2H_2O(l) \rightarrow Ca(OH)_2(aq) + H_2(g)$

Iron reacts on heating in steam.

$3\,Fe(s) + 4H_2O(g) \rightleftharpoons Fe_3O_4(s) + 4H_2(g)$

Copper does not react with water or with steam, even on heating.
  (ii) *Calcium reacts very vigorously with cold dilute hydrochloric acid, forming calcium chloride solution and hydrogen.*

$Ca(s) + 2HCl(aq) \rightarrow CaCl_2(aq) + H_2(g)$

Iron reacts fairly slowly with cold dilute hydrochloric acid, forming iron(II) chloride solution and hydrogen.

$$Fe(s) + 2HCl(aq) \rightarrow FeCl_2(aq) + H_2(g)$$

Copper does not react with dilute hydrochloric acid. The order of reactivity of the three metals is thus calcium, iron, copper.

Example 12.4

Rain water containing carbon dioxide reacts slowly with limestone to form hard water.

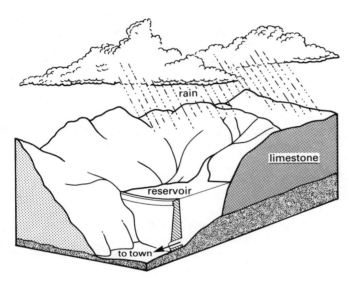

The equation for the formation of this hard water is shown below.

$$CaCO_3(s) + H_2O(l) + CO_2(g) \rightarrow Ca(HCO_3)_2(aq)$$

(a) Why does the amount of hardness in water differ from place to place throughout the world? **(2)**

The rain water will flow through different rocks containing differing amounts of calcium carbonate. The amount of dissolved carbon dioxide will vary from place to place.

(b) Household water has usually been filtered and chlorinated.
   (i) Why are small amounts of chlorine added to household water? **(1)**

To kill bacteria.

   (ii) Why does filtration not remove the hardness from water? **(2)**

*Hardness is caused by **dissolved** calcium salts.*

(c) What would you notice if a small amount of soap (sodium stearate) is shaken with this hard water? **(1)**

Scum would form.

(d) Why should this hard water not be used in a hot water system? **(2)**

Heating causes the reaction above to reverse, thereby precipitating calcium carbonate which will block the pipes.

(e) (i) Name one method that removes the hardness from hard water. **(1)**

Adding washing soda (sodium carbonate).

   (ii) Explain how the method you named removes the hardness from hard water. **(2)**

This precipitates the calcium ions as calcium carbonate.

$$Ca(HCO_3)_2(aq) + Na_2CO_3(aq) \rightarrow CaCO_3(s) + 2NaHCO_3(aq)$$

(SEG, June 1988, Paper 1, Q11)

Example 12.5

A metal X forms a green chloride of formula XCl_2. It is likely that X
A   is a transition metal
B   forms a carbonate with the formula X_2CO_3
C   is in the same group of the periodic table as magnesium
D   reacts violently with cold water
E   is an alkali metal.

The answer is **A**.

Transition metals have coloured ions (see Section 12.5).

Example 12.6

Glass is a mixture of sodium and calcium silicates. Which sodium and calcium salts are used in the making of glass?
A   Carbonates
B   Chlorides
C   Hydrogencarbonates
D   Nitrates
E   Sulphates
The answer is **A**.

(LEAG, June 1988, Paper 1, Q40)

Example 12.7

Limestone, marble, quicklime and slaked lime all contain:
A   Calcium
B   Carbon
C   Hydrogen
D   Sodium
E   Water of crystallisation
The answer is **A**.

(LEAG, June 1988, Paper 1, Q43)

Limestone and marble are both calcium carbonate, quicklime is calcium oxide and slaked lime is calcium hydroxide.

*Example 12.8

(a) One way of getting zinc from the mineral sphalerite is outlined below.

   (i) Apart from zinc, name another element that is present in sphalerite. **(1)**

Sulphur.

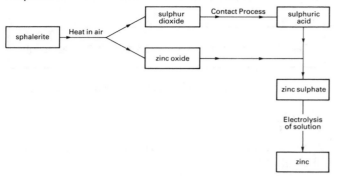

```
Heating sphalerite in air gives sulphur dioxide.
```

(ii) Which element from the air reacts with the heated sphalerite?   **(1)**

Oxygen.

(iii) Explain why the sulphur dioxide formed should not be allowed to escape into the air for economic and environmental reasons.

Economic reasons: It can be used to produce sulphuric acid, thus reducing costs in the Contact Process.   **(2)**

Environmental reasons: Sulphur dioxide is poisonous. It dissolves in water to produce acid rain.   **(2)**

(iv) In this process zinc is produced by the electrolysis of zinc sulphate solution. State the electrode at which the zinc is deposited.   **(1)**

Cathode.

(v) Why is the formation of zinc at the electrode called a *reduction*?   **(1)**

Electrons are gained by the zinc ions.

```
Zn²⁺ + 2 e⁻ → Zn
```
$$Zn^{2+} + 2\,e^- \rightarrow Zn$$

(b) Zinc can also be obtained from zinc sulphate solution by displacement with another metal, M.

$$M + ZnSO_4 \rightarrow MSO_4 + Zn$$

(i) From the Reactivity Series, p. 89, choose **one** metal that could be used as metal M.   **(1)**

A metal above zinc in the series, e.g. magnesium.

(ii) Why could the following two metals **not** be used for this displacement reaction?

Sodium: *Sodium reacts vigorously with water.*   **(1)**

Copper: *Copper is below zinc in the series and so would not displace zinc.*   **(1)**

(iii) Why is this method of displacement **not** used for the industrial extraction of zinc from zinc sulphate solution?   **(2)**

It is too slow and it uses up another more expensive metal.

(c) The amount of metal ores in the Earth's crust is limited. The number of ingots shows how long known reserves will last.

(i) About how many years reserve of zinc remain?   **(1)**

28 years.

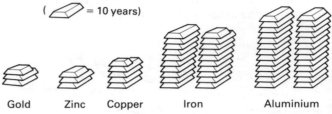

(ii) New resources may be found before this reserve of zinc runs out. Suggest two other possible ways of overcoming the shortage of zinc.

1. *Alloy the zinc with other metals.*   **(1)**
2. *Recycle the zinc.*   **(1)**

(d) Imagine that a new discovery of sphalerite has been found under farmland. One major problem is that the mining of this mineral will produce large quantities of waste rock.

(i) Give one advantage and one disadvantage to the local population of mining the sphalerite.   **(2)**

Advantage	Disadvantage
It will provide more jobs in the area.	*Spoil heaps are unsightly.*

(ii) Give one advantage to the national government of this new discovery of sphalerite.   **(1)**

Zinc ore will not need to be imported, thus improving the balance of payments.

(iii) What should be done to the land once all the sphalerite has been mined?   **(2)**

The land should be filled in and returned to farming.

(SEG, June 1988, Paper 3, Q4)

12.8 Self-test Questions

Question 12.1

Two metals, X and Y, fit into the reactivity series as follows:

    X Na Zn H Y

Which of the following statements is true?

    A   Y will react with hydrochloric acid to give hydrogen.
    B   X will not react with water.
    C   Y will displace X from a solution containing X ions.
    D   The heated oxide of X will be reduced to the metal by hydrogen.
    E   The heated oxide of Y will be reduced to the metal by hydrogen.

(LEAG, June 1988, Paper 1, Q36)

Questions 12.2–12.5 are about the following metals.

    A   Aluminium
    B   Copper
    C   Iron
    D   Magnesium
    E   Sodium

Select from the list above:

Question 12.2

the metal that reacts violently with cold water;   **(1)**

Question 12.3

the metal used to make hot water pipes;   **(1)**

Question 12.4

the metal that forms a protective oxide coat when exposed to air and is used in the manufacture of window frames;   **(1)**

Question 12.5

the metal that forms two different chlorides whose solutions react with sodium hydroxide solution to give precipitates, one coloured reddish-brown, the other green.   **(1)**

(Welsh, June 1988, Paper 1, Q1–4)

Question 12.6

In a limestone area, the main reason for *temporary* hardness in tap water is the presence of dissolved

    A   calcium chloride
    B   calcium hydrogencarbonate
    C   calcium hydroxide
    D   calcium nitrate
    E   calcium sulphate

(LEAG, June 1988, Paper 1, Q32)

Question 12.7

Because it is used in a hard water area, the inside of this copper kettle is covered in scale (calcium carbonate).

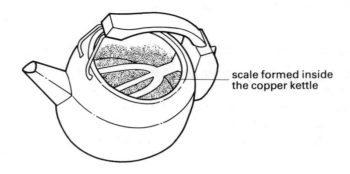

scale formed inside
the copper kettle

(a) What is *hard* water?   (2)
(b) Dilute hydrochloric acid is added to remove the scale (calcium carbonate).
    (i)   What **two** things would you notice happening when the acid is poured onto the scale?   (2)
    (ii) Name **two** products made by the reaction of hydrochloric acid with this scale.   (2)
    (iii) Explain why dilute hydrochloric acid should **not** be used to try to remove scale from
          aluminium kettles.   (2)

(SEG, Winter 1988, Paper 1, Q5)

*Question 12.8

Chromium lies between zinc and iron in the activity series. In its simple chemistry, chromium has a valency (oxidation state) of 3 and forms green compounds.
(a) What will you observe if an excess of powdered chromium is added to aqueous copper(II)
    sulphate?   (3)
(b) Construct the chemical equation for the reaction between chromium and hydrochloric acid.   (2)
(c) Chromium can be manufactured by the chemical reduction of chromium(III) oxide. Suggest a
    suitable reagent and the probable conditions for this reduction.   (2)
(d) (i) Chromium is used to plate iron objects, such as car bumpers. Predict what will happen to
         the iron if a chromium plated car bumper is scratched.
    (ii) Suggest a way in which a car bumper could be plated with chromium.   (3)

(Total 10)
(MEG, June 1989, Paper 3, Q3)

12.9 Answers to Self-test Questions

12.1 E.

> Y is below hydrogen in the reactivity series.

12.2 E.

> $2Na(s) + 2H_2O(l) \rightarrow 2NaOH(aq) + H_2(g)$

12.3 B.
12.4 A.
12.5 C.

> The two chlorides are $FeCl_2$ and $FeCl_3$. These react with sodium hydroxide solution as follows:
> $FeCl_2(aq) + 2NaOH(aq) \rightarrow Fe(OH)_2(s) + 2NaCl(aq)$
> $FeCl_3(aq) + 3NaOH(aq) \rightarrow Fe(OH)_3(s) + 3NaCl(aq)$
> Iron(II) hydroxide is green; iron(III) hydroxide is reddish-brown.

12.6 B.
12.7(a) Hard water is water which does not readily form a lather with soap (see Section 12.3).
  (b) (i) The scale would dissolve in the acid and bubbles of carbon dioxide would be visible.
    (ii) Calcium chloride and carbon dioxide.

> $CaCO_3(s) + 2HCl(aq) \rightarrow CaCl_2(aq) + CO_2(g) + H_2O(l)$
> (scale)

  (iii) The aluminium would dissolve in the hydrochloric acid – aluminium compounds in solution are poisonous.
12.8 (a) The blue solution will turn green and a pink/brown deposit of copper will form.

> $2Cr(s) + 3CuSO_4(aq) \rightarrow Cr_2(SO_4)_3(aq) + 3Cu(s)$

  (b) $2Cr(s) + 6HCl(aq) \rightarrow 2CrCl_3(aq) + 3H_2(g)$
  (c) Any metal above chromium in the activity series will be suitable, e.g. aluminium. The aluminium and the chromium(III) oxide must be heated together.
  (d) (i) The iron will rust.
    (ii) The car bumper is made the cathode in the electrolysis of a chromium salt solution. The anode is made of chromium.

12.10 Grading of Self-test Questions

Questions 12.1 to 12.7 are found in the compulsory part of the examination paper. They are worth a total of 14 marks and the marks/grades will be something like:
11 or more marks ———————— at least C grade
8 marks ———————————— around E grade
6 marks ———————————— around G grade.
    Question 12.8 is on the extended part of the paper designed to gain you an A or B grade. It is not a particularly difficult question and you should be able to get at least 8/10 if you want an A grade and at least 6/10 for a B grade.

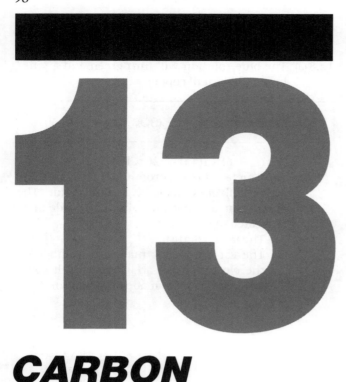

CARBON

13.1 Carbon

Carbon is an element which exhibits allotropy.

Allotropy is the existence of an element in more than one form in the same state.

The condition is important in distinguishing allotropy from straightforward melting and boiling.

Carbon has two allotropes, diamond and graphite. Both consist of pure carbon, which may be proved by burning equal masses of the two substances in excess oxygen when the same mass of carbon dioxide is obtained from each but no other product is formed. Diamond and graphite have widely differing physical properties, these differences being due to variations in the way the atoms are packed together (see Example 13.1).

(a) Reactions and Uses of Carbon

1. Diamond: used in gemstones, cutting tools, rock borers, styluses in record players.
2. Graphite: used as a lubricant, a moderator in atomic reactors, an electrical conductor and in pencil 'leads' (mixed with clay).
3. Carbon is a reducing agent: when carbon is heated with the oxides of the less reactive metals, it reduces them to the metal and is itself oxidised to carbon dioxide:
    $$2\,CuO(s) + C(s) \rightarrow 2Cu(s) + CO_2(g)$$
    (see Section 12.1).

    In industry, coke is used to extract a number of metals such as zinc and iron from their oxide ores.

13.2 Carbon Dioxide, CO_2

Carbon dioxide may be prepared by the action of almost any acid on any carbonate but the reaction most commonly employed is that between dilute hydrochloric acid and marble chips (calcium carbonate).
$$CaCO_3(s) + 2HCl(aq) \rightarrow CaCl_2(aq) + H_2O(l) + CO_2(g)$$

(a) Test for Carbon Dioxide (see Example 13.2)

Carbon dioxide turns lime water milky.
$$Ca(OH)_2(aq) + CO_2(g) \rightarrow CaCO_3(s) + H_2O(l)$$

(b) Properties of Carbon Dioxide

1. Carbon dioxide is a colourless, odourless gas.
2. It is denser than air.
3. It dissolves slightly in water to give an acidic solution.
4. Carbon dioxide does not burn and will only support the combustion of substances which are hot enough to decompose it into its elements.

(c) Uses of Carbon Dioxide

1. In fizzy drinks.
2. In fire extinguishers (see Example 13.4).
3. As a refrigerant.
4. Health salts and baking powder contain sodium hydrogencarbonate and a solid acid such as tartaric acid which react together when water is added to produce carbon dioxide.

13.3 Carbonates

Potassium, sodium and ammonium carbonates are soluble in water, all others being insoluble. The insoluble carbonates can be obtained as precipitates by mixing together solutions containing the required metal ions and carbonate ions.

$$ZnSO_4(aq) + Na_2CO_3(aq) \rightarrow ZnCO_3(s) + Na_2SO_4(aq)$$

Soluble carbonates are prepared from carbon dioxide and the corresponding alkali.

$$CO_2(g) + 2KOH(aq) \rightarrow K_2CO_3(aq) + H_2O(l)$$

All carbonates react with acids to give a salt, water and carbon dioxide (see Example 13.6).

$$CuCO_3(s) + H_2SO_4(aq) \rightarrow CuSO_4(aq) + H_2O(l) + CO_2(g)$$

Carbonates of metals low down in the reactivity series split up on heating to give the metal oxide and carbon dioxide (see Question 13.4).

$$PbCO_3(s) \rightarrow PbO(s) + CO_2(g)$$

13.4 The Carbon Cycle (see data book)

The percentage of carbon dioxide in the atmosphere remains fairly constant. The ways in which carbon atoms circulate in nature are shown in the carbon cycle (see Example 13.6).

13.5 Carbon Monoxide, CO

Carbon monoxide is a product of incomplete combustion of, for example, coal or petroleum. It is extremely poisonous (see Example 13.5).

The gas reduces the oxides of the less active metals on heating (see Example 17.4).

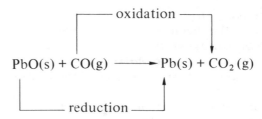

13.6 Worked Examples

Example 13.1

Carbon is an element which exhibits allotropy. The structures of the two allotropes, diamond and graphite, are shown in Fig. 13.1

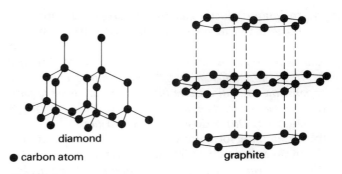

● carbon atom

Fig. 13.1

(a) Explain what is meant by the term 'allotropy'. **(2)**
Allotropy is the existence of an element in more than one form in the same state.
(b) By considering the structures of the allotropes, explain why
   (i) graphite conducts electricity but diamond does not. **(2)**
In diamond, each carbon atom is using its four bonding electrons to form covalent bonds to four other atoms. In graphite, each carbon atom is bonded to only three others, even though four electrons are available for bonding. The extra electrons are free to move from one hexagon to the next within a layer and thus conduct an electric current.
   (ii) both substances have high melting points. **(2)**
This is because they both consist of giant structures of atoms (see Section 4.2), with millions of strong bonds acting throughout the whole of each crystal.

Example 13.2

Marble chips are added to hydrochloric acid in a test tube.
(a) What do you observe? **(1)**
Fizzing as a gas is given off.
(b) What is the chemical name for marble? **(1)**
Calcium carbonate.
(c) Name two other forms of this chemical which occur in nature. **(2)**
Chalk and limestone.
(d) What do you observe if carbon dioxide is passed into lime water for a few seconds? **(1)**

The lime water will go milky.

(e) What is the chemical name for lime water? **(2)**

Calcium hydroxide solution.

(f) Write a word equation for the reaction. **(2)**

Calcium hydroxide + carbon dioxide → calcium carbonate + water.

(g) Write a symbol equation for the reaction. **(2)**

$Ca(OH)_2(aq) + CO_2(g) → CaCO_3(s) + H_2O(l)$

(h) What do you observe if carbon dioxide is passed into lime water for several minutes? **(2)**

The lime water goes milky and then clear again.

(i) There would have been little reaction if sulphuric acid had been added to marble chips. Explain. **(2)**

Calcium sulphate is produced and as this is insoluble it forms a layer around the marble chips and stops the reaction.

Example 13.3

(a) In many places calcium hydrogencarbonate is present in tap water. Explain why this happens. **(3)**

Rain water contains dissolved carbon dioxide (see Example 12.4). If this water passes through chalk or limestone regions, then it will dissolve the calcium carbonate to form calcium hydrogencarbonate.

$CaCO_3(s) + H_2O(l) + CO_2(g) ⇌ Ca(HCO_3)_2(aq)$

(b) Explain the formation of stalactites and stalagmites in caves through which such water drips. **(3)**

The slow evaporation of drops of dilute calcium hydrogencarbonate solution hanging from cave roofs causes the above process to reverse, and this leaves minute deposits of calcium carbonate behind. As a result of this, stalactites form. Where drops of solution fall to the floor and evaporate, stalagmites grow upwards.

Example 13.4

Briefly explain the following:

(a) Carbon dioxide foam or gas can help to extinguish fires. **(2)**

Carbon dioxide does not allow combustion to take place. It is denser than air and blankets the fire.

(b) The large scale demand for limestone can lead to environmental problems. **(3)**

Limestone quarrying produces unsightly holes in the ground.

(Welsh, Summer 1988, Paper 1, Q33)

Example 13.5

The diagram shows how the element silicon is manufactured from the compound silica.

```
SILICA ──────→               ──────→ SILICON
          ELECTRIC
          FURNACE
CARBON ──────→               ──────→ CARBON MONOXIDE
```

(a) Silica contains two elements: silicon (Si) and oxygen (O). The smallest possible quantity of silica has one atom of silicon and two atoms of oxygen.

(i) What is the chemical formula of silica?

SiO_2.

(ii) Suggest a *chemical* name for silica. **(3)**

Silicon(IV) oxide.

(b) (i) Do you think that the manufacture of silicon requires a high or a low temperature? Give a reason for your answer.

High temperature – an electric furnace is needed for heating.

(ii) Write a word equation for the manufacture of silicon.

Silicon(IV) oxide + carbon → silicon + carbon monoxide.

(iii) During this process carbon *removes oxygen* from silica to form silicon. What is this *kind* of reaction called? **(5)**

Reduction.

(c) (i) Give one way in which carbon monoxide is formed in everyday life.

By the incomplete combustion of fuels.

(ii) Give one danger associated with carbon monoxide.

It is poisonous.

Oxygen combines with haemoglobin and is carried round the blood stream as bright red oxyhaemoglobin, which is unstable and readily gives up its oxygen where required. Carbon monoxide combines with haemoglobin to form cherry-red carboxyhaemoglobin. This is much more stable than oxyhaemoglobin and thus the blood can no longer act as an oxygen carrier.

(iii) How can this danger be reduced? **(3)**

By ensuring that there is always adequate oxygen for combustion or by using catalytic converters in cars (see Example 9.7).

(Total 11)

(LEAG, June 1988, Paper 2, Q3)

Example 13.6

(a) The diagram below is of the Carbon Cycle.

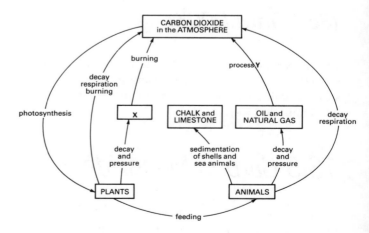

(i) Use your Data Booklet to find the name of substance X; **(1)**

Coal.

the process Y. **(1)**

Burning.

(ii) Which gas, present in air, provides the plants with the carbon they need? **(1)**

Carbon dioxide.

(iii) Name the process that plants use to change this gas into carbon compounds. **(1)**

Photosynthesis.

(iv) How do animals get the carbon compounds they need? **(1)**

Feeding.

You are not expected to *know* the answers to these questions – all the information that you require is in the data book.

(b) The shells of some sea animals form limestone. The amount of calcium carbonate in limestone can be found from the loss of mass when it reacts with an excess of acid.

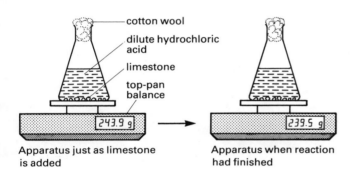

Apparatus just as limestone is added → Apparatus when reaction had finished

The chemical equation for this reaction is:
$$CaCO_3(s) + 2HCl(aq) \rightarrow CaCl_2(aq) + CO_2(g) + H_2O(l)$$

(i) When the acid reacts with the calcium carbonate a fine spray of solution is formed. In this experiment how is the spray of solution stopped from leaving the flask? **(1)**

The cotton wool prevents its escape.

(ii) How would you be able to tell when the reaction had finished? **(1)**

The mass would stop decreasing.

(iii) From the diagrams work out the loss of mass of the flask and its contents. **(1)**

243.9 – 239.5. = 4.4 g.

(iv) What causes the loss of mass that you have worked out? **(2)**

The loss of carbon dioxide to the air.

(c) The percentage of calcium carbonate present in the limestone can be found by following the steps below.

Step 1

The formula mass of carbon dioxide (CO_2) is 44. Work out the formula mass of calcium carbonate given that the relative atomic masses are Ca=40, C=12, O=16 **(1)**

40 + 12 + (3 × 16)
= 100

Step 2

Mass of calcium carbonate = loss of mass of flask and its contents × $\dfrac{\text{formula mass } CaCO_3}{\text{formula mass } CO_2}$

Using the equation above, the loss of mass from (b) (iii) and the formula masses from **Step 1**, work out the mass of calcium carbonate in the limestone. **(2)**

Mass of calcium carbonate = 4.4 × $\dfrac{100}{44}$

= 10g

Step 3

The mass of limestone used was 20 g. Use your answer from **Step 2** to work out the percentage of calcium carbonate in this limestone. **(2)**

% calcium carbonate = $\dfrac{10 \times 100}{20}$

= 50%

(d) (i) Why is limestone added to the blast furnace during the extraction of iron from its ores? **(2)**

The limestone decomposes to give calcium oxide (basic) which reacts with acidic impurities to form slag.

See Example 17.4.

(ii) Give one other use of limestone. **(1)**

In the manufacture of cement.

(SEG, June 1988, Paper 1, Q16)

Example 13.7

Petrol is a mixture of hydrocarbons of the type C_nH_{2n+2}

(a) Explain the presence of the following gases in the exhaust fumes of a car (equations are **not** expected as part of your answer):

(i) carbon dioxide: **(2)**

Complete combustion of a hydrocarbon produces carbon dioxide and water vapour (see Section 18.2).

    (ii) carbon monoxide.   **(2)**

If insufficient oxygen is present, then incomplete combustion occurs and carbon monoxide is formed.

(b) Explain the origins of the following substances which are also present in the exhaust fumes:

    (i)   lead(II) oxide;   **(2)**

Tetraethyl-lead(IV) is added to petrol to prevent premature ignition of the mixture of petrol and air in the cylinder of an engine. When burned, this compound produces lead(II) oxide.

    (ii) oxides of nitrogen such as NO and NO_2.   **(2)**

Oxides of nitrogen are produced when the oxygen and nitrogen in the air combine at the high temperatures produced in the engine.

13.7 Self-test Questions

Question 13.1

Complete the following equations:
(a) zinc carbonate(s) + hydrochloric acid(aq) → _____ + _____ + _____ .
(b) $ZnCO_3(s) \rightarrow$ _____ + _____ .
(c) Copper oxide(s) + carbon monoxide(g) → _____ + _____ .
(d) $Ca(OH)_2(aq) + CO_2(g) \rightarrow$ _____ + _____ .   **(10)**

Question 13.2

A correct statement about charcoal, graphite, diamond and ethanol is that they all:

    A   are allotropes of carbon
    B   have high melting points
    C   are insoluble in water
    D   form carbon dioxide on combustion
    E   decompose on heating to form carbon

                                       (L)

Question 13.3

What type of reaction is occurring in each of the examples given below? Choose from the list **A–D** for your answer (in some cases two letters are needed).
A   thermal decomposition
B   precipitation
C   neutralisation
D   oxidation
(a) The formation of barium sulphate from barium chloride solution and sulphuric acid.
(b) The formation of carbon monoxide from carbon.
(c) Bubbling carbon dioxide into lime water for a few seconds.
(d) The action of heat on copper carbonate.   **(5)**

Question 13.4

Complete the following sentences:
(a) Diamond and graphite resemble each other chemically because _____ .
(b) When carbon dioxide is bubbled into lime water (aqueous calcium hydroxide), a white precipitate is obtained but this redissolves with excess carbon dioxide because _____ .
(c) When copper(II) carbonate is heated, it turns black because _____ .   **(6)**

13.8 Answers to Self-test Questions

13.1(a) Zinc chloride(aq), water(l) and carbon dioxide(g).

(b) $ZnO(s)$ and $CO_2(g)$.

(c) Copper(s) and carbon dioxide(g).

(d) $CaCO_3(s)$ and $H_2O(l)$.

13.2 **D**.

The equations are:
$C(s) + O_2(g) \rightarrow CO_2(g)$ (charcoal, graphite and diamond are all carbon)
$C_2H_5OH(l) + 3O_2(g) \rightarrow 2CO_2(g) + 3H_2O(l)$

13.3 (a) **B**.

(b) **D**.

(c) **B** and **C**.

(d) **A**.

$BaCl_2(aq) + H_2SO_4(aq) \rightarrow BaSO_4(s) + 2HCl(aq)$
$2C(s) + O_2(g) \rightarrow 2CO(g)$
$Ca(OH)_2(aq) + CO_2(g) \rightarrow CaCO_3(s) + H_2O(l)$
$CuCO_3(s) \rightarrow CuO(s) + CO_2(g)$

13.4 (a) they are both allotropes of carbon *or* they contain atoms of one kind only.

(b) calcium carbonate (the white precipitate) reacts further to give calcium hydrogencarbonate which is soluble.

$CaCO_3(s) + CO_2(g) + H_2O(l) \rightleftharpoons Ca(HCO_3)_2(aq)$

(c) Black copper(II) oxide is formed.

$CuCO_3(s) \rightarrow CuO(s) + CO_2(g)$

14 NITROGEN

Topic Guide

14.1 Nitrogen, N_2

Nitrogen forms about 78% of the air and can be prepared from it by removing oxygen and carbon dioxide. Industrially, nitrogen is obtained by the fractional distillation of liquid air (see Section 9.2).

(a) Properties of Nitrogen

1. Nitrogen is a colourless, odourless gas.
2. It is a little less dense than air.
3. It is almost insoluble in water.
4. Nitrogen is generally unreactive. However, it forms nitrogen monoxide when sparked with oxygen, and reacts with hydrogen to give ammonia (see Section 17.5).
$$N_2(g) + O_2(g) \rightleftharpoons 2NO(g)$$
$$N_2(g) + 3H_2(g) \rightleftharpoons 2NH_3(g)$$

(b) Uses of Nitrogen

1. In the manufacture of ammonia.
2. To provide an inert atmosphere, e.g. in flushing out oil tanks.
3. As a refrigerant.

14.2 The Oxides of Nitrogen (see Example 9.7)

Nitrogen monoxide, NO, is a colourless gas which is immediately oxidised to brown fumes of nitrogen dioxide, NO_2, on contact with oxygen.

Both oxides are emitted in car exhaust fumes, causing pollution of the air.

14.3 Ammonia, NH_3

Ammonia is prepared by warming any ammonium salt with any base (see Question 14.1).
$$2NH_4Cl(s) + Ca(OH)_2(s) \rightarrow CaCl_2(s) + 2H_2O(g) + 2NH_3(g)$$

It is manufactured by the Haber process (see Section 17.5).

(a) Tests for Ammonia

Ammonia has a characteristic choking smell and will turn moist universal indicator paper blue. It gives white fumes of ammonium chloride when mixed with hydrogen chloride (see Example 14.2).

$$NH_3(g) + HCl(g) \rightleftharpoons NH_4Cl(s)$$

(b) Properties of Ammonia

1. Ammonia is a colourless gas with a pungent choking smell.
2. It is about half as dense as air.
3. Ammonia is very soluble in water, giving an alkaline solution.

   $$NH_3(aq) + H_2O(l) \rightleftharpoons NH_4^+(aq) + OH^-(aq)$$

   Since it contains hydroxide ions, ammonia solution neutralises acids (giving ammonium salts) and will also precipitate insoluble metallic hydroxides from solutions containing the metal ions (see Section 19.1 and Example 19.4).

(c) Uses of Ammonia

1. To make nitrogenous fertilisers, e.g. ammonium sulphate, ammonium nitrate.
2. To make nitric acid by the Ostwald process (see Section 17.6).
3. Ammonia solution is used in cleaning, as a grease remover.

14.4 Ammonium Salts

Ammonium salts are soluble in water and are prepared by the titration method (see Section 11.5 and Question 14.4). They decompose on heating and some, such as ammonium chloride, sublime (see Question 14.1). They react with sodium hydroxide solution on warming to give ammonia, this reaction being used to test for their presence.

$$NH_4Cl(aq) + NaOH(aq) \rightarrow NaCl(aq) + NH_3(g) + H_2O(l)$$

14.5 Nitric Acid, HNO₃

(a) Properties of Nitric Acid

Dilute nitric acid shows the usual properties of a strong acid (see Section 11.2 and Question 14.2) but it is reduced by metals to one or more of the oxides of nitrogen and does not generally give off hydrogen (see Question 19.5).

(b) Uses of Nitric Acid

1. To make fertilisers, e.g. ammonium nitrate.
2. To make explosives, e.g. TNT.

14.6 Nitrates

All nitrates are soluble in water and are prepared by the titration method (sodium, potassium and ammonium nitrates) or by the insoluble base method (see Section 11.5).

$$KOH(aq) + HNO_3(aq) \rightarrow KNO_3(aq) + H_2O(l)$$
$$PbO(s) + 2HNO_3(aq) \rightarrow Pb(NO_3)_2(aq) + H_2O(l)$$

All nitrates decompose on heating. Nitrates of metals at the top of the reactivity series (potassium, sodium) melt and split up to give the nitrite and oxygen (see Question 14.3).

$$2NaNO_3(l) \rightarrow 2NaNO_2(l) + O_2(g)$$

All other metal nitrates decompose to give the metal oxide, nitrogen dioxide and oxygen.

$$2Cu(NO_3)_2(s) \rightarrow 2CuO(s) + 4NO_2(g) + O_2(g)$$

(a) Test for Nitrates

If a nitrate is warmed with sodium hydroxide solution and aluminium powder is added, ammonia will be given off. (This can be detected by its smell, and by the fact that it turns moist red litmus paper blue.)

14.7 The Nitrogen Cycle

Nitrogen is essential to plants and animals for the production of protein. This element is recirculated in nature as shown in Example 14.4.

14.8 Worked Examples

Example 14.1

(a) (i) Calculate the percentage by mass of nitrogen in ammonium sulphate. **(4)**
   $(NH_4)_2SO_4$

   Relative molecular mass $= (14 + 4) \times 2 + 32$
   $$+ (4 \times 16)$$
   $$= 132$$
   Percentage of nitrogen $= \dfrac{28}{132} \times 100$
   $$= 21.2$$

(b) (ii) Both ammonium sulphate and sodium nitrate are used as fertilisers. Which is the faster acting? Explain your answer. **(4)**

Sodium nitrate. Most plants can take in nitrogen only in the form of nitrates. However, ammonium sulphate can be oxidised to a nitrate by bacteria and so can be used as a fertiliser.

Example 14.2

(a) (i) What is the electron arrangement in a nitrogen atom? **(1)**

2.5

(ii) By means of a drawing, show the electron arrangement in a nitrogen molecule. **(1)**

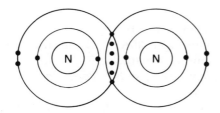

Fig. 14.1

(b) (i) A jet of ammonia is spontaneously flammable in chlorine, producing nitrogen and hydrogen chloride. Write an equation for this reaction. **(2)**

$2NH_3(g) + 3Cl_2(g) \rightarrow N_2(g) + 6HCl(g)$

(ii) What will be observed if excess ammonia is used? **(2)**

White fumes of ammonium chloride are seen since the hydrogen chloride produced will react with excess ammonia.

$6NH_3(g) + 6HCl(g) \rightarrow 6NH_4Cl(s)$
Adding the two equations together gives:
$8NH_3(g) + 3Cl_2(g) \rightarrow N_2(g) + 6NH_4Cl(s)$

Example 14.3

The percentage of ammonia produced from nitrogen and hydrogen under certain conditions of temperature and pressure is given in the graphs in Fig 14.2.

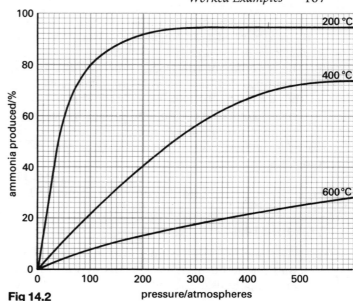

Fig 14.2

Use the graphs to help you answer the following questions.

(a) What happens to the percentage of ammonia produced when:

(i) the temperature is increased? **(1)**

The % is decreased.

(ii) the pressure is increased? **(1)**

The % is increased.

(b) What conditions of temperature and pressure produce the highest percentage of ammonia? **(2)**

200°C and at least 280 atm.

(c) Ammonia solution is used as a fertiliser but has to be pumped into the soil to a level well below the roots of the plants.

Suggest **two** reasons why ammonia solution could not just be sprayed onto the surface of the soil. **(2)**

1. *It would kill the plants.*

2. *Ammonia solution on the surface would evaporate and disperse.*

(d) The table below gives information about nitrogen fertilisers.

Fertiliser	Formula	Mass of one mole of fertiliser	Mass of nitrogen in one mole of fertiliser	% of nitrogen in the fertiliser
ammonia		17	14	82
ammonium nitrate	NH_4NO_3	80		35
ammonium sulphate	$(NH_4)_2SO_4$	132	28	21
urea	CON_2H_4		28	47

(i) Complete the table. **(3)**

Fertiliser	Formula	Mass of one mole of fertiliser	Mass of nitrogen in one mole of fertiliser	% of nitrogen in the fertiliser
ammonia	NH_3	17	14	82
ammonium nitrate	NH_4NO_3	80	*28*	35
ammonium sulphate	$(NH_4)_2SO_4$	132	28	21
urea	CON_2H_4	60	28	47

(ii)   Why do you think that urea is sometimes described as an "organic fertiliser"?   **(1)**

Because it can be produced by living organisms.

(e) The inventor of the Haber Process, Fritz Haber, tried unsuccessfully for years to obtain gold from the sea. If he had found gold in the sea what process could have been used to separate particles of gold from sea water?   **(1)**

Electrolysis or precipitation using a metal higher in the reactivity series.

(Total 11)

(MEG, June 1989, Paper 2, Q10)

Example 14.4

(a) What atmospheric conditions are needed for atmospheric nitrogen to be converted into nitrogen compounds in the soil?   **(1)**

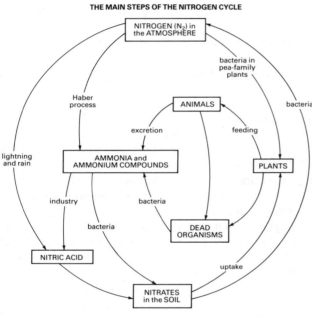

Fig. 14.3

A lightning flash and rain.

> The energy in a lightning flash can cause atmospheric nitrogen and oxygen to combine to produce nitrogen monoxide. This combines with more oxygen to produce nitrogen dioxide which dissolves in water to enter the soil as nitric acid.

(b) Some plants have bacteria in their roots and can absorb nitrogen directly from the atmosphere. Name one such plant.   **(1)**

Any leguminous plant, such as peas, beans or lupins, is a suitable answer.

(c) What class of soluble nitrogen compound found in soil is absorbed through the roots of plants?   **(1)**

Nitrates.

(d) Name a type of nitrogen compound which is found in all plants and animals.   **(1)**

Proteins.

(e) How do animals get the nitrogen compounds they need?   **(1)**

Plants are eaten by animals.

(f) Suggest one way by which soluble nitrogen compounds in the soil are converted to atmospheric nitrogen.   **(1)**

Bacteria in the soil bring about this reaction.

(g) Explain why it is necessary to add artificial fertilisers to the soil.   **(2)**

Man's removal of plants and animals from the land for use as food, together with modern methods of sewage disposal, result in insufficient nitrogen being returned to the soil by decay and excretion. It is essential to restore the balance using artificial fertilisers.

(h) Name one nitrogen-containing compound used as a fertiliser.   **(1)**

Any one of ammonium nitrate, sodium nitrate or ammonium sulphate is a suitable answer.

(i) Name two other elements which are required for healthy plant life.   **(1)**

Potassium and phosphorus.

14.9 Self-test Questions

Question 14.1

(a) The apparatus shown below was assembled and the ammonium chloride was gently heated. It was noticed that litmus paper A started to turn red and litmus paper B became blue; a white solid was seen to form near the cool, open end of the test tube.

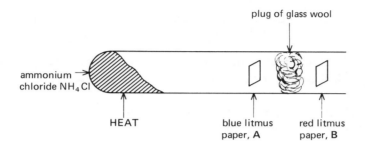

(i) Explain what happened to the ammonium chloride when it was heated and name the white solid formed near the open end of the test tube.

(ii) Explain briefly why the atmosphere in the vicinity of A became acidic while in the vicinity of B it became alkaline.   **(4)**

(b) (i) Name a chemical which reacts with ammonium chloride to form ammonia gas.

(ii) Calculate the volume of ammonia which could be obtained at room temperature and pressure from 10.7 g of ammonium chloride.   **(4)**

(c) Describe briefly **one** simple chemical test which would distinguish between aqueous ammonium chloride and aqueous ammonium sulphate.   **(2)**

Question 14.2

Which of the following is a possible product of the reaction of dilute nitric acid with marble chips?

    A   Calcium
    B   Calcium oxide
    C   Calcium hydroxide
    D   Carbon dioxide
    E   Hydrogen

(L)

Question 14.3

On heating, a metal nitrate decomposed to give a pale yellow residue and oxygen gas. The metal was

    A   Copper
    B   Sodium
    C   Aluminium
    D   Magnesium
    E   Lead

Question 14.4

(a) The nitrogen cycle cannot provide enough fixed nitrogen to produce the food needed to feed the people of the world. Nitrogen from the air is changed artificially into soluble nitrogen compounds, such as ammonium nitrate and ammonium sulphate. These are used as fertilisers.

(i) Complete the table below. The relative atomic masses are N 14, O 16, H 1, S 32.   **(2)**

Fertiliser	Formula	Formula mass in g	% nitrogen
Ammonium nitrate		80	35.0
Ammonium sulphate	$(NH_4)_2SO_4$		21.2

(ii) Use **only** the information in the table to give **one** reason why ammonium nitrate would probably be the better of these two fertilisers.   **(1)**

(iii) What are *fertilisers*?   **(2)**

(iv) Describe how you would make some crystals of ammonium sulphate starting from ammonia gas and any other apparatus or chemicals you may need.   **(4)**

(b) A packet of the fertiliser *Growfast* is shown below.

(i) What do the letters NPK tell you about the elements that the fertiliser contains?   **(3)**

(ii) Give a simple test you could use to show that *Growfast* contains ammonium salts.   **(2)**

NPK FERTILISER

17 . 17 . 17

GROWFAST

EEC FERTILISER

17 . 17 . 17

Test	Result

(c) The fertiliser *Growfast* used to be sold in paper bags. Today it is sold in poly(ethene) bags.

(i) Give **one** advantage of using a plastic bag rather than a paper bag.   **(1)**

(ii) Give another example of a material that is now often replaced by plastic material.   **(1)**

(iii) Give **one** advantage the plastic material has over the material you have chosen in part (ii).   **(1)**

```
        H    H                          H    H
        |    |                          |    |
   H —  C —  C — OH              H —  C —  C — H
        |    |                          |    |
        H    H                          H    H


        H    H                     H    H    H
        |    |                     |    |    |
        C =  C                H —  C —  C —  C — H
        |    |                     |    |    |
        H    H                     H    H    H
```

(iv) Put a ring around the molecule that is used to make poly(ethene).   **(1)**

(v) Name the molecule you have chosen in part (iv).   **(1)**

(d) Plastics such as poly(ethene) are difficult to get rid of.

(i) Why is poly(ethene) difficult to get rid of?   **(2)**

(ii) One method of getting rid of poly(ethene) could be by burning. Explain why this method may **not** be safe.   **(2)**

(SEG, Winter 1988, Paper 1, Q13)

14.10 Answers to Self-test Questions

$M_r (NH_4Cl) = 53.5$; molar volume of a gas at room temperature and pressure $= 24 \ dm^3 \ mol^{-1}$.

14.1 (a) (i) The ammonium chloride sublimed (see Section 1.4). On heating, ammonium chloride dissociates to give ammonia and hydrogen chloride, but these gases recombine on cooling. The white solid is thus ammonium chloride.
$$NH_4Cl(s) \rightleftharpoons NH_3(g) + HCl(g)$$
(ii) Ammonia, being less dense than hydrogen chloride, diffuses more quickly through the glass wool plug so that it will reach litmus paper B before the hydrogen chloride does, leaving hydrogen chloride around A.

(b) (i) Sodium hydroxide.

In fact, any base will do. The equation is
$$NH_4Cl(s) + NaOH(s) \rightarrow NaCl(s) + H_2O(g) + NH_3(g)$$

(ii) 1 mol NH_4Cl gives 1 mol NH_3
53.5 g NH_4Cl gives 24 dm^3 NH_3
10.7 g NH_4Cl gives $24 \times \dfrac{10.7}{53.5}$ dm^3 NH_3

$= 4.8 \ dm^3$

(c) If barium chloride solution is added, aqueous ammonium sulphate gives a white precipitate of barium sulphate.

$$(NH_4)_2SO_4(aq) + BaCl_2(aq) \rightarrow BaSO_4(s) + 2NH_4Cl(aq)$$

14.2 **D.**

Marble chips (calcium carbonate) react with nitric acid to give carbon dioxide.
$$CaCO_3(s) + 2HNO_3(aq) \rightarrow Ca(NO_3)_2(aq) + H_2O(l) + CO_2(g)$$

14.3 **B.**

All the other nitrates give nitrogen dioxide as well as oxygen.

14.4

Fertiliser	Formula	Formula mass in g	% nitrogen
Ammonium nitrate	NH_4NO_3	80	35.0
Ammonium sulphate	$(NH_4)_2SO_4$	132	21.2

(ii) Ammonium nitrate contains a greater percentage of nitrogen.
(iii) Substances containing the chemical elements needed for healthy plant growth. They are needed to compensate for the deficiencies of poor soil.
(iv) Ammonia gas is passed into dilute sulphuric acid until the solution is neutral. The solution is heated to the point of crystallisation and then poured into a conical flask, which is stoppered and the solution allowed to cool. The crystals are filtered off, washed with a little distilled water and dried.

(b) (i) The fertiliser contains nitrogen, phosphorus and potassium.
(ii) The fertiliser can be heated with sodium hydroxide solution. If it contains ammonium salts, the fertiliser will give off ammonia (which turns litmus paper blue).

e.g. $(NH_4)_2SO_4(aq) + 2NaOH(aq) \rightarrow$
$Na_2SO_4(aq) + 2H_2O(l) + 2NH_3(g)$

(c) (i) The plastic bag is stronger (OR waterproof).
(ii) Iron.
(iii) The plastic will not rust.
(iv)

(v) Ethene.
(d) (i) It is non-biodegradable and will not rot away.
(ii) It could produce carbon monoxide which is poisonous.

This question is in the compulsory part of the paper and tests a range of skills – your ability to use the data given, your knowledge of chemistry both within the laboratory and within the global environment. The total number of marks for this question is 23 and you should gain at least 18 marks for a grade C or above, at least 14 marks for a grade E and around 10 marks for a grade G.

15

OXYGEN AND SULPHUR

Topic Guide

15.1 Oxygen, O_2

Oxygen is the most abundant element in the Earth's crust; it also forms 21% of the atmosphere.

Oxygen is prepared in the laboratory by adding hydrogen peroxide solution to manganese(IV) oxide. The manganese(IV) oxide acts as a catalyst.
$$2H_2O_2(aq) \rightarrow 2H_2O(l) + O_2(g)$$

It is a product of the electrolysis of dilute sulphuric acid (see Section 6.2).

Oxygen is manufactured by the fractional distillation of liquid air (see Section 9.2).

(a) Test for Oxygen

Oxygen relights a glowing splint.

(b) Properties of Oxygen

1. Oxygen is a colourless, odourless gas.
2. It is a little more dense than air.
3. It is slightly soluble in water.
4. Oxygen reacts with most elements to give their oxides, e.g. sodium burns with a yellow flame to give sodium oxide.
   $$4Na(s) + O_2(g) \rightarrow 2Na_2O(s)$$
   Sulphur burns with a bright blue flame to give mainly sulphur dioxide.
   $$S(s) + O_2(g) \rightarrow SO_2(g)$$

(c) Uses of Oxygen

1. In steel making to remove impurities from cast iron (see Section 17.2).
2. In oxy-acetylene blowpipes which are used for cutting and welding steel.
3. As an aid to breathing, e.g. in hospitals and climbing.
4. In rocket fuels.

15.2 Oxides

Oxides are compounds of oxygen with one other element, e.g. sodium oxide, Na_2O. There are several different types of oxide and these are discussed in Example 15.2.

15.3 Metal Hydroxides

A **metal hydroxide** is made up of metal ions and hydroxide ions (OH^-). Most metal hydroxides are insoluble in water and may be prepared by precipitation (see Section 11.5), e.g.

$FeCl_3(aq) + 3NaOH(aq) \rightarrow Fe(OH)_3(s) + 3NaCl(aq)$

Soluble hydroxides can be formed by the addition of the metal oxide to water (see Example 15.1).

All metal hydroxides dissolve in acids to give a salt and water only but the amphoteric hydroxides (e.g. aluminium, zinc and lead hydroxides) dissolve in alkalis as well (see Question 15.1).

$Cu(OH)_2(s) + H_2SO_4(aq) \rightarrow CuSO_4(aq) + 2H_2O(l)$

The hydroxides of potassium and sodium are stable to heat but those of metals below sodium in the reactivity series decompose into the corresponding oxide and water on heating, e.g.

$Cu(OH)_2(s) \rightarrow CuO(s) + H_2O(l)$

15.4 Sulphur

Sulphur is extracted from underground deposits by the Frasch process (see Example 15.3). It is also present as an impurity in crude oil and natural gas.

(a) Properties of Sulphur

1. Sulphur is a yellow, brittle, non-metallic solid with a relatively low melting point.
2. When heated, sulphur combines with most metals to form sulphides and with non-metals such as oxygen, chlorine and hydrogen, e.g.
   $Zn(s) + S(s) \rightarrow ZnS(s)$

(b) Uses of Sulphur

1. To make sulphuric acid.
2. To vulcanise (harden) rubber.

15.5 Sulphur Dioxide, SO₂

Sulphur dioxide is formed by burning sulphur and fuels containing sulphur compounds.

$S(s) + O_2(g) \rightarrow SO_2(g)$

(a) Properties of Sulphur Dioxide

1. Sulphur dioxide is a colourless, poisonous gas.
2. It has a characteristic choking smell.
3. It is about twice as dense as air.
4. Sulphur dioxide is very soluble in water. It reacts with water to give a solution of sulphurous acid, H_2SO_3, which is oxidised to give sulphuric acid, a major component of acid rain (see Example 15.4).

(b) Uses of Sulphur Dioxide

1. As an intermediate in the production of sulphuric acid.
2. As a bleaching agent.
3. To preserve food.

15.6 Sulphuric Acid, H₂SO₄

Sulphuric acid is manufactured by the Contact Process (see Section 17.4 and Example 15.5).

(a) Properties of Concentrated Sulphuric Acid (see Example 15.6)

1. Sulphuric acid is a colourless, oily liquid. It is highly corrosive.
2. It is **hygroscopic** (it absorbs water vapour from the atmosphere). This makes it useful for drying gases (see Question 15.4). When poured into water, an exothermic reaction occurs.
3. It is a **dehydrating agent** (it can remove chemically combined water or the elements of water from other compounds) (see Example 15.6).
4. Concentrated sulphuric acid is a powerful oxidising agent.
5. Dilute sulphuric acid behaves as a typical strong acid (see Section 11.2, Example 15.6 and Question 15.3).

15.7 Sulphates

These are prepared as described in Section 11.5.

(a) Test for Sulphates

If dilute hydrochloric acid followed by a few drops of barium chloride solution is added to a sulphate solution, a white precipitate of barium sulphate is obtained, e.g.

$Na_2SO_4(aq) + BaCl_2(aq) \rightarrow BaSO_4(s) + 2NaCl(aq)$.

15.8 Worked Examples

Example 15.1

Oxygen can be prepared by adding hydrogen peroxide solution to manganese(IV) oxide. The manganese(IV) oxide is recovered unchanged in mass at the end of the reaction.

(a) What is the function of the manganese(IV) oxide in this reaction?   **(1)**

The manganese(IV) oxide acts as a catalyst.

Sodium and sulphur both burn in oxygen and the product of each reaction is soluble in water.

(b) Name the product formed when each element burns in oxygen.   **(2)**

Sodium oxide. Sulphur dioxide.

The equations for these reactions are

$4Na(s) + O_2(g) \rightarrow 2Na_2O(s)$

$S(s) + O_2(g) \rightarrow SO_2(g)$

(c) Give the names and approximate pH values of the two aqueous solutions.   **(3)**

Sodium hydroxide pH 13. Sulphurous acid pH 4.

The equations for these reactions are

$Na_2O(s) + H_2O(l) \rightarrow 2NaOH(aq)$
$SO_2(g) + H_2O(l) \rightleftharpoons SO_2(aq)$
$SO_2(aq) + H_2O(l) \rightleftharpoons H_2SO_3(aq)$

When zinc combines with oxygen the compound formed is insoluble in water but dissolves in both dilute hydrochloric acid and in sodium hydroxide solution.

(d) What is the word used to describe the behaviour of the zinc compound? **(1)**

Amphoteric.

See Example 15.2.

(e) Describe in outline the commercial preparation of oxygen from the air. **(3)**

Oxygen is manufactured by the fractional distillation of liquid air (see Section 9.2).

(f) Give two large-scale uses of oxygen. **(2)**

In steel making and as an aid to breathing in hospitals or climbing.

Example 15.2

Classify the following oxides as acidic, basic or amphoteric:

(i) aluminium oxide,

Amphoteric.

(ii) sulphur dioxide,

Acidic.

(iii) magnesium oxide. **(3)**

Basic.

There are several types of oxide:

(a) Acidic oxides are usually the oxides of non-metals. They react with bases to form salts and with alkalis to form salts and water only. Many of them combine with water to form acids.

(b) Basic oxides are the oxides of metals. They react with acids to form salts and water only. If they dissolve in water they form alkalis.

(c) Amphoteric oxides are the oxides of certain metals in the middle groups of the periodic table, e.g aluminium, zinc and lead. They have the properties of both acidic and basic oxides, i.e. they react with both alkalis and acids to form salts and water only.

(d) Neutral oxides are oxides of a few non-metals. They react with neither acids nor bases.

Example 15.3

(a) Sulphur is extracted from underground deposits by the Frasch process. Three concentric pipes, A, B and C, are sunk down to the deposits as shown in Fig. 15.1.

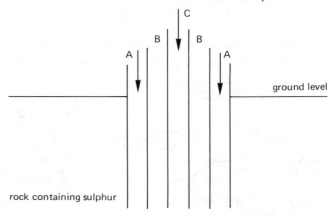

Fig. 15.1

Water at 170°C is pumped down the outer pipe.

(i) Explain how it is possible to obtain water with a temperature of 170°C. **(1)**

Water boils at 100°C at 1 atm pressure. If the pressure is increased, the boiling point of the water is raised.

(ii) What is the water used for? **(1)**

The water is used to melt the sulphur.

(iii) Hot compressed air is passed down tube C. What happens in tube B? **(1)**

A froth of water, air and molten sulphur is forced up the middle pipe and is led off to settling tanks where the sulphur separates out.

(b) Give **TWO** large-scale uses of sulphur. **(2)**

To make sulphuric acid and to harden rubber.

Example 15.4

Rain falling near some power stations is often slightly acidic. This 'acid' rain may be seen to affect some city statues and buildings but not others. Explain this observation. **(2)**

Coal-burning power stations generate sulphur dioxide which dissolves in water to form sulphurous acid and, by oxidation, sulphuric acid ('acid' rain). The 'acid' rain will attack those building materials which react with acids, e.g. marble.

Acid rain also has an effect on vegetation and animals. Smokeless fuels generate less smoke and tar but produce more sulphur dioxide than the same mass of coal.

Example 15.5

(a) You are the Managing Director of the Brimstone Company which manufactures and markets sulphuric acid.

The company has recently discovered extensive deposits of sulphur on the surface of the island of Smallbrook and purchased the rights to mine the sulphur. The island lies about 50 miles west of the industrial mainland.

Apart from a range of hills in the north-east the island is mainly flat. The roads are poor and there is no railway. The prevailing wind blows from the east.

A, B, and C are tiny fishing villages. D is a small market town. The rest of the island is largely uninhabited with a few small farms. The price of land is low compared with that on the mainland.

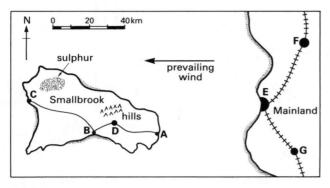

Fig. 15.2

On the mainland, E is a major port with good road and rail communications to all main industrial centres, such as F and G. Your company has no buildings or trade in this area.

To exploit the deposits your company proposes to build a new sulphuric acid plant.

Write a short report to the Board of Directors recommending a site for the new plant. You should indicate clearly where the plant is to be built (it may be on the island or on the mainland), listing the advantages and disadvantages of your chosen site under the following headings:

1. Other chemical resources.
2. Pollution problems.
3. Economic/transport aspects.   **(7)**

There are various possible positions for the sulphuric acid plant. You do not have to agree with the examiner! Marks will be obtained for your reasons for choosing a particular position, i.e. for listing the advantages and disadvantages of the chosen site.

One possible position would be near E.

1. **Other chemical resources.** *In addition to the sulphur, the main chemical resources needed are air and water. These are available anywhere along the coast, both on the island and on the mainland. Sulphur will have to be shipped from the island to the mainland and so this is a disadvantage of this site. Small amounts of catalyst (vanadium(V) oxide) and initially some concentrated sulphuric acid (to dissolve the sulphur trioxide) will also be needed but it will be easier to get them to E rather than the island.*
2. **Pollution problems.** *This is a disadvantage of site E. The prevailing wind blows from the east and so will blow any fumes/acid rain over towards the island.*
3. **Economic/transport aspects.** *This is where I think that site E definitely has an advantage. Admittedly sulphur has to be shipped in but it will weigh less than the sulphuric acid that is made from it. Site E has good road and rail communications to all main industrial areas and so the sulphuric acid can easily be*

transported to where it is required. If the sulphuric acid were made on the island it would have to be shipped out to major industrial areas. Smallbrook has only a small population and so, although it would probably be possible to employ sufficient local people to extract the sulphur, it might be difficult to get a large enough workforce to produce the sulphuric acid as well.

This question does not ask you for details of the manufacture of sulphuric acid but obviously you need to know which chemical resources are required. To help you with your revision, try to write down the details of the Contact process – if you get stuck, Example 17.6 should help you.

(b) It is the first time your company has had any activity near the sea. List two mineral resources to be found in the sea and the uses to which they might be put.   **(3)**

Two mineral resources to be found in the sea are sodium chloride and magnesium chloride. Sodium chloride is used in the preparation and preserving of food and in the production of a large number of sodium compounds, e.g. sodium hydroxide and sodium carbonate. Magnesium chloride is used to produce magnesium, a metal of low density which is used in alloys.

(Total 10)
(MEG, June 1988, Paper 3, Q6)

Example 15.6

Fig. 15.3

(a) What property of sulphuric acid does the hazard sign in Fig. 15.3 indicate?   **(1)**
It is corrosive.

(b) What are the hazards involved in the storage and transportation of sulphuric acid?   **(3)**
Water must be excluded since the reaction between water and sulphuric acid is highly exothermic and hence dangerous. Sulphuric acid is a powerful oxidising agent and reacts vigorously with many substances, often producing sulphur dioxide which is a poisonous gas.

(c) Describe how sulphuric acid reacts with each of the following. State whether concentrated or dilute acid is used.

(i) copper(II) sulphate crystals;

Concentrated sulphuric acid converts blue crystals of copper (II) sulphate-5-water to the white anhydrous salt. It is behaving as a dehydrating agent.

$$CuSO_4.5H_2O(s) \rightarrow CuSO_4(s) + 5H_2O(l)$$

(ii) sugar;

Concentrated sulphuric acid will remove the elements of water (i.e. hydrogen and oxygen atoms in the ratio 2 : 1) from sugar. The mixture gets hot, swells up and leaves a black mass of carbon.

$$C_{12}H_{22}O_{11}(s) \rightarrow 12C(s) + 11H_2O(l)$$

The sulphuric acid is acting as a dehydrating agent here as well.

NB. Do not confuse dehydration with drying. A drying agent only removes water that is not chemically combined.

    (iii) magnesium. **(2 each)**

Dilute sulphuric acid is behaving here as a typical strong acid. Magnesium effervesces with dilute sulphuric acid to produce hydrogen.

$$Mg(s) + H_2SO_4(aq) \rightarrow MgSO_4(aq) + H_2(g)$$

15.9 Self-test Questions

Question 15.1

(a) Describe what happens if a few drops of sodium hydroxide solution are added to:
   (i) copper(II)sulphate solution;
   (ii) aluminium sulphate solution.   **(2)**
(b) What happens if excess sodium hydroxide solution is added?   **(2)**
(c) Explain your answer to (b).   **(2)**

Question 15.2

From the list

    A ammonia   **D** nitrogen
    B chlorine   **E** sulphur dioxide
    C hydrogen   choose the gas which is

(a) used to preserve food,
(b) prepared by the distillation of liquid air,
(c) soluble in water to give an alkaline solution,
(d) obtained as a by-product when fossil fuels are burned,
(e) used in the manufacture of margarine.   **(1 each)**

Question 15.3

Dilute sulphuric acid reacts with

    A copper to give copper(II) sulphate and hydrogen,
    B iron to give iron(II) sulphate and hydrogen,
    C magnesium carbonate to give magnesium oxide, carbon dioxide and sulphur dioxide.
    D zinc to give zinc sulphate and water,
    E zinc oxide to give zinc sulphate and hydrogen.

Question 15.4

Arrangements for drying a gas with concentrated sulphuric acid could include:

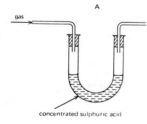 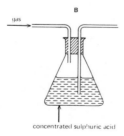 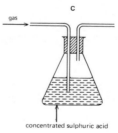 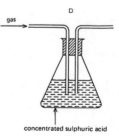

15.10 Answers to Self-test Questions

15.1(a) (i) A blue precipitate of copper(II) hydroxide is formed.
   (ii) A white precipitate of aluminium hydroxide is formed.
 (b) The copper(II) hydroxide remains unchanged but the aluminium hydroxide dissolves.
 (c) Aluminium hydroxide is amphoteric and so reacts with excess alkali. Copper(II) hydroxide is basic.

15.2(a) **E.**   (d) **E.**
 (b) **D.**   (e) **C.**
 (c) **A.**

15.3 **B.**

The relevant equations are:
$$Fe(s) + H_2SO_4(aq) \rightarrow FeSO_4(aq) + H_2(g)$$
$$MgCO_3(s) + H_2SO_4(aq) \rightarrow MgSO_4(aq) + CO_2(g) + H_2O(l)$$
$$Zn(s) + H_2SO_4(aq) \rightarrow ZnSO_4(aq) + H_2(g)$$
$$ZnO + H_2SO_4(aq) \rightarrow ZnSO_4(aq) + H_2O(l)$$
Copper is below hydrogen in the reactivity series and so does not react with dilute sulphuric acid.
Concentrated sulphuric acid oxidises copper and is itself reduced to sulphur dioxide:
$$Cu(s) + 2H_2SO_4(l) \rightarrow CuSO_4(s) + 2H_2O(l) + SO_2(g).$$

15.4 **C.**

THE HALOGENS

16.1 Hydrogen Chloride, HCl

Hydrogen chloride is a colourless gas with a pungent, choking smell. It gives steamy fumes in moist air and is very soluble in water, forming hydrochloric acid. This is a strong acid (see Section 11.4 and also Example 16.1 and Question 16.1). Hydrogen chloride is manufactured by burning hydrogen in chlorine.

$$H_2(g) + Cl_2(g) \rightarrow 2HCl(g)$$

Concentrated hydrochloric acid is easily oxidised to chlorine, e.g. by manganese(IV) oxide.

16.2 Chlorides

All of the common metallic chlorides are soluble in water, except those of silver and lead. They are prepared as described in Section 11.5 (see also Example 16.3).

$$Pb(NO_3)_2(aq) + 2NaCl(aq) \rightarrow PbCl_2(s) + 2NaNO_3(aq)$$
$$CuO(s) + 2HCl(aq) \rightarrow CuCl_2(aq) + H_2O(l)$$

(a) Test for Chlorides

Chlorides in solution react with silver nitrate solution in the presence of dilute nitric acid to give a white precipitate of silver chloride (see Example 16.1).

$$NaCl(aq) + AgNO_3(aq) \rightarrow AgCl(s) + NaNO_3(aq)$$

16.3 Chlorine, Cl_2

Chlorine is prepared in the laboratory by the oxidation of concentrated hydrochloric acid by a strong oxidising agent such as manganese(IV) oxide.

Chlorine is manufactured by the electrolysis of sodium chloride solution using a titanium anode and a steel cathode (see Section 17.3 and Example 17.5).

(a) Test for Chlorine

Chlorine bleaches moist universal indicator paper.

(b) Properties of Chlorine

1. Chlorine is a greenish-yellow gas with a characteristic pungent, choking smell.
2. It is poisonous.
3. It is about twice as dense as air.
4. Chlorine is slightly soluble in water. It reacts with water to give an acidic solution.
5. Chlorine combines with most metals, non-metals and with hydrogen to give the corresponding chloride, particularly on heating (see Example 16.3).
$$2Na(s) + Cl_2(g) \rightarrow 2NaCl(s)$$
$$H_2(g) + Cl_2(g) \rightarrow 2HCl(g)$$
6. Chlorine is an extremely powerful oxidising agent (see Example 16.3).

(c) Uses of Chlorine

1. In the manufacture of plastics (e.g. PVC), anaesthetics, insecticides (e.g. DDT), solvents and aerosol propellants, all of which are chlorinated organic compounds.
2. As a bleach in the pulp and textile industries.
3. In the treatment of sewage and in the purification of water.

16.4 A Comparison of the Halogens (see Question 6.4)

Atoms of the halogens all have 7 electrons in their outermost shells and therefore behave similarly (see Example 16.6).

The melting points and boiling points increase down the group so that fluorine is a yellow gas, chlorine a greenish-yellow gas, bromine a reddish-brown liquid and iodine a black solid. All the halogens combine with a large number of metals and non-metals and with hydrogen.

$$2Fe(s) + 3Br_2(g) \rightarrow 2FeBr_3(s)$$

In general, the reactions of fluorine are the most vigorous and those of iodine are the least vigorous. For example, bromine water, like chlorine water, is acidic but only about 1% of the dissolved bromine actually reacts with the water. Iodine is virtually insoluble in water but does show slight acidic properties by dissolving in sodium hydroxide solution.

The size of the atoms increases from fluorine to iodine. Thus fluorine, which has the smallest atoms, is the best electron attractor (i.e. oxidising agent) of these four elements and iodine the feeblest. Once the extra electron has been gained it will be more firmly held in a small ion such as fluoride than in a large ion. Thus it is possible for a change such as:
$$Cl_2(g) + 2I^-(aq) \rightarrow I_2(aq) + 2Cl^-(aq)$$
to occur (see Example 16.5).

16.5 Worked Examples

Example 16.1

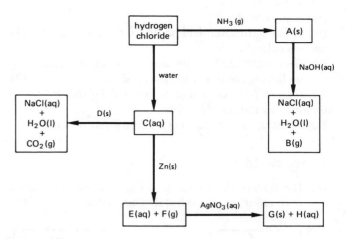

Fig. 16.1

(a) Name the compounds A to H. **(8)**

Hydrogen chloride gas reacts with ammonia to give white fumes of ammonium chloride (A).

$$NH_3(g) + HCl(g) \rightleftharpoons NH_4Cl(s)$$

Ammonium chloride reacts with sodium hydroxide solution to give ammonia (B).

$$NH_4Cl(s) + NaOH(aq) \rightarrow NaCl(aq) + H_2O(l) + NH_3(g)$$
This is a test for ammonium salts.

C is hydrochloric acid.
D is sodium carbonate.

$$Na_2CO_3(s) + 2HCl(aq) \rightarrow 2NaCl(aq) + H_2O(l) + CO_2(g)$$

Zinc reacts with hydrochloric acid to give zinc chloride (E) and hydrogen (F).

$$Zn(s) + 2HCl(aq) \rightarrow ZnCl_2(aq) + H_2(g)$$

Silver nitrate solution reacts with zinc chloride solution to give a white precipitate of silver chloride (G) and a solution of zinc nitrate (H).

$$ZnCl_2(aq) + 2AgNO_3(aq) \rightarrow 2AgCl(s) + Zn(NO_3)_2(aq)$$

(b) Describe a test by which you could identify:
  (i) gas B;
Ammonia turns universal indicator paper purple (see Section 14.3).
  (ii) gas F. **(2)**
Hydrogen 'pops' when a flame is applied (see Section 10.4).

Example 16.2

(a) What are the essential processes involved in the purification of rock salt to give common salt?   **(3)**

(i) Solution.

(ii) Filtration.

(iii) Evaporation.

(b) What is the chemical name for common salt?   **(1)**

Sodium chloride.

(c) Give one advantage and one disadvantage of including common salt in our diet.   **(2)**

Advantage: It is an essential mineral for health OR it improves the flavour of our food.

Disadvantage: It can lead to high blood pressure.

Example 16.3

(a) The hazard signs shown in Fig. 16.2 are associated with chlorine gas. What do they mean?   **(2)**

(i) 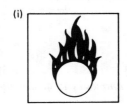   (ii)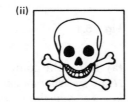

Fig. 16.2

(i) Oxidising.

(ii) Toxic.

(b) What reaction takes place when chlorine is passed over heated iron wool?   **(2)**

Iron wool catches fire in chlorine to give thick brown fumes of iron(III) chloride.

$2Fe(s) + 3Cl_2(g) \rightarrow 2FeCl_3(s)$

(c) How would you distinguish between a solution in water of the salt prepared in (b) and the product formed when iron filings are added to dilute sulphuric acid?   **(2)**

Sodium hydroxide solution produces a precipitate of red/ brown iron(III) hydroxide with iron(III) chloride solution but a precipitate of green iron(II) hydroxide when added to iron(II) sulphate solution (from the iron filings and dilute sulphuric acid).

$FeCl_3(aq) + 3\,NaOH(aq) \rightarrow 3NaCl(aq) + Fe(OH)_3(s)$
$\qquad\qquad\qquad\qquad\qquad\qquad\qquad$ *red/brown*
$FeSO_4(aq) + 2NaOH(aq) \rightarrow Na_2SO_4(aq) + Fe(OH)_2(s)$
$\qquad\qquad\qquad\qquad\qquad\qquad\qquad\qquad$ *green*

(d) The addition of chlorine water to aqueous iron(II) sulphate results in the appearance of a yellow colour and the disappearance of the chlorine smell. Explain this reaction.   **(2)**

Chlorine is an oxidising agent, oxidising green Fe^{2+} to yellow Fe^{3+}. The chlorine molecules are reduced to chloride ions.

The ionic equation is:
$2Fe^{2+}(aq) + Cl_2(aq) \rightarrow 2Fe^{3+}(aq) + 2Cl^-(aq)$

Example 16.4

(a) How would you show that an aqueous solution contained

 (i) chlorine?

A piece of litmus paper placed in the solution will be bleached if chlorine is present.

 (ii) chloride ions?   **(4)**

If silver nitrate solution acidified with nitric acid is added to the solution, a white precipitate of silver chloride is formed if chloride ions are present.

(b) What is the difference between a chlorine atom and a chloride ion?   **(1)**

A chloride ion is charged and is formed by the addition of an electron to a chlorine atom.

Example 16.5

(a) Chlorine is obtained commercially by the electrolysis of molten sodium chloride.

 (i) Write down the equation for the production of chlorine at the appropriate electrode, and name the type of chemical reaction taking place.   **(5)**

$2Cl^-(l) - 2e \rightarrow 2Cl(g)$
$\qquad\qquad\quad \downarrow$
$\qquad\qquad Cl_2(g)$

Chlorine is liberated at the anode (see Section 6.2). Since electrons are lost, oxidation is taking place.

 (ii) Give two important uses of chlorine.   **(2)**

In the manufacture of plastics and in the purification of water.

(b) Bromine and iodine are members of the same group of the periodic table as chlorine. Describe tests by which these three elements could be arranged in an order of activity.   **(6)**

If chlorine water is added to an aqueous solution of sodium bromide containing a little 1,1,1-trichloroethane, then the chlorine, being more reactive than bromine, will displace it from the solution. The bromine produces an orange colouration with 1,1,1-trichloroethane. A similar experiment using bromine water and an aqueous solution of sodium iodide produces a violet colouration in the 1,1,1-trichloroethane due to the displacement of iodine.

Thus the order of activity is:

chlorine

bromine

iodine.

Example 16.6

Fluorine, chlorine, bromine and iodine are all in Group VII of the periodic table. What does this tell you about:

(a) the electronic structures of atoms of bromine and iodine;   **(1)**

Both atoms will have 7 electrons in their outermost shells.

(b) the molecular formula of bromine and iodine;   **(1)**

The molecular formulae of bromine and iodine will be similar to that of chlorine, i.e. Br_2 and I_2.

(c) the formula of sodium bromide;   **(1)**

NaBr (similar to NaCl).

(d) the solubility of silver iodide?   **(1)**

It will be insoluble in water (like silver chloride).

16.6 Self-test Questions

*Question 16.1

Hydrogen chloride is a gas which is denser than air and dissolves easily in water.
(a) Describe how you could show that hydrogen chloride is very soluble in water.　　　　(2)
(b) Give the tests you could use to show that when hydrogen chloride reacts with water the resulting solution contains both hydrogen ions ($H^+(aq)$) and chloride ions ($Cl^-(aq)$).　　　　(4)

	Test	Result
Hydrogen ions ($H^+(aq)$)		
Chloride ions ($Cl^-(aq)$)		

(c) Hydrochloric acid is formed when hydrogen chloride is bubbled through water. Describe an experiment in which hydrochloric acid acts as a typical acid. You should name any reagents used, give any observations and write a balanced chemical equation for the reaction.　　　　(4)

(SEG, June 1988, Paper 3, Q6)

Question 16.2

Within a Group of the periodic table, the order of chemical reactivity of non-metals decreases down the Group. From this it follows that:

　A　Chlorine will displace fluorine from potassium fluoride solution.
　B　Bromine will displace chlorine from potassium chloride solution and iodine from potassium iodide solution.
　C　Iodine will displace chlorine from potassium chloride solution and bromine from potassium bromide solution.
　D　Chlorine will displace bromine from potassium bromide solution and iodine from potassium iodide solution.
　E　Iodine will displace fluorine from potassium fluoride solution.

16.7 Answers to Self-test Questions

16.1(a) I would perform the fountain experiment. A round-bottomed flask is filled completely with hydrogen chloride. A bung and glass tube are inserted in the mouth of the flask. The flask is inverted with the open end of the tube below the surface of water. The water rises up the tube and eventually enters the flask when it sprays up like a fountain (this process can be speeded up by pouring a little propanone on the base of the flask).

(c) When hydrochloric acid is added to magnesium, bubbles are seen and hydrogen (pops in a flame) is given off.
$$Mg(s) + 2HCl(aq) \rightarrow MgCl_2(aq) + H_2(g)$$

> There are several reactions that could have been given here. See Section 11.2 for other typical reactions of acids.

16.2 **D**.

> Any element will displace a less reactive one from a solution containing its ions.

(b)	Test	Result
Hydrogen ions (H⁺(aq))	Universal indicator paper	Goes red
Chloride ions (Cl⁻(aq))	Silver nitrate solution + nitric acid added	White precipitate obtained

17 SOME INDUSTRIAL PROCESSES

Topic Guide

17.1 Introduction

Industrial processes are designed to manufacture products as economically as possible, taking into account both the speed and the cost of operation.

Chemical works should ideally be sited near the source of raw materials and the users of the products, or near to a good transport system. Control of pollution is an important factor to take into account, even though it can add a considerable amount to the cost involved.

In recent years the realisation that the earth's resources are not limitless has led to an increase in the recycling of materials. For example, scrap steel and aluminium can be reprocessed and made into new items.

17.2 Extraction of Metals

The method of extracting a metal from its compounds depends upon the position of the metal in the reactivity series. Electrolysis is the only economic way of reducing ions of metals near the top of the series: for example, aluminium is obtained by electrolysing a solution of aluminium oxide in molten cryolite (see Example 17.3). Metals such as this could not be manufactured cheaply until the means of generating large amounts of electricity had been invented.

For metals lower down in the series, chemical reduction is used. The commonest reducing agent is coke (impure carbon, made by heating coal in the absence of air). Iron is manufactured by heating its ore, often impure iron(III) oxide, with limestone and coke in a blast furnace (see Example 17.4).

The blast furnace produces *cast iron*, which is hard and brittle owing to the presence of impurities such as carbon, sulphur and phosphorus. Steel is stronger and more flexible than iron. It is made by removing the impurities from cast iron and then adding carbon and other elements such as chromium in the correct proportions to give the required product.

Oxygen is blown onto the surface of molten cast iron in a converter of the type shown in Fig. 17.1. It oxidises the non-metallic impurities to acidic oxides, which escape as gases or combine with the basic lining of the converter to form slag. Other elements are then added to give the type of steel required.

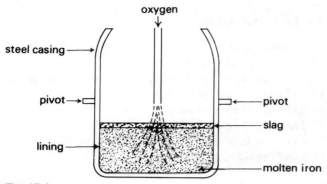

Fig. 17.1

17.3 Manufacture of Sodium Hydroxide and Chlorine

These two important chemicals are manufactured by the electrolysis of brine (sodium chloride solution) (see Example 17.5).

17.4 Manufacture of Sulphuric Acid

Sulphuric acid is manufactured from sulphur, air and water in the Contact Process (see Examples 15.5 and 17.6).

17.5 Manufacture of Ammonia

Nitrogen from the air and hydrogen from water and natural gas (methane) are combined under special conditions in the Haber process to make ammonia (see Example 17.7).

17.6 Manufacture of Nitric Acid

Nitric acid is made in the Ostwald process, where ammonia is catalytically oxidised by the oxygen of the air (see Example 17.8).

17.7 Worked Examples

Example 17.1

Which of the metals listed below is most likely to be extracted by electrolysis of its molten chloride?
A   Calcium
B   Copper
C   Iron
D   Silver
E   Zinc
The answer is **A**.

(AEB, 1982)

> Calcium is high up in the reactivity series – electrolysis is used to extract these elements.

*Example 17.2

The diagram shows some ways in which air plays an important part in industry.

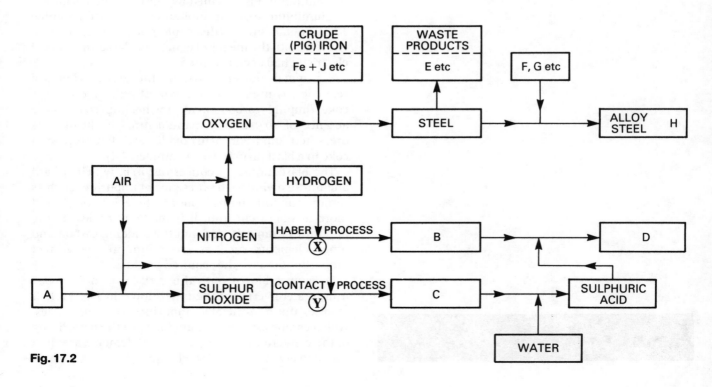

Fig. 17.2

(a) (i) Give the name of the process by which air is separated into oxygen and nitrogen.

Fractional distillation.

(ii) Give the name of one other important product of this process. **(3)**

Argon.

(b) Give the names of possible substances which might be represented by the letters A to D. **(4)**

A *Sulphur.*   B *Ammonia.*

C *Sulphur trioxide.*   D *Ammonium sulphate.*

(c) What are the catalysts X and Y used in the two named processes? **(2)**

X *Iron.*   Y *Vanadium*(V) *oxide.*

(d) (i) Give the name of a possible waste product E.

Carbon dioxide.

(ii) Give the names of two metallic elements, F and G, which might be used to make alloy steel.

F *Chromium.*   G *Nickel.*

(iii) Give an example of an alloy steel H. **(4)**

Stainless steel.

(e) Give one **other** industrial or commercial use for nitrogen and oxygen, and in each case explain why air is not a suitable substitute. **(4)**

Oxygen is used in rocket fuels.

Air is not suitable for this purpose because nitrogen does not support combustion and would be carried as extra mass.

Nitrogen is used for "flushing" out oil tanks.

Air is not suitable for this purpose because air/oil mixtures are explosive. **(Total 17)**

(LEAG, June 1988, Paper 3, Q4)

*Example 17.3

(a)

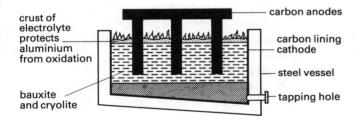

crust of electrolyte protects aluminium from oxidation — carbon anodes
— carbon lining cathode
— steel vessel
bauxite and cryolite — tapping hole

The diagram shows the method used to extract aluminium by the electrolysis of molten purified bauxite. The bauxite is mixed with cryolite, which is also a compound containing aluminium. The cryolite is not electrolysed in the process.

(i) Give the name and formula of the aluminium compound which is the main ingredient of bauxite. **(1)**

Aluminium oxide, Al_2O_3.

(ii) Give equations for the reactions occurring at the two electrodes. **(2)**

Anode: $6O^{2-} - 12e^- \rightarrow 6O$

$$\downarrow$$

$$3O_2$$

Cathode: $4Al^{3+} + 12e^- \rightarrow 4Al$

(iii) Why do the anodes have to be replaced from time to time? **(1)**

Because they react with the oxygen to give carbon dioxide.

(iv) What is the purpose of adding cryolite to the bauxite and how does this help in energy conservation in the process? **(2)**

Cryolite reduces the melting point of the bauxite. Less electricity is used to keep the electrolyte molten.

(v) The world supplies of bauxite are likely to be exhausted within 30 years. What is being done to try to prolong the lifetime of these supplies? **(2)**

Aluminium is recycled. Aluminium is alloyed with other metals.

(b) Alloys of aluminium are used in the manufacture of aircraft.

(i) What is meant by an *alloy*? **(1)**

A mixture of a metal with other elements, usually metals.

(ii) State **four** properties of aluminium alloys which make them useful in the manufacture of aircraft. **(2)**

Low density.

Strong.

Unreactive.

Malleable.

(c) Aluminium and carbon form a compound aluminium carbide. 10.8 g of aluminium carbide contains 8.1 g of aluminium.

$[A_r(C) = 12 \quad A_r(Al) = 27]$

(i) Calculate the mass of carbon combined with 8.1 g of aluminium.

$10.8 - 8.1 = 2.7 g$

(ii) Calculate the relative numbers of moles of aluminium and carbon in aluminium carbide.

Mol Al $= \dfrac{8.1}{27} = 0.3$ Mol C $= \dfrac{2.7}{12} = 0.225$

(iii) Deduce the empirical (simplest) formula of aluminium carbide. **(4)**

0.3 mol Al combines with 0.225 mol C

1.33 mol Al combines with 1 mol C

4 mol Al combines with 3 mol C

∴ Empirical formula $= Al_4C_3$

(Welsh, June 1988, Paper 2, Q5)

*Example 17.4

(a) Aluminium is extracted by electrolysis.

(i) Explain why aluminium is **not** extracted by reducing aluminium oxide with carbon (coke). **(2)**

Aluminium is above carbon in the reactivity series and so the reaction would not work.

See Section 12.1.

(ii) Describe an experiment by which you could show that aluminium comes above iron in the reactivity series. **(3)**

A mixture of aluminium and iron oxide is heated. A vigorous reaction takes place and aluminium oxide and iron are formed.

$$2Al(s) + Fe_2O_3(s) \rightarrow Al_2O_3(s) + 2Fe(s)$$

    (iii) Why is aluminium less likely to corrode than iron in damp air? **(2)**

Aluminium is covered with a surface layer of oxide which protects it from further reaction.

(b) Iron is extracted by reducing iron(III) oxide with carbon (coke) in a blast furnace.

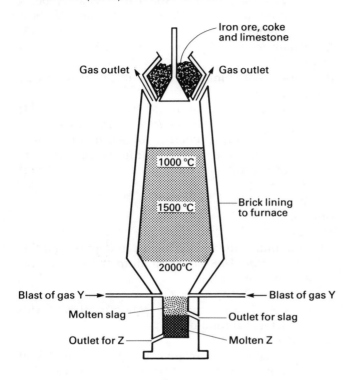

    (i) What is gas Y? **(1)**

Air.

    (ii) What is molten Z? **(1)**

Iron.

(c) In the blast furnace the coke is used to provide the heat energy and the reducing agent (carbon monoxide).

    (i) Write a balanced chemical equation for the burning of coke in excess air. **(2)**

$$C(s) + O_2(g) \rightarrow CO_2(g)$$

    (ii) Write a balanced chemical equation for the formation of carbon monoxide from the coke. **(2)**

$$C(s) + CO_2(g) \rightarrow 2CO(g)$$

$$\text{or } 2C(s) + O_2(g) \rightarrow 2CO(g)$$

    (iii) Why is carbon monoxide called a *reducing agent*? **(1)**

It removes the oxygen from the iron(III) oxide.

$$Fe_2O_3(s) + 3CO(g) \rightarrow 2Fe(l) + 3CO_2(g)$$

(d) Sand (SiO_2), is an impurity in the raw materials. The sand is removed from the blast furnace by reacting it with calcium oxide to form a liquid slag.

$$CaO(s) + SiO_2(s) \rightarrow CaSiO_3(l)$$

    (i) Describe how calcium oxide is formed in the blast furnace. **(2)**

The limestone decomposes on heating.

$$CaCO_3(s) \rightarrow CaO(s) + CO_2(g)$$

    (ii) Why does the oxide of calcium react with the oxide of silicon? **(2)**

Calcium oxide is basic; silicon oxide is acidic.

    (iii) Why would problems be caused if the sand were not removed by this reaction? **(2)**

The sand would mix with the iron and make it brittle.

                  (SEG, June 1988, Paper 3, Q2)

Example 17.5

The diagram below shows one form of the diaphragm cell for the industrial production of sodium hydroxide by the electrolysis of sodium chloride solution (brine).

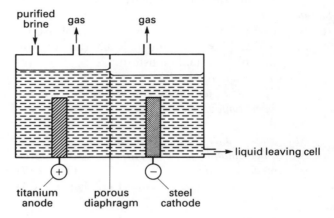

(a) A gas is formed at both the anode and cathode. In **each** case
    (i) state the name of the gas formed,
    (ii) explain by means of an equation how the gas is formed,
    (iii) state one large scale use of the gas.

ANODE
    (i) *Name of gas: Chlorine*
    (ii) *Equation:* $2Cl^-(aq) - 2e^- \rightarrow 2Cl(g) \rightarrow Cl_2(g)$
    (iii) *Large scale use: In the manufacture of plastics, e.g. PVC.* **(3)**

CATHODE
    (i) *Name of gas: Hydrogen*
    (ii) *Equation:* $2H^+(aq) + 2e^- \rightarrow 2H(g) \rightarrow H_2(g)$
    (iii) *Large scale use: In the manufacture of hydrogen chloride.* **(3)**

The liquid leaving the cell is sodium hydroxide solution since these ions (Na^+, OH^-) have not been discharged.

(b) Explain why sodium chloride is used on roads in the winter. **(1)**

It makes water freeze at a lower temperature.

(c) (i) Explain briefly how a sample of soap could be made in the laboratory from sodium hydroxide. **(2)**

Castor oil and sodium hydroxide are boiled together. Salt is added to precipitate the soap which is filtered off and washed with a little distilled water.

    (ii) Why do soaps give a scum when added to hard water? **(2)**

Soap reacts with the calcium ions in the water to form a precipitate(scum).

    (iii) Why are detergents preferred to soaps in the washing of clothes? **(1)**

They do not form scum.

> Their calcium salts are soluble.

(Welsh, June 1988, Paper 1, Q37)

*Example 17.6

Sulphur dioxide is produced by the burning of sulphur and certain other sulphur compounds for the manufacture of sulphuric acid. The modern Contact Process for this is so efficient that very little sulphur dioxide escapes into the atmosphere. Sulphur dioxide is also produced by other industries as an unwelcome by-product and is liberated to the atmosphere where it is a major cause of 'acid rain'.

(a) In the Contact Process, sulphur dioxide is reacted with dry air to convert it into sulphur trioxide which is then absorbed in 98% sulphuric acid. The reaction conditions are chosen to give a high yield of sulphur trioxide at an economic rate of reaction.

    (i) State the reaction conditions used in the formation of sulphur trioxide. Give a reason for any one of these. **(3)**

450°C, a catalyst of vanadium(V) oxide and a pressure slightly above atmospheric to force the gases through the plant.

    (ii) Give an equation for the formation of sulphur trioxide. **(1)**

$$2SO_2(g) + O_2(g) \rightleftharpoons 2SO_3(g)$$

    (iii) Explain why sulphur trioxide is absorbed in 98% sulphuric acid and not in water. Give an equation for the reaction occurring between sulphur trioxide and sulphuric acid. **(2)**

Sulphur trioxide is not absorbed in water because the reaction is too violent and inefficient.

$$SO_3(g) + H_2SO_4(l) \rightarrow H_2S_2O_7(l)$$

> Water is then added to give sulphuric acid:
> $H_2S_2O_7(l) + H_2O(l) \rightarrow 2H_2SO_4(l)$.

    (iv) The overall process produces a large quantity of heat energy. Why does this help to make the production of sulphuric acid relatively cheap? **(1)**

It is used to heat the incoming gases (sulphur dioxide and oxygen).

    (v) Why are sulphuric acid plants often sited near ports? **(1)**

Because the sulphur must be imported.

(b) Which one of the following hazard symbols, A, B, C, would you expect to find on a bottle of concentrated sulphuric acid? Explain your reasoning. **(2)**

 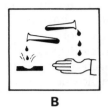 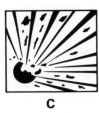

    A   **B**   **C**

B *It is corrosive.*

(c) (i) Explain why all rain is acidic. **(1)**

All rain contains dissolved carbon dioxide.

    (ii) If all rain is acidic, what do you understand by the phrase 'acid rain'? **(1)**

Rain that contains more harmful acidic oxides, e.g. SO_2, NO_2.

    (iii) Name **one** industry said to be a major contributor towards 'acid rain' and explain briefly how this pollution arises. **(2)**

The electricity industry. Coal burning power stations produce sulphur dioxide.

    (iv) Why do emissions from some industries in Western Europe cause particular problems hundreds of miles away in Scandinavia? **(1)**

The prevailing winds blow the sulphur dioxide to Scandinavia.

(Welsh, June 1988, Paper 2, Q6)

Example 17.7

(a) Ammonia is manufactured from hydrogen and nitrogen by the Haber process.

    (i) What are the raw materials for the process? **(3)**

Air, water and natural gas (methane).

    (ii) Write an equation for the synthesis of ammonia, and state the three essential conditions for an acceptable yield of ammonia. **(3)**

$N_2(g) + 3H_2(g) \rightleftharpoons 2NH_3(g)$
The plant operates at about 500°C and 250 atm pressure.
A catalyst of iron is used to speed up the reaction.

(b) Describe, with a diagram, how ammonia may be safely dissolved in water in the laboratory. **(3)**

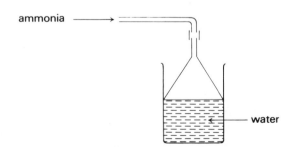

Ammonia is so soluble in water that precautions have to be taken to prevent sucking back. In the funnel arrangement water rises in the funnel but the level in the beaker drops. Air enters under the rim of the funnel and equalises the pressure inside and outside the apparatus so that the water drops back again. The funnel must be almost as wide as the beaker if the system is to work efficiently.

Example 17.8

Nitric acid, HNO_3, is made from ammonia in three stages.

Stage 1 A mixture of ammonia and air is passed over a platinum gauze catalyst when nitrogen oxide is formed by an exothermic reaction.

$4NH_3(g) + 5O_2(g) \rightleftharpoons 6H_2O(g) + 4NO(g)$

Stage 2 The nitrogen oxide is cooled and mixed with air to give nitrogen dioxide.

$4NO(g) + 2O_2(g) \rightarrow 4NO_2(g)$

Stage 3 The nitrogen dioxide forms nitric acid when dissolved in water in the presence of air.

$4NO_2(g) + 2H_2O(l) + O_2(g) \rightarrow 4HNO_3(aq)$

(a) Air is used to provide the necessary oxygen for the process. Give the names of TWO other gases which must inevitably be present in the reaction vessel from this source.   **(1)**

Nitrogen, carbon dioxide.

(b) What percentage of the air is oxygen?   **(1)**

21%.

See Section 9.1

(c) Suggest ONE reason why the platinum catalyst used is in the form of a gauze.   **(1)**

The gauze has a greater surface area than a lump of platinum of the same mass and is thus more effective.

(d) When the reaction vessel is first being brought into service, the catalyst is heated electrically. Explain why this heating is stopped once the reactor is in full operation.   **(1)**

The chemical reaction in Stage 1 takes place on the catalyst surface and is exothermic, so it keeps the catalyst hot.

(e) Why is the temperature used in Stage 1 reasonably *high*?   **(1)**

So that the reaction proceeds at a reasonable rate.

(f) What volume of ammonia, measured at room temperature and atmospheric pressure, is needed to produce 63 kg of nitric acid? (1 mol of molecules of any gas occupies 24 dm^3 at room temperature and atmospheric pressure. Relative atomic masses: H = 1 N = 14 O = 16)   **(2)**

1 mol of nitric acid is made from 1 mol of ammonia (see equations)

∴ 63 g of nitric acid is made from 24 dm^3 of ammonia at room temperature and pressure

∴ 63 kg of nitric acid is made from 24 000 dm^3 of ammonia at room temperature and pressure.

(g) A pressure of up to 10 atmospheres is often used in Stage 1. Suggest a reason for compressing the gases.   **(1)**

Compressing the gases increases their concentrations and therefore increases the rate of the reaction.

(h) State ONE large-scale use of nitric acid.   **(1)**

To make fertilisers such as ammonium nitrate.

17.8 Self-test Questions

Question 17.1

In the manufacture of aluminium, the reaction occurring at the cathode of the cell is:

A $Al^+ + e^- \rightarrow Al$
B $Al^{3+} - 3e^- \rightarrow Al$
C $Al^{3+} + 3e^- \rightarrow Al$
D $Al \rightarrow Al^{3+} + 3e^-$
E $Al + 3e^- \rightarrow Al^{3+}$

Question 17.2

The production of iron in the blast furnace requires an iron ore and

A coke, limestone and calcium silicate only
B air, limestone and calcium silicate only
C air, coke and limestone only
D air, coke and calcium silicate only
E air, coke, limestone and calcium silicate

(NISEC)

Question 17.3

The bar chart shows the yearly consumption of sodium hydroxide in Western Europe from 1975 to 1982.

(a) In 1983, the yearly consumption was found to be 76 million tonnes. Show this value on the chart   **(1)**

(b) In which year was the consumption at a maximum?   **(1)**

(Welsh, June 1988, Paper 1, Q27)

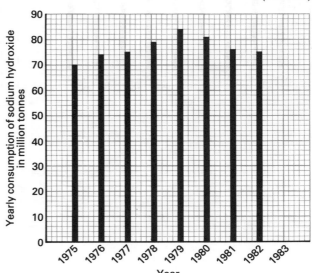

*Question 17.4

Read the passage below and use it to answer the questions that follow.

In a process for the manufacture of sodium carbonate, ammonia gas is bubbled through concentrated aqueous sodium chloride (brine) until no more ammonia will dissolve. Carbon dioxide is then bubbled through the solution and sodium hydrogencarbonate (which is soluble in water but almost insoluble in brine) is precipitated.

$Na^+(aq) + HCO_3^-(aq) \rightarrow NaHCO_3(s)$

Ammonium chloride is left in solution and the mixture is separated. Ammonia gas is regained from this solution by heating with calcium oxide, and recycled. The sodium hydrogencarbonate is heated to give sodium carbonate, carbon dioxide and water.

(a) Name a readily available mineral from which calcium oxide may be obtained.   **(1)**
(b) Construct the chemical equation for the reaction of ammonium chloride with calcium oxide. **(1)**
(c) Suggest how the sodium hydrogencarbonate is separated from the ammonium chloride.   **(1)**
(d) Construct the chemical equation for the action of heat on sodium hydrogencarbonate.   **(1)**
(e) Give one large scale use of sodium carbonate.   **(1)**
(f) Suggest another material involved in this process which could be recycled.   **(1)**

(Total 6)

(MEG, June 1988, Paper 3, Q2)

17.9 Answers to Self-test Questions

17.1 **C.**
17.2 **C.**
17.3 (a)

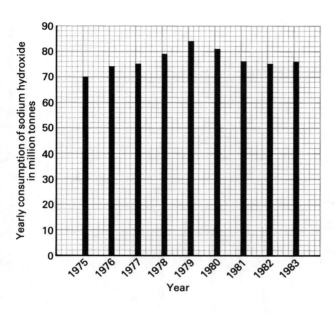

(b) 1979.

17.4 (a) Limestone – calcium carbonate.

$$CaCO_3(s) \rightarrow CaO(s) + CO_2(g)$$

(b) $2NH_4Cl(aq) + CaO(s) \rightarrow CaCl_2(aq) + 2NH_3(g) + H_2O(l)$
(c) The sodium hydrogencarbonate is precipitated. It can be filtered off, washed and dried.
(d) $2NaHCO_3(s) \rightarrow Na_2CO_3(s) + H_2O(g) + CO_2(g)$
(e) Making glass.
(f) Carbon dioxide.

This question concerns a process which is not covered by your syllabus but many of the answers are to be found in the text. For example, in part (b) you are told that ammonia is one of the products, and in part (d) you are given all of the products. In part (c), you are told that the sodium hydrogencarbonate is formed as a precipitate – this is the clue to the method of separation. You will need at least 4/6 marks to be in line for a grade A and something like 3/6 for a grade B for this question which is from the extension part of the paper.

18

ORGANIC CHEMISTRY

Topic Guide

18.1 Introduction

Organic chemistry is the chemistry of carbon compounds, excluding carbonates and the oxides of carbon. Many of these compounds are associated with the living world, e.g. proteins and sugars are organic compounds. There are a very large number of organic compounds since carbon atoms can join together in many different ways to form rings and chains of atoms. These compounds can be divided into families known as **homologous series,** in which all the members can be represented by the same general formula. The members have similar chemical properties and the physical properties change gradually as the relative molecular mass changes.

Isomerism is the existence of two or more compounds with the same molecular formula but different structures, the different forms being called *isomers*.

For example, butane and methylpropane, whose structures are given below, are isomers.

butane   methylpropane

18.2 The Alkanes

The alkanes are hydrocarbons, i.e. compounds containing hydrogen and carbon only. They form a homologous series of general formula C_nH_{2n+2}, their molecules containing only single covalent bonds.
Compounds which have molecules containing only single covalent bonds are said to be **saturated**.

Examples include:

$$H-\underset{\underset{H}{|}}{\overset{\overset{H}{|}}{C}}-H \qquad H-\underset{\underset{H}{|}}{\overset{\overset{H}{|}}{C}}-\underset{\underset{H}{|}}{\overset{\overset{H}{|}}{C}}-H \qquad H-\underset{\underset{H}{|}}{\overset{\overset{H}{|}}{C}}-\underset{\underset{H}{|}}{\overset{\overset{H}{|}}{C}}-\underset{\underset{H}{|}}{\overset{\overset{H}{|}}{C}}-H \qquad H-\underset{\underset{H}{|}}{\overset{\overset{H}{|}}{C}}-\underset{\underset{H}{|}}{\overset{\overset{H}{|}}{C}}-\underset{\underset{H}{|}}{\overset{\overset{H}{|}}{C}}-\underset{\underset{H}{|}}{\overset{\overset{H}{|}}{C}}-H$$

methane   ethane   propane   butane

Alkanes are obtained commercially from petroleum.

Like all hydrocarbons, alkanes burn in a plentiful air supply to form carbon dioxide and water. In a limited air supply, carbon monoxide or even carbon may be produced because of incomplete combustion. Alkanes take part in *substitution* reactions, e.g. methane reacts with chlorine or bromine in the presence of light (see Example 18.1).

$$CH_4(g) + Cl_2(g) \rightarrow HCl(g) + CH_3Cl(g)$$
$$\text{chloromethane}$$

18.3 The Alkenes

The alkenes form a homologous series of general formula C_nH_{2n}, their molecules containing a double bond, e.g.

$$\underset{H}{\overset{H}{>}}C=C\underset{H}{\overset{H}{<}} \qquad \underset{H}{\overset{H}{>}}C=C\underset{H}{\overset{H}{<}}$$

ethene   propene

Compounds which have molecules containing double or triple covalent bonds are said to be **unsaturated**.

One of the two bonds in a double bond is easily broken and as a result alkenes are very reactive. They take part in *addition* reactions (see Example 18.3).

When ethene is shaken with a solution of bromine in 1,1,1-trichloroethane, the reddish-brown colour of the bromine disappears almost immediately and 1,2-dibromoethane is obtained as the organic product.

$$\underset{H}{\overset{H}{>}}C=C\underset{H}{\overset{H}{<}} + Br_2 \longrightarrow H-\underset{\underset{Br}{|}}{\overset{\overset{H}{|}}{C}}-\underset{\underset{Br}{|}}{\overset{\overset{H}{|}}{C}}-H$$

Polymerisation is the process in which many small molecules join together to make one large one, e.g.

Molecules of ethene (the monomer) join together in chains to form polythene (the polymer). One of the bonds in the C=C bond breaks and the molecules undergo an addition reaction. This process is called *addition polymerisation* (see Examples 18.1 and 18.6).

Plastics can be divided into two main classes according to their behaviour when heated – thermoplastics or thermosetting plastics (see Example 18.2).

Alkenes are converted into a wide range of products, e.g. plastics, ethanol, ethane-1,2-diol (antifreeze) and CFCs (chlorofluorocarbons – ozone unfriendly compounds).

18.4 Petroleum and Coal

Petroleum was produced underground by the combined effects of heat, pressure and bacteria on the remains of marine animals and plants which died many millions of years ago. It is composed chiefly of hydrocarbons and is the source of most organic compounds used in manufacturing processes. Liquid petroleum is fractionally distilled in tall fractionating towers. Each fraction contains groups of hydrocarbons with boiling points within a particular range, rather than pure samples of individual compounds (see Example 18.5).

Table 18.1

THE MAIN FRACTIONS FROM CRUDE OIL   (LIQUID PETROLEUM)

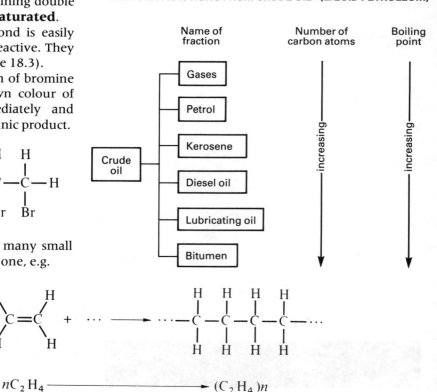

$$\cdots + \underset{H}{\overset{H}{>}}C=C\underset{H}{\overset{H}{<}} + \underset{H}{\overset{H}{>}}C=C\underset{H}{\overset{H}{<}} + \cdots \longrightarrow \cdots-\underset{\underset{H}{|}}{\overset{\overset{H}{|}}{C}}-\underset{\underset{H}{|}}{\overset{\overset{H}{|}}{C}}-\underset{\underset{H}{|}}{\overset{\overset{H}{|}}{C}}-\underset{\underset{H}{|}}{\overset{\overset{H}{|}}{C}}-\cdots$$

$$nC_2H_4 \longrightarrow (C_2H_4)n$$

There is little demand for the heavier oils, and they are usually converted to more useful products by cracking.

Cracking is the thermal decomposition of alkanes of high relative molecular mass to give a mixture of alkanes and alkenes of lower relative molecular mass, e.g.

$$C_{10}H_{22} \rightarrow C_2H_4 + C_8H_{18}$$

Coal was formed in a similar way to petroleum by the underground compression of vegetable matter. It consists mainly of carbon, together with compounds containing hydrogen, oxygen, nitrogen and sulphur. Burning coal pollutes the atmosphere with smoke and harmful gases such as sulphur dioxide. However, *destructive distillation* of coal (heating coal in the absence of air) gives useful products from which many organic chemicals can be obtained.

Petroleum and coal are non-renewable energy resources, i.e they cannot be replaced. At the present rate, coal could last for at least 200 years but our oil reserves could dry up within 30 years (see Example 18.4 and Question 18.8).

18.5 The Alcohols

The alcohols form a homologous series of general formula $C_nH_{2n+1}OH$ e.g.

methanol   ethanol

Ethanol is manufactured by the hydration of ethene.

$$C_2H_4(g) + H_2O(g) \xrightarrow[\text{phosphoric(V) acid catalyst}]{300°C, 65 \text{ atm}} CH_3CH_2OH(g)$$

It is also prepared by fermentation of aqueous glucose solutions using yeast which contains the enzyme zymase. Enzymes are complex organic catalysts. After filtering, the solution can be concentrated using fractional distillation (see Example 18.6 and Question 18.9).

$$C_6H_{12}O_6(aq) \rightarrow 2C_2H_5OH(aq) + 2CO_2(g)$$

Fermentation is the slow decomposition of an organic substance brought about by micro-organisms and usually accompanied by the evolution of heat and a gas.

The simple alcohols are colourless liquids which are miscible with water.

(a) Chemical Properties of the Alcohols

1. The alcohols burn in air to form carbon dioxide and water.

$$C_2H_5OH(l) + 3O_2(g) \rightarrow 2CO_2(g) + 3H_2O(g)$$

2. Alcohols are oxidised to acids with acidified potassium dichromate(VI).

(b) Uses of the Alcohols

1. As solvents.
2. As fuels.
3. In beers, wines and spirits. Beer is made by the fermentation of the starch in barley; wine is made in a similar way by the fermentation of the sugars in grapes. Distillation of these dilute solutions produced by fermentation increases the alcohol content and yields spirits. During fermentation it is important to exclude air because oxidising bacteria may enter and convert the ethanol to ethanoic acid (vinegar). This accounts for the 'souring' of wine exposed to the air (see Question 18.9).

18.6 Ethanoic Acid

Ethanoic acid has the formula

It is prepared by the oxidation of ethanol using acidified potassium dichromate(VI) solution.

$$CH_3CH_2OH(l) \xrightarrow{2[O]} CH_3COOH(l) + H_2O(l)$$

Ethanoic acid is a colourless liquid which is completely miscible with water. A 5% solution of ethanoic acid is used as vinegar. It is a weak acid, showing all the typical properties of an acid (see Section 11.2), e.g. it reacts with sodium hydroxide solution to give sodium ethanoate and water.

$$CH_3COOH(aq) + NaOH(aq) \rightarrow CH_3COONa(aq) + H_2O(l)$$

Soaps are the sodium or potassium salts of long-chained carboxylic acids (e.g. octadecanoic acid) which are prepared by boiling animal fats or vegetable oils (which are esters) with sodium hydroxide solution (see Example 17.5). This process is called saponification. Soapless detergents are made from petroleum and consist of molecules which are similar in form and action to those of soap. Unlike soap, their calcium and magnesium salts are soluble in water and thus do not form scum.

18.7 Worked Examples

Example 18.1

(a) (i) What is understood by the term *unsaturated hydrocarbon*?   **(2)**

Hydrocarbons are compounds containing carbon and hydrogen only. If the compound is unsaturated, its molecules contain double or triple covalent bonds.

(ii) Name one unsaturated hydrocarbon and draw its structural formula.   **(1)**

Ethene.

(iii) Name or write the formula of the product formed when bromine and the unsaturated hydrocarbon combine. **(1)**

1,2-dibromoethane.

In this reaction two bromine atoms add on across the double bond.

(iv) Name **one** *saturated* hydrocarbon and draw its structural formula. **(2)**

Ethane.

(v) What would be the products of the reaction between 1 mol of this hydrocarbon and 1 mol of bromine? **(2)**

Bromoethane and hydrogen bromide.

(b) (i) Which of the two named hydrocarbons can be converted to a polymer? Name the polymer and draw its structure. **(3)**

Unsaturated hydrocarbons can be converted to polymers, i.e. ethene can be polymerised to give polythene.

(ii) Explain what is meant by polymerisation. **(2)**

Polymerisation is the process in which many small molecules join together to make one large one. One of the bonds in each carbon-to-carbon double bond breaks and then the molecules add together to make the polymer.

(iii) State one environmental disadvantage of a polymer such as polythene. **(1)**

It does not rot away naturally in the environment, i.e. it is non-biodegradable.

(iv) Would burning be a suitable way of disposing of a plastic such as PVC? Explain your answer. **(2)**

No. On burning, PVC releases hydrogen chloride. This has a choking smell and dissolves in rain water to give hydrochloric acid, another component of acid rain (see Example 15.4).

Example 18.2

Buta-1,3-diene forms a polymer according to the equation

$$n\mathrm{CH_2 = CH - CH = CH_2} \rightarrow [\mathrm{CH_2 - CH = CH - CH_2}]_n$$

(a) Explain this reaction. **(3)**

This is an addition polymerisation process. In this process, the molecules of the monomer (buta-1,3-diene) join together to form the polymer. The empirical formula of the polymer is the same as that of the monomer.

(b) What does the n on the left-hand side of the equation stand for? **(1)**

n is a large whole number, usually several hundred.

(c) Give one chemical test which would show that the product still contains double bonds. **(3)**

A solution of bromine in 1,1,1-trichloroethane is rapidly decolourised.

(d) How could it be demonstrated that a polymer is a thermoplastic rather than a thermosetting polymer? **(2)**

Thermoplastics are those that soften on heating and harden on cooling, the process being repeatable any number of times. Thermosetting plastics soften on being heated the first time after manufacture and thus can be moulded. This heating causes cross-linking to occur between the long-chained macromolecules, and results in the setting up of a rigid three-dimensional network which cannot be softened by subsequent reheating. Thus, studying the effect of heat on a plastic will demonstrate that it is a thermoplastic rather than a thermosetting polymer.

Example 18.3

Give the name or molecular formula for the product of reaction of ethene (ethylene) with each of the following:

(a) bromine; **(1)**

$C_2H_4Br_2$ *or 1,2-dibromoethane*

(b) steam in the presence of a hot phosphoric acid catalyst; **(1)**

C_2H_5OH *or ethanol*

(c) hydrogen with a suitable catalyst; **(1)**

C_2H_6 *or ethane*

> The conditions needed are a nickel catalyst and a temperature of 200°C. See Example 10.7.

(d) more ethene. **(1)**

$(C_2H_4)_n$ *or polythene.*

Example 18.4

(a) What is a fossil fuel? **(2)**

Petroleum and coal are fossil fuels. They are formed from decaying remains of marine animals and plants which died millions of years ago (see Section 18.4).

(b) Give the name and formula of the main compound found in natural gas. **(2)**

Methane, CH_4

(c) Name two areas where petroleum can be found. **(2)**

North Sea, Arabian Gulf.

(d) Petroleum is a mixture of many hydrocarbons. How could you separate kerosene from liquid petroleum? (Table 18.1 may help.) **(1)**

Fractional distillation.

(e) Give one use of
 (i) kerosene,

Fuel for jet engines.

 (ii) bitumen. **(2)**

On roads.

(f) Suggest one hazard involved in the storage of natural gas or petroleum. **(2)**

These substances have low boiling points and are highly flammable. They must be kept away from all flames or sparks.

(g) What does the hazard sign in Fig. 18.1 indicate? **(1)**

Fig. 18.1

Highly flammable.

(h) Give two adverse effects of coal mining on the environment. **(2)**
 (i) *subsidence of the land,*
 (ii) *spoil heaps.*

> In addition, breathing in coal dust affects miners' lungs.

(i) What information does the graph in Fig. 18.2 give you? **(4)**

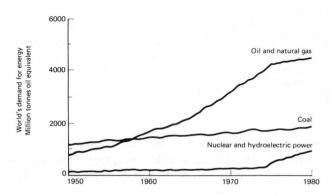

Fig. 18.2

It tells us that the demand for all forms of energy has increased. Although the demand for coal has increased only slightly, oil and natural gas are supplying a larger proportion of our energy needs. In recent years, there has been a large increase in nuclear power and hydroelectricity and a slowing in the increase in use of oil. This corresponds to the large increase in oil prices in the 1970s.

(j) Suggest two other energy sources. **(2)**

Sunlight (by means of solar panels).

Rotting vegetable waste. This produces methane, which is made use of in sewage works where sludge digestion is often used to provide sufficient fuel for the works.

Example 18.5

Crude oil was separated into four different fractions using the apparatus drawn below.

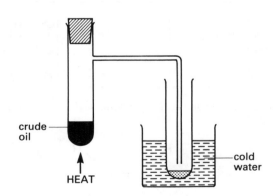

(a) (i) What essential piece of apparatus is missing?

A thermometer.

> A thermometer should be inserted through the rubber bung in order to measure the boiling range of each fraction.

 (ii) Name the process used to separate crude oil into the four fractions. **(2)**

Fractional distillation.

(b) (i)   Complete the table below.

Name of hydrocarbon	Formula	Boiling point
	CH_4	−160°C
ethane	C_2H_6	− 93°C
propane		− 45°C
butane	C_4H_{10}	1°C

(2)

The missing name is methane; the missing formula is C_3H_8.

(ii) The two products of burning any of the hydro-carbons in a plentiful supply of air are: **(2)**

carbon dioxide and water.

(Total 6)

e.g. $CH_4(g) + 2O_2(g) \rightarrow CO_2(g) + 2H_2O(g)$

(MEG, Nov. 1988, Paper 2, Q6)

*Example 18.6

(a) Alkenes are the starting materials for polymers.
(i)   Complete the following table.   **(4)**

Name of alkene	ethene	propene
Molecular formula	C_2H_4	
Structural formula of alkene	H H | | C = C | | H H	
Name of polymer made from the alkene		poly(propene)
Structural formula of polymer		⎡CH₃ H⎤ | | −|C — C|− | | ⎣H H⎦ n

Propene has the molecular formula C_3H_6; the structural formula is

$$
\begin{array}{c}
H \qquad\qquad H \\
\diagdown \quad\; / \\
C = C \\
H \diagup \;\; \diagdown \; H \\
C \\
/ \;\; \diagdown \\
H \qquad H
\end{array}
$$

The polymer made from ethene is called poly(ethene) and its structural formula is

$$
\begin{array}{c}
\left[\begin{array}{cc} H & H \\ | & | \\ C & C \\ | & | \\ H & H \end{array}\right]_n
\end{array}
$$

(ii) What does *n* mean in the structural formula of poly(propene)?   **(1)**

A large whole number.

(iii) What do the structures of all alkenes have in common?   **(2)**

A carbon – carbon double bond.

(iv) Give a simple test that could be used to show the presence of an alkene in a mixture with alkanes present.   **(2)**

Test	Result
Addition of bromine water.	Immediate decolourisation of the solution.

(v) How does industry manufacture large quantities of ethene?   **(2)**

By the cracking of petroleum
e.g. $C_{10}H_{22} \rightarrow C_8H_{18} + C_2H_4$
The molecules split when heated with a catalyst.

(b) Ethanol can be made by the addition of water to ethene. Ethanol can also be made by fermentation of sugars.

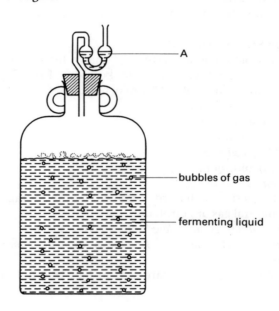

(i)   Name the gas produced during the fermentation shown above.   **(1)**

Carbon dioxide.

$C_6H_{12}O_6(aq) \rightarrow 2C_2H_5OH(aq) + 2CO_2(g)$

(ii) This gas escapes through the piece of apparatus labelled A. What is the main purpose of this piece of apparatus?   **(1)**

To stop air entering the apparatus.

Air oxidises the ethanol to ethanoic acid.

(iii) What must be added to a sugar solution to make it ferment?   **(1)**

Yeast.

(iv) At about what temperature does fermentation take place at its fastest rate? **(1)**

30°C.

(v) Explain your choice of temperature given in (iv). **(2)**

Too low or too high a temperature will kill the yeast.

(vi) Why can drinking ethanol be a possible danger to humans? **(2)**

Excess ethanol affects the liver and also slows down reaction times so that a traffic accident could occur.

(vii) Ethanol can be used as a fuel. Write a balanced chemical equation for the combustion of ethanol in air. **(2)**

$C_2H_5OH(l) + 3O_2(g) \rightarrow 2CO_2(g) + 3H_2O(g)$

(SEG, June 1988, Paper 3, Q5)

Example 18.7

Which of the following methods would you use to separate a concentrated solution of ethanol from a fermented liquid?

A Crystallisation

B Evaporation

C Filtration

D Fractional distillation

E Paper chromatography

The answer is **D**.

(LEAG, June 1988, Paper 1, Q26)

18.8 Self-test Questions

Question 18.1

Which of the following is the formula for propane?

  A C_2H_4
  B C_2H_6
  C C_3H_6
  D C_3H_8
  E C_4H_{10}

(LEAG, June 1988, Paper 1, Q49)

Questions 18.2–18.6 concern the following compounds of carbon:

  A   Butane   D   Ethene
  B   Carbon dioxide   E   Methane
  C   Carbon monoxide

Choose from **A** to **E**, the compound which

Question 18.2

is the main constituent of natural gas

Question 18.3

contains a double bond between carbon atoms

Question 18.4

could NOT be used as a fuel

Question 18.5

can be polymerised

Question 18.6

is formed by the incomplete combustion of natural gas.

(LEAG, June 1988, Paper 1, Q16–20)

*Question 18.7

Polythene [poly(ethene)] is produced in two forms with different densities:
(i)   low density: 0.92 g/cm^3: LDPE
(ii) high density: 0.96 g/cm^3: HDPE
On average 300 000 tonnes of LDPE –
the low density form – are produced in the
UK each year.

The uses of LDPE are shown in the pie
chart.

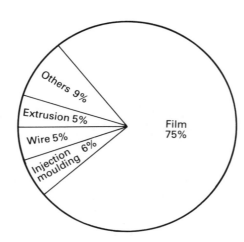

HDPE is made by dissolving ethene in a solvent such as heptane and adding a suitable catalyst. This reaction is strongly exothermic. The HDPE, which is insoluble, is removed and converted into pellets.

(a) How is ethene obtained on a large scale? **(2)**

(b) Choose a reaction, other than polymerisation, that uses a catalyst. Give the name(s) of the reagent(s), the product(s) and the catalyst. **(3)**

(c) (i) C_7H_x is the formula for heptane. What is the value of x? **(1)**

   (ii) You suspect that some ethene remains, unpolymerised, in the solvent.
   Describe a chemical test you could perform to find out if any ethene remains.
   Name the reagent you would use. State what you would see if ethene was present.
   Construct the chemical equation for the reaction. **(3)**

(d) Calculate, in tonnes, the average amount of LDPE used for injection moulding each year. **(1)**

(Total 10)

(MEG, June 1989, Paper 3, Q2)

Question 18.8

(a) The pie chart shows the proportions of different energy sources used by one country.

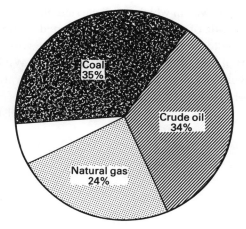

   (i)   Show the other energy sources (nuclear (6%) and hydroelectric (1%)) on the pie chart. **(2)**

   (ii) Put each of the energy sources from the completed pie chart under the correct heading in the table below. **(2)**

Renewable energy source	Non-renewable energy source

   (iii) Explain the difference between *renewable* and *non-renewable* sources of energy. **(2)**

(b) (i)   How is petrol obtained from crude oil? **(2)**

   (ii) Kerosene is also obtained from crude oil. What type of transport uses kerosene as its fuel? **(1)**

   (iii) Suggest **one** thing that is likely to happen as the supply of crude oil begins to run out. **(1)**

(c) Replacing steel car bodies by those made from aluminium or aluminium alloys would save fuel. Give **one** reason for each of the following statements. **(3)**

Statement	Reason for statement
Using aluminium or its alloys for a car body would save fuel.	
An aluminium car body would probably last longer than a steel car body.	
Aluminium is rarely used to make car bodies.	

(SEG, Winter 1988, Paper 1, Q14)

Question 18.9

(a) A dilute aqueous solution of ethanol can be produced in the laboratory by the fermentation of glucose.
    (i) Give a brief account of the way in which this is carried out. **(3)**
    (ii) Give the name and formula of the other product formed in the reaction. **(1)**

(b) The formation of ethanol by fermentation is the basis of the wine-making industry. If wine is left open to the air, the pH of the solution gradually decreases. What is the reason for this? **(2)**

(c) Ethanol is used as a solvent. Explain the meaning of solvent and give one example of the commercial use of ethanol as a solvent. **(2)**

(Welsh, June 1988, Paper 1, Q36)

18.9 Answers to Self-test Questions

18.1 **D**.
18.2 **E**.
18.3 **D**.

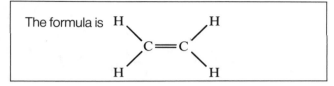

The formula is

18.4 **B**.
18.5 **D**.
18.6 **C**.
18.7(a) Cracking of petroleum,
e.g. $C_{10}H_{22} \rightarrow C_8H_{18} + C_2H_4$
(b) Ethene reacts with hydrogen to give ethane. The catalyst is nickel at 200°C.

$$C_2H_4 + H_2 \xrightarrow[200°C]{Ni} C_2H_6$$

(c) (i) 16.

Alkanes have the formula C_nH_{2n+2}. If $n = 7$, then $2n+2 = 16$.

(ii) Bromine water immediately changes from orange to colourless if ethene is present.
$C_2H_4 + Br_2 \rightarrow C_2H_4Br_2$
(d) Injection moulding uses 6% of 300,000 tonnes of LDPE. This is $\dfrac{6}{100} \times 300,000$
= 18000 tonnes

18.8(a) (i)

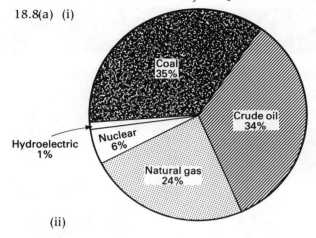

(ii)

Renewable energy source	Non-renewable energy source
Hydroelectric	Coal
	Crude oil
	Natural gas
	Nuclear

(iii) A renewable energy source is one such as ethanol which can easily and quickly be made from sugar. A non-renewable energy source is one that takes millions of years to form and so cannot easily be remade (e.g. fossil fuels such as coal).
(b) (i) By fractional distillation.
(ii) Jet aeroplanes.
(iii) Petrol will be blended with ethanol as fuel for cars.
(c) The 3 reasons are:
Aluminium is less dense than iron and so the car would be lighter.
Aluminium does not rust as iron does.
Aluminium is more expensive than iron (OR aluminium is less strong than iron).
18.9(a) (i) A glucose solution is mixed with yeast and kept at 30°C for several days away from the air.
(ii) Carbon dioxide, CO_2.
(b) In the presence of air, ethanol is changed to ethanoic acid. Acids have low pH values.
(c) A solvent is a substance which will dissolve another one (the solute). Ethanol is used as a solvent for lacquers, varnishes and perfumes.

CHEMICAL ANALYSIS

19.1 Tests for Cations and Anions

This section has been restricted to the detection of the following ions: NH_4^+, K^+, Na^+, Ca^{2+}, Al^{3+}, Zn^{2+}, Fe^{2+}, Fe^{3+}, Cu^{2+}, CO_3^{2-}, SO_4^{2-}, NO_3^- and Cl^-.

Ion	Experiment	Observation
CO_3^{2-}	Add dil. HCl.	Immediate effervescence (CO_2 – lime water milky)
Cl^-	Dissolve in distilled water (dil. HNO_3 if insoluble in water). Acidify with dil. HNO_3 and add a few drops of $AgNO_3$ solution.	Thick white precipitate (of AgCl), soluble in excess ammonia solution
SO_4^{2-}	Dissolve in distilled water (dil. HCl if insoluble in water). Acidify with dil. HCl and add a little $BaCl_2$ solution.	Thick white precipitate (of $BaSO_4$)
Ca^{2+}	Dissolve in distilled water. Add NaOH solution until *just* alkaline (test with indicator paper), then fill up the tube and tip its contents into a second tube.	White precipitate, insoluble in excess alkali ($Ca(OH)_2$)
Al^{3+}, Zn^{2+}		White precipitate, soluble in excess alkali ($Al(OH)_3$), ($Zn(OH)_2$)
Cu^{2+}		Pale blue precipitate ($Cu(OH)_2$)
Fe^{2+}		Dirty green precipitate ($Fe(OH)_2$)
Fe^{3+}		Red-brown precipitate ($Fe(OH)_3$)
NH_4^+	Heat if no precipitate.	NH_3 (smell, alkaline gas)
NO_3^-	Add a *little* Al powder if no smell.	NH_3
Ca^{2+}, Al^{3+}	Repeat above test using NH_3 solution in place of the NaOH solution.	White precipitate, insoluble in excess alkali ($Ca(OH)_2$), ($Al(OH)_3$)
Zn^{2+}		White precipitate, soluble in excess alkali ($Zn(OH)_2$)

Ion	Experiment	Observation
Cu^{2+}		Pale blue precipitate ($Cu(OH)_2$), giving royal blue solution with excess alkali
Fe^{2+}		Dirty green precipitate ($Fe(OH)_2$)
Fe^{3+}		Red-brown precipitate ($Fe(OH)_3$)
K^+	Dip a platinum wire into conc. HCl in a watch glass and then heat the *end* of the wire in a flame. Repeat if necessary until the wire does not colour the flame. Then dip the wire into the acid again, touch it on the powdered solid and replace it in the flame. Clean the wire after use.	Lilac flame (red through blue glass)
Na^+		Golden yellow flame
Ca^{2+}		Brick-red flame
Cu^{2+}		Green-blue flame

19.2 Worked Examples

Example 19.1

Two experiments were carried out on a substance X (Fig. 19.1).

Experiment 1

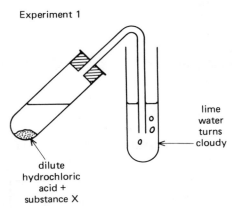

lime water turns cloudy

dilute hydrochloric acid + substance X

Fig. 19.1

Experiment 2

platinum wire

lilac flame colour

concentrated hydrochloric acid + substance X

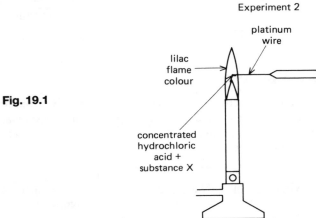

(a) Which gas is turning the lime water (calcium hydroxide solution) cloudy?
Carbon dioxide.

(b) **From experiment 1 alone**, what can be learned about the identity of X?
X is a carbonate (or hydrogencarbonate).

(c) **From experiment 2 alone**, what can be learned about the identity of X? **(3)**
X is a compound of potassium.

(SEB)

Example 19.2

Describe briefly how **each** of the following procedures could be carried out:

(a) To prove by a physical test that a sample of a colourless liquid is pure water. **(2)**
Test its boiling point – it should be 100°C if the liquid is water.

> Note: it would be possible for another liquid to have a boiling point of 100°C. A chemical test is needed in addition to the physical test to prove conclusively that a liquid is pure water. Such a test would be the use of cobalt(II) chloride paper (blue → pink) or anhydrous copper(II) sulphate (white → blue).

(b) To prove by a chemical test that
  (i) a sample of river water contains chloride (Cl^-) ions, **(2)**
Add dilute nitric acid and silver nitrate solution. A white precipitate indicates Cl^- ions.

> $Ag^+(aq) + Cl^-(aq) \rightarrow AgCl(s)$

  (ii) a sample of cooking oil is unsaturated, i.e. contains compounds with carbon–carbon double bonds.
Add bromine water. Immediate decolourisation shows that the cooking oil is unsaturated.

> See Section 18.3.

(c) The preparation of a crystalline sample of hydrated copper(II) sulphate, $CuSO_4.5H_2O$, from an aqueous solution of copper(II) sulphate. **(3)**
Heat the solution to the point of crystallisation. Put the solution in a conical flask, stopper it and allow the solution to cool. Filter off the crystals, wash and dry them.

(Welsh, June 1988, Paper 1, Q32)

*Example 19.3

(a) A laboratory technician places an order for five chemicals which are all solids. When the order is delivered it is found that the labels have come off the bottles. The order was for:
Copper(II) chloride
Lead(II) carbonate
Magnesium sulphate
Sodium nitrate
Zinc nitrate.

Plan and explain a method by which you could identify each bottle correctly, using **only** test tubes, water, indicator paper, a splint and a lighted bunsen. **(5)**

Copper(II) chloride is green and so this solid can be identified immediately. Lead(II) carbonate is the only insoluble solid and so the addition of water to each solid should enable lead(II) carbonate to be identified. The three remaining solids are heated separately in test tubes and any vapours evolved are tested with a glowing splint. The splint should be relit with both sodium nitrate and zinc nitrate (oxygen is evolved) but in the case of zinc nitrate a brown gas is evolved as well (this is nitrogen dioxide). The remaining solid is magnesium sulphate.

(b) In an experiment to determine the number of molecules of water of crystallisation in one molecule of hydrated nickel chloride a student recorded the following results:

Mass of container empty	8.88 g
Mass of container with hydrated salt	10.07 g
Mass of container and salt after first heating	9.55 g
Mass of container and salt after second heating	9.53 g

(i) Name a suitable container.
Crucible.

(ii) Suggest two precautions, one to increase accuracy and the other to ensure safety, which the student should have been taking while heating the salt. Explain the purpose of your precautions.

The container and contents should be heated to constant mass. This ensures that the reaction has finished. The salt will tend to spit out of the container which should therefore be heated slowly and the student should wear safety spectacles.

(iii) Why was the container with its contents reheated and reweighed?
This is an attempt to drive off all the water of crystallisation.

(iv) Calculate the value of x in $NiCl_2 . xH_2O$
(relative molecular mass: $NiCl_2$ = 130) **(5)**

	$NiCl_2$	H_2O
No. of grams	$9.53 - 8.88$ = 0.65	$10.07 - 9.53$ = 0.54
No. of moles	$\dfrac{0.65}{130}$ = 0.005	$\dfrac{0.54}{18}$ = 0.03
÷ *by smallest*	1	6

∴ $x = 6$

(Total 10)
(MEG, June 1988, Paper 3, Q8)

Example 19.4

Suggest a name and formula for each of the compounds **A** to **E** below.

(a) The green crystalline solid **A** dissolved in water to give a pale green solution. One portion of this solution was treated with aqueous ammonia and a green precipitate **B** was formed. A second portion of the solution of **A** gave a white precipitate **C** with barium chloride solution that was not soluble in dilute hydrochloric acid. **(8)**

*C is barium sulphate, $BaSO_4$, so **A** is a sulphate.*
B is iron(II) hydroxide, $Fe(OH)_2$.
A must be iron(II) sulphate, $FeSO_4$.

$$FeSO_4(aq) + 2NH_4OH(aq) \rightarrow Fe(OH)_2(s) + (NH_4)_2SO_4(aq)$$
$$FeSO_4(aq) + BaCl_2(aq) \rightarrow BaSO_4(s) + FeCl_2(aq)$$

(b) A white solid **D** dissolved in water exothermically to give a strongly alkaline solution. When the solution of **D** was added to copper(II) sulphate solution, a blue precipitate **E** was formed. Substance **D** gave a golden yellow flame colour. **(8)**
*D is sodium hydroxide, $NaOH$, and **E** is copper(II) hydroxide, $Cu(OH)_2$.*

$$CuSO_4(aq) + 2NaOH(aq) \rightarrow Cu(OH)_2(s) + Na_2SO_4(aq)$$

Examples 19.5–19.8 are about the following salts:
A   Ammonium nitrate
B   Calcium carbonate
C   Potassium chloride
D   Sodium carbonate
E   Zinc sulphate
Select from the list above:

Example 19.5

the salt which can be used to neutralise acid soils; **(1)**
*The answer is **B**.*

$$e.g. \; CaCO_3(s) + 2HCl(aq) \rightarrow CaCl_2(aq) + H_2O(l) + CO_2(g)$$

Example 19.6

the salt, which on heating with sodium hydroxide solution, gives off a gas that turns moist universal indicator paper blue; **(1)**
*The answer is **A**.*

$$NH_4NO_3(aq) + NaOH(aq) \rightarrow NH_3(g) + H_2O(l) + NaNO_3(aq)$$

Example 19.7

the salt which can be used to soften hard water;   **(1)**
The answer is **D**.

The carbonate ions precipitate the calcium ions in the water as calcium carbonate.
$Na_2CO_3(aq) + CaSO_4(aq) \rightarrow CaCO_3(s) + Na_2SO_4(aq)$

Example 19.8

the salt which in solution reacts with dilute hydrochloric acid and barium chloride solution to give a white precipitate.   **(1)**
The answer is **E**.

This is a test for sulphates.
$ZnSO_4(aq) + BaCl_2(aq) \rightarrow BaSO_4(s) + ZnCl_2(aq)$

(Welsh, June 1988, Paper 1, Q9–12)

19.3 Self-test Questions

Question 19.1

Sodium hydroxide solution produces a reddish-brown precipitate when added to a solution of

    A   aluminium sulphate
    B   copper(II) sulphate
    C   iron(II) sulphate
    D   iron(III) sulphate
    E   magnesium sulphate

Question 19.2

When solid X is heated, it gives off a brown gas. X could be

    A   Ammonium chloride
    B   Lead(II) nitrate
    C   Lead(IV) oxide
    D   Potassium nitrate
    E   Sodium bromide

Question 19.3

A white solid, X, is analysed, and the results are shown in the table below.

Test	Results
A platinum wire is dipped in concentrated hydrochloric acid then touched on to X and held in a Bunsen flame.	A lilac flame is seen.
Dilute nitric acid and aqueous silver nitrate are added to a solution of X.	There is a white precipitate.

X is therefore

    A   potassium chloride
    B   calcium chloride
    C   potassium carbonate
    D   calcium sulphate
    E   sodium chloride

(LEAG, June 1988, Paper 1, Q33)

Question 19.4

A solid Y gave:
    (i) a red flame colour
    (ii) an alkaline gas on warming with aqueous sodium hydroxide
    (iii) vigorous effervescence with dilute hydrochloric acid
The ions present in Y are:

    A Ca^{2+}, NH_4^+, CO_3^{2-}
    B Ca^{2+}, NH_4^+, SO_4^{2-}
    C K^+, NH_4^+, CO_3^{2-}
    D K^+, NH_4^+, SO_4^{2-}
    E Na^+, Ca^{2+}, Cl^-

(LEAG, June 1988, Paper 1, Q44)

*Question 19.5

An analyst was required to determine the composition of an alloy of copper, silver (Ag) and gold (Au). The **finely powdered alloy** was warmed with an excess of moderately concentrated nitric acid which dissolved two of the metals.

$$3Cu(s) + 8HNO_3(aq) \rightarrow 3Cu(NO_3)_2(aq) + 2NO(g) + 4H_2O(l)$$
$$3Ag(s) + 4HNO_3(aq) \rightarrow 3AgNO_3(aq) + NO(g) + 2H_2O(l)$$

When no further reaction was apparent the mixture was **diluted with water** and filtered, and the residue (A) was washed, dried and weighed (see below).

Excess hydrochloric acid was then added to the filtrate.

$$AgNO_3(aq) + HCl(aq) \rightarrow AgCl(s) + HNO_3(aq)$$

The white precipitate (B) was removed by filtration, washed, dried and weighed (see below).

The filtrate was then mixed with excess sodium hydroxide solution to give a precipitate (C),

$$Cu(NO_3)_2(aq) + 2NaOH(aq) \rightarrow Cu(OH)_2(s) + 2NaNO_3(aq)$$

after which the mixture was boiled until the precipitate was completely black.
$$Cu(OH)_2(s) \rightarrow CuO(s) + H_2O(l)$$
The black powder (D) was removed by filtration, washed, dried and weighed.
These results were recorded:

> Mass of residue A = 0.20 g
> Mass of precipitate B = 0.40 g
> Mass of residue D = 0.65 g

Calculate the composition of the alloy. Comment on EITHER (a) the two expressions printed in **heavy type** OR (b) the accuracy of your answer.

(Relative atomic masses: O = 16.0, Cl = 35.5, Cu = 63.5, Ag = 108.0)   **(10)**

(LEAG, June 1988, Paper 3, Q7)

Question 19.6

Which piece of apparatus should be used to measure exactly 27.6 cm^3 of dilute sulphuric acid?

  A   100 cm^3 beaker
  B   50 cm^3 pipette
  C   100 cm^3 measuring cylinder
  D   50 cm^3 burette
  E   100 cm^3 conical flask

(LEAG, June 1988, Paper 1, Q35)

Question 19.7

Statements (a)–(i) describe *pure* substances at room temperature and atmospheric pressure. Select from the list below one substance in each case which fits the description. You may use the same substance as many times as you wish. (Black, white or grey are not regarded as colours.)

copper(II) sulphate crystals	copper	gold
mercury	bromine	chalk
air	hydrogen	ethanol
copper(II) oxide	chlorine	bread
sea water	water	ammonia

(a) a coloured solid compound;
(b) a white solid compound;
(c) a black solid compound;
(d) a colourless liquid compound;
(e) a colourless gaseous compound;

(f) a coloured solid element;
(g) a liquid element;
(h) a colourless gaseous element;
(i) a coloured gaseous element.

(9)

(LEAG, Jan. 1989, Paper 2, Q1)

19.4 Answers to Self-test Questions

19.1 D.

Fe$_2$(SO$_4$)$_3$ (aq) + 6NaOH(aq) → 2Fe(OH)$_3$(s) + 3Na$_2$SO$_4$ (aq)

19.2 B.

Lead(II) nitrate gives off nitrogen dioxide on heating.

19.3 A.

The first test indicates the presence of the potassium ion whilst the second is a test for the chloride ion.

19.4 A.

The first test indicates the presence of the calcium ion; the second is a test for the ammonium ion. Of the possible anions given, only the carbonate will fizz with hydrochloric acid.

19.5 A is gold. Therefore the mass of gold is 0.20 g.
B is silver chloride. The mass of silver chloride is 0.40 g.

$$\text{Mass of silver} = \frac{108}{143.5} \times 0.40 \text{ g} = 0.30 \text{ g}$$
$$(M_r \text{ (AgCl)} = 143.5)$$

D is copper(II) oxide. The mass of copper(II) oxide is 0.65 g.

$$\text{Mass of copper} = \frac{63.5}{79.5} \times 0.65 \text{ g} = 0.52 \text{ g}$$
$$(M_r \text{(CuO)} = 79.5)$$

The composition of the alloy is approximately 2 parts gold to 3 parts silver to 5 parts copper.
(a)   An alloy is a mixture of a metal with one or more other elements, usually metals. If the alloy is finely powdered it has been ground up so that it will react completely.
    Diluted with water: in this reaction water is added so that the acid is less concentrated than before and safer to handle.
OR (b) Of the three metals, the mass of gold will be the most accurate. The mass of silver is less accurate since all of the silver ions may not have been precipitated as silver chloride. The mass of the copper is the least accurate; all of the copper ions may not have been precipitated as copper hydroxide and the conversion of copper hydroxide to copper oxide may be incomplete. The accuracy of all the masses depends on how much solid is lost during the filtering, washing and drying process.

19.6 **D.**

19.7 (a) Copper(II) sulphate crystals.
    (b) Chalk.
    (c) Copper(II) oxide.
    (d) Water or ethanol.
    (e) Ammonia.
    (f) Copper or gold.
    (g) Mercury or bromine.
    (h) Hydrogen.
    (i) Chlorine.

20

THE LAST HURDLE

Topic Guide

No doubt you bought this book in the first place to try to improve your grade in the GCSE Chemistry Examination. We hope that you have found it to be of use. If you have worked steadily through each chapter, looked at the Worked Examples and then tested yourself using the Questions, then you should by now be feeling a lot more confident.

This last chapter consists solely of Self-test Questions. The questions are of all types and cover many different topics. We suggest that you use these questions for revision purposes. Go through the questions and then mark them carefully. This should tell you which topics you need to revise more thoroughly.

The rest is up to you!

20.1 Self-test Questions

Question 20.1

Some properties of four chemical elements are shown in the table below. The elements are labelled by letters which are **not** chemical symbols.

Element	Melting point /°C	Boiling point /°C	Conduction of electricity	Effect of heating in air
A	3,600	4,200	yes	Gas given off which turns limewater milky
B	− 101	− 34	no	none
C	1,063	2,850	yes	none
D	− 7	58	no	none

Note: Each letter may be used once, more than once, or not at all for your answers to part (a).

(a) Which letter represents an element which is

    (i)   a gas at room temperature, **(1)**

    (ii) a liquid at room temperature, **(1)**

    (iii) a metal, **(1)**

    (iv) the one with the largest temperature range for its liquid state, **(1)**

    (v) an allotrope of carbon? **(1)**

(b) Name the allotrope in (a)(v) above **(1)**

(Welsh, June 1988, Paper 1, Q29)

Questions 20.2 – 20.5 concern the following statements about the experiment shown in the diagram. The laboratory temperature and pressure remained constant throughout.

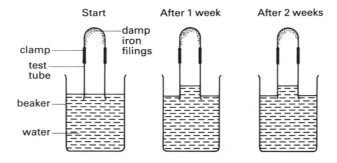

    A   The water rises inside the test tube.

    B   The water levels do not change between week 1 and week 2.

    C   Some of the iron filings change colour.

    D   The water level in the beaker falls slightly.

    E   A lighted splint cannot burn in the gas left in the test tube at the end of the experiment.

    Select, from **A** to **E**, the statement which shows that:

Question 20.2

the experiment has finished at the end of week 1

Question 20.3

the volume of gas inside the test tube becomes less

Question 20.4

a new compound is made

Question 20.5

the gas inside the tube at the end is not air

(LEAG, June 1989, Paper 1, Q7-10)

Question 20.6

The equation:

$$NaOH(aq) + HCl(aq) \rightarrow NaCl(aq) + H_2O(l)$$

sodium · · · · hydrochloric · · · sodium · · · · water
hydroxide · · · · · · acid · · · · · · · · chloride

represents

    A   addition
    B   dehydration
    C   crystallisation
    D   neutralisation
    E   precipitation

(LEAG, June 1989, Paper 1, Q26)

Question 20.7

An element has an atomic number of 12. An atom of this element contains

    A   4 protons
    B   6 protons
    C   8 protons
    D   12 protons
    E   24 protons

(LEAG, June 1989, Paper 1, Q29)

Question 20.8

From the chemicals listed below, choose the one which produces acid rain.

    A   Argon
    B   Carbon monoxide
    C   Chlorine
    D   Hydrogen
    E   Sulphur dioxide

(LEAG, June 1989, Paper 1, Q39)

Question 20.9

Iron is obtained using a blast furnace. The raw materials that enter the top of a furnace are iron ore, limestone and

    A   basic slag
    B   coke
    C   crude oil
    D   hot air
    E   lime

(LEAG, June 1989, Paper 1, Q40)

Question 20.10

Which of these compounds is most likely to be obtained by cracking octadecane, $C_{18}H_{38}$?

    A $C_{36}H_{74}$
    B $C_{36}H_{70}$
    C C_8H_{16}
    D   CO
    E CO_2

(LEAG, June 1989, Paper 1, Q42)

Question 20.11

The alcohol methanol, CH_3OH, is widely used as a fuel and as a solvent. Methanol can be made by heating carbon monoxide and hydrogen at 300°C under a pressure of 300 atmospheres.

$$CO(g) + 2H_2(g) \rightarrow CH_3OH(g)$$

When methanol is produced in this way, heat is produced.
(a) What word is used to describe a reaction with this type of energy change? **(1)**
(b) (i) State TWO ways in which this reaction could be speeded up.
    (ii) State one way in which this reaction could be slowed down. **(3)**
(c) (i) The reaction is reversible. Rewrite the equation to show this.
    (ii) If methanol is decomposed in this way, what kind of energy change would occur? **(2)**
(d) Carbon monoxide and hydrogen are both dangerous chemicals. State one danger associated with each. **(2)**
(e) (i) Suggest why methanol can be used as a fuel.
    (ii) Give TWO advantages it might have over coal. **(3)**

(Total 11)
(LEAG, June 1989, Paper 2, Q4)

*Question 20.12

Gunpowder is made up of three finely ground ingredients. This equation shows what happens when gunpowder burns or explodes.

$$2KNO_3(s) + 3C(s) + S(s) \rightarrow K_2S(s) + 3CO_2(g) + N_2(g)$$

(a) (i) Give the names of the THREE ingredients of gunpowder.
    (ii) Why are the ingredients finely ground? **(4)**
(b) Gunpowder is not used in rifles because it produces smoke and leaves a residue in the barrel of the gun. What does the equation suggest that the residue might be?
    (i) Give the formula of this compound.
    (ii) Give the names of the elements in it. **(2)**
(c) In the late nineteenth century, two powerful explosives were produced called nitroglycerin and guncotton. This equation describes what happens when nitroglycerin explodes.

$$4C_3H_5N_3O_9(l) \rightarrow 12CO_2(g) + 10H_2O(g) + 6N_2(g) + O_2(g) + \text{nitroglycerin}$$

    (i) In what way do the physical states of nitroglycerin and gunpowder differ?
    (ii) Why is the symbol (g), and not (l), used after H_2O? **(3)**

(d) The other explosive, guncotton, was used in shells and torpedoes but was not entirely suitable for use in cartridges (to fire bullets etc.) because it left a deposit of carbon. When the two explosives nitroglycerin and guncotton were mixed, however, the explosive cordite was made and this did not leave a residue.

    (i) What product of the explosion of nitroglycerin would tend to react with the carbon residue from guncotton?

    (ii) What compound would be likely to form as a result?

    (iii) What chemical process would have happened in the formation of this compound?

    (iv) Why would this leave no residue? **(4)**

(e) Coal and charcoal are neither explosive nor easy to ignite, yet clouds of coal dust represent a hazard in mines. Explain. **(1)**

(Total 14)

(LEAG, June 1989, Paper 3, Q1)

*Question 20.13

This question concerns the manufacture of iron by the blast furnace process.

   A manufacturer buys some iron ore. On analysis it proves to contain 80% iron(III) oxide (Fe_2O_3) and 20% silica (SiO_2).

(Relative atomic masses: C = 12, O = 16, Si = 28, Fe = 56)

(a) (i) *In every 1000 g of ore*, what mass is iron(III) oxide, Fe_2O_3?

    (ii) How many moles of iron(III) oxide, Fe_2O_3, does this represent?

    (iii) If this oxide is reduced according to the equation:

$$Fe_2O_3(s) + 3CO(g) \rightarrow 2Fe(l) + 3CO_2(g)$$

how many moles of carbon monoxide molecules, CO, will be required?

    (iv) If only 25% of all the carbon monoxide in the furnace is used, and 75% passes out unchanged, how many moles of carbon monoxide molecules, CO, will be required to reduce all the iron(III) oxide, Fe_2O_3, in 1000 g of ore?

    (v) How many moles of coke (assumed to be 100% carbon) must be added to produce this quantity of carbon monoxide, CO, if carbon monoxide is the only product from the coke?

    (vi) What mass of coke would this be?

    (vii)If the manufacturer buys 1000 tonnes of ore, what mass of coke must be mixed with the *whole purchase* of iron ore when added to the blast furnace? **(9)**

(b) Limestone is also added to the blast furnace. Assuming that the reaction of the limestone in removing the silica is 100% efficient, calculate, as in part (a), the quantity of limestone which must be added to the 1000 tonnes of ore.

$$CaCO_3(s) \rightarrow CaO(s) + CO_2(g)$$
$$CaO(s) + SiO_2(s) \rightarrow CaSiO_3(l)$$

Begin,

In 1000 g of ore, the mass of SiO_2 is . . . **(7)**

(Total 16)

(LEAG, June 1989, Paper 3, Q3)

*Question 20.14

The compound urea is used as a fertiliser. The gases ammonia, NH_3, and carbon dioxide, CO_2, are heated together under pressure to form solid urea, $(NH_2)_2CO$, and another product.
(a) Calculate the percentage of nitrogen in urea.
   (Relative atomic masses: H = 1.00, C = 12.0, N = 14.0, O = 16.0)
   Insert your answer in Table 20.1.   **(3)**
(b) (i) Complete and balance the equation below and include state symbols.
       $NH_3 + CO_2 \rightarrow (NH_2)_2CO +$
   (ii) Calculate the mass of urea formed from 880 g carbon dioxide.
       (Relative atomic masses: H = 1.00, C = 12.0, N = 14.0, O = 16.0)   **(7)**
(c) A farmer whose land was too acidic and short of nitrogen decided to apply a mixture of lime (calcium hydroxide) and ammonium nitrate. Do you think this is a good idea? Give reasons for your answer.   **(2)**
(d) Some comparisons between urea and ammonium nitrate are given in the table:

Table 20.1

	Ammonium nitrate	Urea
Chemical formula	NH_4NO_3	$(NH_2)_2CO$
pH of dilute solution	4.5	7
percentage of nitrogen	35	
Melting point (°C)	170	133

Suggest two reasons why urea may be a better fertiliser than ammonium nitrate.   **(2)**
                                                                                       (Total 14)
                                                                       (LEAG, June 1989, Paper 3, Q5)

*Question 20.15

Using only the chemicals listed below and common laboratory apparatus, describe carefully how you would prepare a sample of dry copper metal. Include in your answer relevant observations and equations.
Powdered copper(II) carbonate
Powdered zinc
Dilute sulphuric acid
Distilled water

                                                                                              (10)
                                                                      (LEAG, June 1989, Paper 3, Q10)

*Question 20.16

Caesium(Cs) is an element with an atomic number of 55. It has a mass number and relative atomic mass of 133. It occurs in the first Group of the periodic table.
(a) Using the above data, write what you can about the structure of an atom of caesium.
(b) Show, using outer electrons only, how you would expect an atom of caesium to combine with an atom of chlorine.
(c) Predict, with reasons, TWO physical properties of the compound caesium chloride.   **(Total 10)**
                                                                      (LEAG, June 1989, Paper 3, Q11)

*Question 20.17

Sodium chloride is separated from sea water. The salt is used to make a concentrated solution of brine. The electrolysis of brine produces hydrogen, chlorine and sodium hydroxide solution. The cathodes are made of steel and the anodes of titanium.
(a) How is sodium chloride separated from sea water? **(1)**
(b) (i) If there is a leak of gas from the electrolysis cell, how can you tell whether it is chlorine or hydrogen? **(3)**
  (ii) If there is a leak of liquid, how can you tell whether it is brine or sodium hydroxide solution? **(3)**
(c) Hydrogen gas is used as a fuel or reacted with chlorine to form hydrogen chloride. Hydrogen chloride can be absorbed in water to produce hydrochloric acid.
  (i) Give a balanced chemical equation for the reaction of hydrogen with chlorine. **(2)**
  (ii) Dry hydrogen chloride does not change the colour of dry, blue litmus paper. However, a solution of hydrogen chloride in water changes the colour of the litmus paper to red. Explain this difference. **(2)**
(d) Steel is much cheaper than titanium. Suggest why steel is **not** used for the anodes as well as the cathodes. **(1)**
(e) Explain the following. You must give equations for any reactions that take place.
    The titanium and steel electrodes conduct electricity and are not chemically changed. The sodium chloride solution (brine) conducts electricity and is chemically changed. **(7)**
(SEG, Summer 1989, Paper 3, Q5)

*Question 20.18

Hydrocarbons are used as starting materials for making many substances.
(a) Complete the table.
    (Relative atomic masses: C=12, H=1) **(7)**

Hydrocarbon	Formula	Relative molecular mass	Structural formula
		44	H H H H—C—C—C—H H H H
propene	C_3H_6		
		30	

(b) Suggest how you could show that diesel fuel contains several different alkanes and is not a single alkane. **(2)**
(c) Hydrocarbons have many uses, such as in diesel fuel, and for the manufacture of fertilisers and poly(ethene) bags. A farmer uses all of these when applying fertiliser to the land. Explain what pollution problems the farmer could cause when carrying out this process. **(5)**
(d) Suggest how **one** pollution problem you describe in part (c) could be lessened or prevented. **(2)**
(SEG, Summer 1989, Paper 3, Q6)

20.2 Answers to Self-test Questions

20.1 (a) (i) **B.**
        (ii) **D.**
        (iii) **C.**
        (iv) **C.**
        (v) **A.**
    (b) Graphite.

> **A** must be graphite because it gives carbon dioxide on heating and also conducts electricity. The only other element to conduct electricity is **C** and so **C** must be the metal.

20.2 **B.**
20.3 **A.**
20.4 **C.**
20.5 **E.**
20.6 **D.**

> Neutralisation is when an acid and base react to give a salt and water only.

20.7 **D.**

> Atomic number = number of protons.

20.8 **E.**
20.9 **B.**
20.10 **C.**

> See Section 18.4.
> Cracking always produces smaller chains of carbon atoms.

20.11 (a)   Exothermic.
      (b) (i) Increase the pressure and use a catalyst (or increase the temperature).
           (ii) Decrease the temperature.

> See Section 8.1.

      (c) (i) $CO(g) + 2H_2(g) \rightleftharpoons CH_3OH(g)$
          (ii) Endothermic.
      (d) (i) Carbon monoxide is poisonous.
          (ii) Hydrogen/air mixtures are explosive.
      (e) (i) It produces heat when it burns.
          (ii) Methanol produces less pollution on combustion – it forms water and carbon dioxide. It is easier to transport.

20.12 (a) (i) Potassium nitrate, carbon and sulphur.
          (ii) This increases the surface area of the reactants and ensures thorough mixing, thus giving a rapid reaction.
      (b) (i) K_2S.
          (ii) Potassium and sulphur.
      (c) (i) Nitroglycerin is a liquid and gunpowder is a solid.
          (ii) At the high temperature of the reaction, H_2O is gaseous and not liquid.
      (d) (i) The oxygen.
          (ii) Carbon dioxide.
          (iii) Combustion, oxidation.
          (iv) Carbon dioxide is gaseous.
      (e) Coal dust has a very large surface area and is intimately mixed with air; this means that any spark produces a rapid reaction.

20.13 (a) (i) 80% of 1000 g = 800 g
          (ii) Molar mass of $Fe_2O_3 = (2 \times 56) + (3 \times 16)$
                 $= 160 \text{ g mol}^{-1}$
             Moles of $Fe_2O_3 = \dfrac{800}{160} = 5$

> See Section 5.1.

          (iii) Moles of CO = 3 × moles of Fe_2O_3 = 15
          (iv) Moles of CO required = 4 × 15 = 60
          (v) 1 mole of coke produces 1 mole of carbon monoxide
               Moles of coke needed = 60
          (vi) Mass of coke = 60 × 12 g = 720 g
          (vii) 720 tonnes
      (b) In 1000 g of ore, the mass of SiO_2 is 200 g
           Molar mass of $SiO_2 = 28 + (2 \times 16)$
                 $= 60 \text{ g mol}^{-1}$

           Moles of $SiO_2 = \dfrac{200}{60} = 3.33$

           1 mole of limestone gives 1 mole of calcium oxide which reacts with 1 mole of silica
           Moles of limestone needed = 3.33
           Molar mass of limestone = 40 + 12 + (3 × 16)
                 $= 100 \text{ g mol}^{-1}$
           Mass of limestone needed = 3.33 × 100 g
                 = 333 g

           Mass of limestone added to 1000 tonnes of ore = 333 tonnes

20.14 (a) Molar mass of urea = 2 × (14 + 2) + 12 + 16
                 $= 60 \text{ g mol}^{-1}$

           $\%N = \dfrac{2 \times 14}{60} \times 100 = 46.7$

See Section 5.1.

(b) (i) $2NH_3(g) + CO_2(g) \rightarrow (NH_2)_2CO(s) + H_2O(g)$

    (ii) 1 mol CO_2 gives 1 mol $(NH_2)_2CO$

Molar mass of $CO_2 = 12 + (2 \times 16)$
$$= 44 \text{ g mol}^{-1}$$
Molar mass of $(NH_2)_2CO = 60 \text{ g mol}^{-1}$
44 g CO_2 gives 60 g $(NH_2)_2CO$
∴ 880 g CO_2 gives 1200 g $(NH_2)_2CO$

(c) No, since ammonium nitrate and calcium hydroxide react together to produce ammonia.
$$Ca(OH)_2 + 2NH_4NO_3 \rightarrow Ca(NO_3)_2 + 2NH_3 + 2H_2O$$

(d) Urea contains a greater percentage of nitrogen. It also forms a neutral solution whereas ammonium nitrate forms an acidic solution.

20.15 Some dilute sulphuric acid is heated in a beaker. Copper(II) carbonate is added until no more bubbles are seen. Any excess solid is filtered off. This produces blue copper(II) sulphate solution.
$$CuCO_3(s) + H_2SO_4(aq) \rightarrow CuSO_4(aq) + CO_2(g) + H_2O(l)$$
Excess powdered zinc is then added to the copper(II) sulphate solution. This produces a reddish-brown precipitate of copper which can be filtered off from the resulting colourless solution of zinc sulphate. Any unreacted zinc can be removed by stirring the solid with dilute sulphuric acid which reacts with the zinc to produce zinc sulphate solution and hydrogen; the copper does not react. The copper is then filtered off, washed with distilled water and dried.
$$Zn(s) + CuSO_4(aq) \rightarrow ZnSO_4(aq) + Cu(s)$$

See Sections 11.5 and 12.1.

20.16 (a) A caesium atom must contain 55 protons, 55 electrons and 78 neutrons. The electrons are arranged in energy levels with one electron in the outermost energy level.

See Section 2.4 – the number of neutrons = 133 – 55

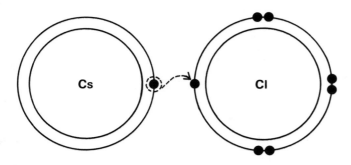

(b) When an atom of caesium combines with one of chlorine, the outermost electron in the caesium atom is transferred to the chlorine atom so that each ion formed contains a stable octet of eight electrons in their outermost shells.

See Section 4.1.

(c) Caesium chloride is ionic. This means that it will have a high melting point and will conduct electricity when molten.

See Section 4.2.

20.17 (a) The water is evaporated off.

    (b) (i) The gas could be tested with moist indicator paper. If it is chlorine, then the indicator paper will be bleached. If it is hydrogen, the indicator paper will not change.

       (ii) Again, indicator paper can be used. Brine will have a pH of 7 whereas sodium hydroxide solution is alkaline.

    (c) (i) $H_2(g) + Cl_2(g) \rightarrow 2HCl(g)$

       (ii) Acidic properties are only shown when water is present. When hydrogen chloride dissolves in water, it reacts with it to produce ions (H^+) which affect the litmus paper.

See Section 11.2.

(d) Chlorine is produced at the anodes and this reacts with steel.

(e) Steel and titanium are metals which contain free electrons to carry the current. These electrons can move within the metal without altering its structure. Sodium chloride solution contains ions. These ions move to the oppositely charged electrodes, pick up or lose electrons and become atoms and molecules as shown below.

At anode $\qquad$ At cathode
$2Cl^-(aq) \rightarrow 2Cl(g) + 2e^- \dashrightarrow 2e^- + 2H^+(aq) \rightarrow 2H(g)$
$\qquad\qquad\downarrow \qquad\qquad\qquad\qquad\qquad\qquad \downarrow$
$\qquad\qquad Cl_2(g) \qquad\qquad\qquad\qquad\qquad H_2(g)$

In a metal the current is carried by the electrons whereas in a solution the current is carried by the ions.

See Section 6.1.

20.18   (a)   The first hydrocarbon is propane with the formula C_3H_8. Propene has a relative molecular mass of 42 and the structural formula:

The last hydrocarbon is ethane, formula C_2H_6, and structural formula:

> See Sections 18.2 and 18.3.

(b)   A pure substance boils at a constant temperature. Diesel fuel boils over a range of temperatures, showing that it consists of several different alkanes.

(c)   The farmer will use diesel fuel in his tractor. Combustion of diesel fuel produces carbon dioxide (Greenhouse effect – see Example 9.7) and also pollutants such as carbon monoxide. Fertilisers are put on the land to promote healthy plant growth. However, if they drain into rivers they pollute them (see Section 10.3 and Example 10.6). Poly(ethene) bags are non-biodegradable; they will not rot and so are difficult to dispose of. Burning them will produce pollution problems (carbon monoxide).

(d)   Replace the tractor by a horse; there would then be less need for an inorganic fertiliser and no pollution from diesel fuel either!

20.3 Grading of Self-test Questions

Questions 20.1 to 20.11 are found in the compulsory part of the examination paper. They are worth a total of 26 marks and you should be looking to get at least 18 marks to gain a grade C or above. Around 15 marks is equivalent to something like a grade E whilst less than 10 marks will gain you at most a G grade. The remaining questions in this chapter are to be found on the harder extension paper designed to differentiate between A and B grades. These questions are worth a total of 99 marks. You should get a grade A if you obtain at least 75 marks and a B grade if you obtain around 55 marks or more.

Index

Macmillan Work Out Series

For GCSE examinations
Accounting
Biology
Business Studies
Chemistry
Computer Studies
English Key Stage 4
French (cassette and pack available)
Geography
German (cassette and pack available)
Modern World History
Human Biology
Core Maths Key Stage 4
Revise Mathematics to further level
Physics
Religious Studies
Science
Social and Economic History
Spanish (cassette and pack available)
Statistics

For A Level examinations
Accounting
Biology
Business Studies
Chemistry
Economics
English
French (cassette and pack available)
Mathematics
Physics
Psychology
Sociology
Statistics